# Summary of Contents

D0572263

# THE CSS ANTHOLOGY
## 101 ESSENTIAL TIPS, TRICKS & HACKS

BY **RACHEL ANDREW**
**3RD EDITION**

# The CSS Anthology: 101 Essential Tips, Tricks & Hacks

by Rachel Andrew

Copyright © 2009 SitePoint Pty Ltd

**Managing Editor**: Chris Wyness        **Technical Director**: Kevin Yank

**Technical Editor**: Andrew Tetlaw     **Cover Design**: Alex Walker

**Editor**: Kelly Steele

**Printing History**:                   **Latest Update**: July 2009

 First Edition: November 2004

 Second Edition: May 2007

 Third Edition: July 2009

## Notice of Rights

## Notice of Liability

## Trademark Notice

Published by SitePoint Pty Ltd

Web: www.sitepoint.com

Email: business@sitepoint.com

ISBN 978-0-9805768-0-1

Printed and bound in Canada

## About the Author

Rachel Andrew is a director of web solutions provider edgeofmyseat.com and a web developer. When not writing code, she writes *about* writing code and is the author of several SitePoint books, including *HTML Utopia: Designing Without Tables Using CSS* and *Everything You Know About CSS Is Wrong!*, which promote the practical use of web standards alongside other everyday tools and technologies. Rachel takes a common sense, real world approach to web standards, with her writing and teaching being based on the experiences she has in her own company every day.

Rachel lives in the UK with her partner Drew and daughter Bethany. When not working, they can often be found wandering around the English countryside hunting for geocaches and nice pubs that serve Sunday lunch and a good beer.

## About the Technical Editor

Andrew Tetlaw has been tinkering with web sites as a web developer since 1997. At SitePoint he is dedicated to making the world a better place through the technical editing of SitePoint books, kits, articles, and newsletters. He is also a busy father of five, enjoys coffee, and often neglects his blog at http://tetlaw.id.au/.

## About the Technical Director

As Technical Director for SitePoint, Kevin Yank keeps abreast of all that is new and exciting in web technology. Best known for his book, *Build Your Own Database Driven Website Using PHP & MySQL*, he also co-authored *Simply JavaScript* with Cameron Adams and *Everything You Know About CSS Is Wrong!* with Rachel Andrew. In addition, Kevin hosts the *SitePoint Podcast* and writes the *SitePoint Tech Times*, a free email newsletter that goes out to over 240,000 subscribers worldwide.

Kevin lives in Melbourne, Australia and enjoys speaking at conferences, as well as visiting friends and family in Canada. He's also passionate about performing improvised comedy theater with Impro Melbourne (http://www.impromelbourne.com.au/) and flying light aircraft. Kevin's personal blog is *Yes, I'm Canadian* (http://yesimcanadian.com/).

## About SitePoint

SitePoint specializes in publishing fun, practical, and easy-to-understand content for web professionals. Visit http://www.sitepoint.com/ to access our blogs, books, newsletters, articles, podcasts, and community forums.

*For Bethany*

# Table of Contents

## Chapter 3  CSS and Images

## Chapter 4    Navigation . . . . . . . . . . . . . . . . . . . . . . . . 89

# Preface

Apart from writing books like this one, I write code. I make my living by building web sites and applications as, I'm sure, many readers of this book do. I use CSS to complete jobs every day, and I know what it's like to struggle to make CSS work when the project needs to be finished the next morning.

When I talk to designers and developers who avoid using CSS, or use CSS only for simple text styling, I hear over and over again that they just lack the time to learn this whole new way of working. After all, tables and spacer GIFs function, they do the job, and they pay the bills.

I was lucky. I picked up CSS very early in the piece, and started to play with it because it interested me. As a result of that early interest, my knowledge grew as the CSS techniques themselves were developed, and I can now draw on nine years' experience building CSS layouts every time I tackle a project.

In this book, I've tried to pass on the tricks and techniques that allow me to quickly and easily develop web sites and applications using CSS.

Pages and pages of theory are nowhere to be found in this book. What you'll find are solutions that will enable you to do the cool stuff today, but should also act as starting points for your own creativity. In my experience, it's far easier to learn by doing than by reading, so while you can use this book to find solutions that will help you get that client web site up and running before the deadline, please experiment with these examples and use them as a means to learn new techniques.

The book was designed to let you quickly find the answer to the particular CSS problem with which you're struggling at any given point in time. There's no need to read it from cover to cover—just grab the technique you need, or that interests you, and you're set to go. Along with each solution, I've provided an explanation to help you understand why the technique works. This knowledge will allow you to expand on, and experiment with, the technique in your own time.

I hope you enjoy this book! It has been great fun to write, and my hope is that it will be useful as a day-to-day reference, as well as a tool that helps give you the confidence to explore new CSS techniques.

# Who Should Read this Book?

This book is aimed at people who need to work with CSS—web designers and developers who've seen the cool CSS designs out there, but are short on the time to wade through masses of theory and debate in order to create a site. Each problem is solved with a working solution that can be implemented as it is or used as a springboard to creativity.

As a whole, this book isn't a tutorial; while Chapter 1 covers the very basics of CSS, and the early chapters cover simpler techniques than those that follow, you'll find the examples easier to grasp if you have a basic grounding in CSS.

# What's Covered in this Book?

**Chapter 1: *Making a Start with CSS***

This chapter follows a different format to the rest of the book—it's simply a quick CSS tutorial for anyone who needs to brush up on the basics of CSS. If you've been using CSS in your own projects, you might want to skip this chapter and refer to it on a needs basis, when you want to look into basic concepts in more detail.

**Chapter 2: *Text Styling and Other Basics***

This chapter covers techniques for styling and formatting text in your documents; font sizing, colors, and the removal of annoying extra whitespace around page elements are explained as the chapter progresses. Even if you're already using CSS for text styling, you'll find some useful tips here.

**Chapter 3: *CSS and Images***

Combining CSS and images can create powerful visual effects. This chapter looks at the ways in which you can do this, covering background images on various elements, and positioning text with images, among other topics.

**Chapter 4: *Navigation***

We all need navigation and this chapter explains how to create it, CSS-style. The topics of CSS replacements for image-based navigation, CSS *tab* navigation, combining background images with CSS text to create attractive and accessible menus, and using lists to structure navigation in an accessible way are addressed in this chapter.

### Chapter 5: *Tabular Data*

While the use of tables for layout should be avoided wherever possible, tables should be used for their real purpose: the display of tabular data, such as that contained in a spreadsheet. This chapter will demonstrate techniques for the application of tables to create attractive and usable tabular data displays.

### Chapter 6: *Forms and User Interfaces*

Whether you're a designer or a developer, it's likely that you'll spend a fair amount of time creating forms for data entry. CSS can help you to create forms that are attractive and usable; this chapter shows how we can do that while bearing the key accessibility principles in mind.

### Chapter 7: *Cross-browser Techniques*

How can we deal with older browsers, browsers with CSS bugs, and alternative devices? These questions form the main theme of this chapter. We'll also see how to troubleshoot CSS bugs—and where to go for help—as well as discussing the ways you can test your site in as many browsers as possible.

### Chapter 8: *Accessibility and Alternative Devices*

It's all very well that our pages look pretty to the majority of our site's visitors—but what about that group of people who rely upon assistive technology, such as screen magnifiers and screen readers? Or those users who prefer to navigate the Web using the keyboard rather than a mouse, for whatever reason? In this chapter, we'll see how we can make our site as welcoming and accessible as possible for *all* users, rather than just able-bodied visitors with perfect vision.

### Chapter 9: *CSS Positioning and Layout*

In this chapter, we explore the use of CSS to create beautiful and accessible pages. We cover a range of different CSS layouts and a variety of techniques, which can be combined and extended upon to create numerous interesting page layouts.

# The Book's Web Site

Located at http://www.sitepoint.com/books/cssant3/, the web site that supports this book will give you access to the following facilities.

## The Code Archive

As you progress through this book, you'll note file names above many of the code listings. These refer to files in the code archive, a downloadable ZIP file that contains all of the finished examples presented in this book. Simply click the **Code Archive** link on the book's web site to download it.

## Updates and Errata

No book is error-free, and attentive readers will no doubt spot at least one or two mistakes in this one. The Corrections and Typos page on the book's web site will provide the latest information about known typographical and code errors, and will offer necessary updates for new releases of browsers and related standards.[1]

# The SitePoint Forums

If you'd like to communicate with other designers about this book, you should join SitePoint's online community.[2] The CSS forum, in particular, offers an abundance of information above and beyond the solutions in this book, and a lot of fun and experienced web designers and developers hang out there.[3] It's a good way to learn new tricks, have questions answered in a hurry, and just have a good time.

# The SitePoint Newsletters

In addition to books like this one, SitePoint publishes free email newsletters, including *The SitePoint Tribune*, *The SitePoint Tech Times*, and *The SitePoint Design View*. Reading them will keep you up to date on the latest news, product releases, trends, tips, and techniques for all aspects of web development. If nothing else, you'll read useful CSS articles and tips, but if you're interested in learning other

---

[1] http://www.sitepoint.com/books/cssant2/errata.php
[2] http://www.sitepoint.com/forums/
[3] http://www.sitepoint.com/launch/cssforum/

technologies, you'll find them especially valuable. Sign up to one or more SitePoint newsletters at http://www.sitepoint.com/newsletter/.

# The SitePoint Podcast

Join the SitePoint Podcast team for news, interviews, opinion, and fresh thinking for web developers and designers. They discuss the latest web industry topics, present guest speakers, and interview some of the best minds in the industry. You can catch up on the latest and previous podcasts at http://www.sitepoint.com/podcast/ or subscribe via iTunes.

# Your Feedback

If you're unable to find an answer through the forums, or if you wish to contact us for any other reason, the best place to write is books@sitepoint.com. We have an email support system set up to track your inquiries, and friendly support staff members who can answer your questions. Suggestions for improvements, as well as notices of any mistakes you may find are especially welcome.

# Acknowledgments

Firstly, I'd like to thank the SitePoint team for making this book a reality, and for being easy to communicate with despite the fact that our respective time zones saw me going to bed as they started work each day.

To those people who are really breaking new ground in the world of CSS, those whose ideas are discussed throughout this book, and those who share their ideas and creativity with the wider community, thank you.

Thanks to Drew for his support and encouragement, for being willing to discuss CSS concepts as I worked out my examples for the book, for making me laugh when I was growing annoyed, and for putting up with our entire lack of a social life. Finally, thanks must go to my daughter Bethany, who is very understanding of the fact that her mother is constantly at a computer, and who reminds me of what's important every day. You both make so many things possible, thank you.

# Conventions Used in This Book

You'll notice that we've used certain typographic and layout styles throughout this book to signify different types of information. Look out for the following items.

## Markup Samples

Any markup—be that HTML or CSS—will be displayed using a fixed-width font like so:

```
<h1>A perfect summer's day</h1>
<p>It was a lovely day for a walk in the park. The birds
were singing and the kids were all back at school.</p>
```

If the markup forms part of the book's code archive, the name of the file will appear at the top of the program listing, like this:

*example.css*

```
.footer {
  background-color: #CCC;
  border-top: 1px solid #333;
}
```

If only part of the file is displayed, this is indicated by the word *excerpt*:

*example.css (excerpt)*

```
  border-top: 1px solid #333;
```

If additional code is to be inserted into an existing example, the new code will be displayed in bold:

```
function animate() {
  new_variable = "Hello";
}
```

Also, where existing code is required for context, rather than repeat all the code, a vertical ellipsis will be displayed:

```
function animate() {
    ⋮
    return new_variable;
}
```

Some lines of code are intended to be entered on one line, but we've had to wrap them because of page constraints. A ➡ indicates a line break that exists for formatting purposes only, and should be ignored.

```
URL.open("http://www.sitepoint.com/blogs/2007/05/28/user-style-she
➡ets-come-of-age/");
```

## Tips, Notes, and Warnings

### Hey, You!

Tips will give you helpful little pointers.

### Ahem, Excuse Me ...

Notes are useful asides that are related—but not critical—to the topic at hand. Think of them as extra tidbits of information.

### Make Sure You Always ...

... pay attention to these important points.

### Watch Out!

Warnings will highlight any gotchas that are likely to trip you up along the way.

# Making a Start with CSS

Cascading Style Sheets sound intimidating. The name alone conjures up images of cryptic code and syntax too difficult for the layperson to grasp. In reality, however, CSS is one of the simplest and most convenient tools available to web developers. In this first chapter, which takes a different format than the rest of the book, I'll guide you through the basics of CSS and show you how it can be used to simplify the task of managing a consistently formatted web site. If you've already used CSS to format text on your sites, you may want to skip this chapter and jump straight to the solutions that begin in Chapter 2.

## How do I define styles with CSS?

The basic purpose of CSS is to allow the designer to define **style declarations** (formatting details such as fonts, element sizes, and colors), and to apply those styles to selected portions of HTML pages using **selectors**—references to an element or group of elements to which the style is applied.

# Solution

Let's look at a basic example to see how this is done. Consider the following HTML document outline:

```
<!DOCTYPE html PUBLIC "-//W3C//DTD XHTML 1.0 Strict//EN"
    "http://www.w3.org/TR/xhtml1/DTD/xhtml1-strict.dtd">
<html xmlns="http://www.w3.org/1999/xhtml" lang="en-US">
  <head>
    <title>A Simple Page</title>
    <meta http-equiv="content-type"
        content="text/html; charset=utf-8" />
  </head>
  <body>
    <h1>First Title</h1>
    <p>A paragraph of interesting content.</p>

    <h2>Second Title</h2>
    <p>A paragraph of interesting content.</p>

    <h2>Third title</h2>
    <p>A paragraph of interesting content.</p>
  </body>
</html>
```

This document contains three headings (in bold above), which have been created using <h1> and <h2> tags. Without CSS styling, the headings will be rendered using the browser's internal style sheet—the h1 heading will be displayed in a large font size, and the h2 headings will be smaller than the h1, but larger than paragraph text. The document that uses these default styles will be *readable*, if a little plain. We can use some simple CSS to change the look of these elements:

```
<!DOCTYPE html PUBLIC "-//W3C//DTD XHTML 1.0 Strict//EN"
    "http://www.w3.org/TR/xhtml1/DTD/xhtml1-strict.dtd">
<html xmlns="http://www.w3.org/1999/xhtml" lang="en-US">
  <head>
    <title>A Simple Page</title>
    <meta http-equiv="content-type"
        content="text/html; charset=utf-8" />
    <style type="text/css">
      h1, h2 {
        font-family: sans-serif;
```

```
        color: #3366CC;
    }
  </style>
  </head>
  <body>
    <h1>First Title</h1>
    <p>A paragraph of interesting content.</p>

    <h2>Second Title</h2>
    <p>A paragraph of interesting content.</p>

    <h2>Third title</h2>
    <p>A paragraph of interesting content.</p>
  </body>
</html>
```

All the magic lies between the `<style>` tags in the `head` of the document, where we specify that a light blue, sans-serif font should be applied to all `h1` and `h2` elements in the document. Regarding the syntax—I'll explain it in detail in a moment. It's unnecessary to add to the markup itself—changes to the style definition at the top of the page will affect all three headings, as well as any other headings that might be added to the page at a later date.

 **HTML or XHTML?**

Throughout this book I'll use the term HTML to refer generally to web page documents, markup, and code examples. You can take that as meaning HTML and/or XHTML unless stated otherwise.

Now that you have an idea of what CSS does, let me explain the different ways in which you can use CSS styles in your HTML documents.

## Inline Styles

The simplest method of adding CSS styles to your web pages is to use **inline styles**. An inline style is applied to a HTML element via its `style` attribute, like this:

```
<p style="font-family: sans-serif; color: #3366CC;">
  Amazingly few discotheques provide jukeboxes.
</p>
```

An inline style has no selector; the style declarations are applied to the parent element—in the above example the <p> tag.

Inline styles have one major disadvantage: it's impossible to reuse them. For example, if we wanted to apply the style above to another p element, we'd have to type it out again in that element's style attribute. And if the style needed changing further on, we'd have to find and edit every HTML tag where the style was copied. Additionally, because inline styles are located within the page's markup, it makes the code difficult to read and maintain.

## Embedded Styles

Another approach you can take to applying CSS styles to your web pages is to use the style element, as I did in the first example we looked at. Using this method, you can declare any number of CSS styles by placing them between the opening and closing <style> tags, as follows:

```
<style type="text/css">
  ⋮ CSS Styles…
</style>
```

The <style> tags are placed inside the head element. The type attribute specifies the language that you're using to define your styles. CSS is the only style language in wide use, and is indicated with the value text/css.

While it's nice and simple, the <style> tag has one major disadvantage: if you want to use a particular set of styles throughout your site, you'll have to repeat those style definitions within the style element at the top of every one of your site's pages.

A more sensible alternative is to place those definitions into a plain text file, then link your documents to that file. This external file is referred to as an external style sheet.

## External Style Sheets

An **external style sheet** is a file (usually given a **.css** filename) that contains a web site's CSS styles, keeping them separate from any one web page. Multiple pages can link to the same **.css** file, and any changes you make to the style definitions in that file will affect all the pages that link to it. This achieves the objective of creating site-wide style definitions that I mentioned above.

To link a document to an external style sheet (say, **styles.css**), we simply place a `link` element within the document's `head` element:

```
<link rel="stylesheet" type="text/css" href="styles.css" />
```

Remember our original example in which three headings shared a single style rule? Let's save that rule to an external style sheet with the filename **styles.css**, and link it to the web page like so:

```
<!DOCTYPE html PUBLIC "-//W3C//DTD XHTML 1.0 Strict//EN"
    "http://www.w3.org/TR/xhtml1/DTD/xhtml1-strict.dtd">
<html xmlns="http://www.w3.org/1999/xhtml" lang="en-US">
<head>
<title>A Simple Page</title>
<meta http-equiv="content-type"
    content="text/html; charset=utf-8" />
<link rel="stylesheet" type="text/css" href="styles.css" />
</head>
<body>
<h1>First Title</h1>
<p>…</p>

<h2>Second Title</h2>
<p>…</p>

<h2>Third Title</h2>
<p>…</p>
</body>
</html>
```

The value of the `rel` attribute must be `stylesheet` and the `type` must be `text/css`. The `href` attribute indicates the location and name of the style sheet file.

The linked **styles.css** file contains the style definition:

```
h1, h2 {
  font-family: sans-serif;
  color: #3366CC;
}
```

As with an image file, you can reuse this **styles.css** file in any pages in which it's needed. It will save you from re-typing the styles, as well as ensuring that your headings display consistently across the entire site.

## CSS Syntax

A style sheet is a collection of style definitions. Every CSS style definition, or rule, has two main components:

- A list of one or more **selectors**, separated by commas, define the element or elements to which the style will be applied.
- The **declaration block**, surrounded by curly braces {...}, specifies what the style actually does.

The declaration block contains one or more **style declarations** and each one sets the value of a specific **property**. Multiple declarations are separated by a semi-colon (;). A property declaration is made up of the property name and a value, separated by a colon (:). You can see all of these elements labeled in Figure 1.1.

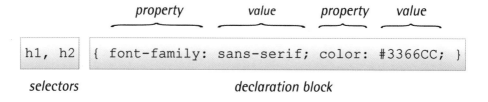

Figure 1.1. The components of a CSS rule: a list of selectors and a declaration block

Property declarations set the values for fonts, colors, and other settings that should be applied by the style. The solutions throughout the book focus mainly on the different properties and the values they can take.

Figure 1.1 also illustrates that a style rule can be written in a single line. Some CSS authors prefer to indent their style rules to aid readability, while others choose to write their rules on one line to save space. The following shows the same style rule written both ways:

```
h1, h2 {
  font-family: sans-serif;
  color: #3366CC;
}

h1, h2 { font-family: sans-serif; color: #3366CC; }
```

The formatting makes no difference at all; it's totally up to you how you write your style sheet.

# What are CSS Selectors and how do I use them effectively?

In the following example, the selectors are h1 and h2, which means that the style should apply to all h1 and h2 elements:

```
h1, h2 {
  font-family: sans-serif;
  color: #3366CC;
}
```

## Solution

In this section, I'll describe the basic CSS2.1 selector types that are in common use today and give you some examples of each.

### Type Selectors

The most basic form of selector is a **type selector**, which we've already seen. By naming a particular HTML element, you can apply a style rule to every occurrence of that element in the document. Type selectors are often used to set the basic styles that will appear throughout a web site. For example, the following style rule might be used to set the default paragraph font for a web site:

```
p {
  font-family: Tahoma, Verdana, Arial, Helvetica, sans-serif;
  font-size: 1em;
  color: #000000;
}
```

Here we set the font, size, and color for all p (paragraph) elements in the document.

## Class Selectors

Assigning styles to elements is all well and good, but what happens if you want to assign different styles to identical elements that occur in various places within your document? This is where CSS **classes** come in.

Consider the following style, which turns all the paragraph text blue on a page:

```
p {
  color: #0000FF;
}
```

Great! But what would happen if you had a sidebar on your page with a blue background? If the text in the sidebar were to display blue as well it would be invisible. What you need to do is define a class for your sidebar text, then assign a CSS style to that class.

To create a paragraph of the sidebar class, first add a class attribute to the opening tag:

```
<p class="sidebar">This text will be white, as specified by the
    CSS style definition below.</p>
```

Now we can write the style for this class:

```
p {
  color: #0000FF;
}
.sidebar {
  color: #FFFFFF;
}
```

This second rule uses a class selector to indicate that the style should be applied to any element with a `class` value of the `sidebar`. The period (`.`) at the beginning indicates that we're naming a `class`, instead of a HTML element.

Now, what would happen if there were links in your sidebar? By default, they'd be rendered just like any other links in your page; however, add a `class="sidebar"` attribute to the link element, and they'll turn white, too:

```
<p class="sidebar">This text will be white, <a class="sidebar"
    href="link.html">and so will this link</a>.</p>
```

That's fairly neat, but what if you wanted to make the links stand out a bit more? Perhaps you want to display them in bold text? Adding the `bold` text declaration to the `sidebar` class style will turn your whole sidebar bold, which defeats the purpose. You need a CSS selector that selects links of the `sidebar` class only, and by combining a type selector with a class selector, you can do exactly that:

```
p {
  color: #0000FF;
}
.sidebar {
  color: #FFFFFF;
}
a.sidebar:link, a.sidebar:visited {
  font-weight: bold;
}
```

Note that we've also used the `:link` and `:visited` pseudo-classes here—we'll look at pseudo-classes in more detail later in this chapter.

If you were to add these style rules to your style sheet and reload the page in your browser, you'd see that your sidebar links display in a font that's white *and* bold—both of the styles that we defined above for the `sidebar` class are applied to our sidebar links. If we were to specify a different color in the third style rule, however, links would adopt that new color, because the third selector is more specific, and CSS style rules are applied in order of increasing selector specificity.

Incidentally, the process of applying multiple styles to a single page element is called **cascading**, and is where Cascading Style Sheets gained their name. We'll learn more about selector specificity and the cascade at the end of this chapter.

## ID Selectors

In contrast with class selectors, **ID selectors** are used to select one particular element, rather than a group of elements. To use an ID selector, first add an id attribute to the element you wish to style. It's important that the ID is unique within the HTML document:

```
<p id="tagline">This paragraph is uniquely identified by the ID
   "tagline".</p>
```

To reference this element by its ID selector, we precede the id with a hash (#). For example, the following rule will make the above paragraph white:

```
#tagline {
   color: #FFFFFF;
}
```

ID selectors can be used in combination with other selector types. The following style, for example, applies to elements with a class of new appearing within the paragraph that has an id of tagline:

```
#tagline .new {
   font-weight: bold;
   color: #FFFFFF;
}
```

The selector in the above example is actually known as a descendant selector, and we learn about those in the very next section.

## Descendant Selectors

If your sidebar consisted of more than just one paragraph of text, you *could* add the class to every opening <p> tag in the sidebar. However, it would be much neater to apply a class of sidebar to a container element, and set the color of every p element within that container to white, with a single CSS style rule. This is what **descendant selectors** are for.

Here's the new selector:

```
p {
   color: #0000FF;
}
.sidebar p {
   color: #FFFFFF;
}
```

And here's the updated HTML:

```
<div class="sidebar">
  <p>This paragraph will be displayed in white.</p>
  <p>So will this one.</p>
</div>
```

As you can see, a descendant selector comprises a list of selectors (separated by spaces) that matches a page element (or group of elements) *from the outside in*. In this case, because our page contains a div element that has a class of sidebar, the descendant selector .sidebar p refers to all p elements inside that div.

## Child Selectors

The descendant selector matches all elements that are descendants of the parent element, including elements that are *not direct* descendants.

Consider the following markup:

```
<div class="sidebar">
  <p>This paragraph will be displayed in white.</p>
  <p>So will this one.</p>
  <div class="tagline">
    <p>If we use a descendant selector, this will be white too.
       But if we use a child selector, it will be blue.</p>
  </div>
</div>
```

In this example, the descendant selector we saw in the previous section, `.sidebar p`, would match all the paragraphs that are nested within the `div` element with the class sidebar *as well as* those inside the `div` with the class `tagline`. But if instead you only wanted to style those paragraphs that were *direct* descendants of the `sidebar div`, you'd use a **child selector**. A child selector uses the > character to specify a direct descendant.

Here's the new selector, which sets the text color to white for those paragraphs directly inside the `sidebar div` (but not those within the `tagline div`):

```
p {
  color: #0000FF;
}
.sidebar>p {
  color: #FFFFFF;
}
```

 **Internet Explorer 6 Doesn't Support the Child Selector**

Unfortunately, IE6 falls short of supporting the child selector, so if this style is essential to the layout of your page, you'll need to find an alternative way to target the element.

## Adjacent Selectors

An adjacent selector will only match an element if it's adjacent to another specified element. Therefore, if we have HTML:

```
<h2>This is a title</h2>
<p>This paragraph will be displayed in white.</p>
<p>Ths paragraph will be displayed in black.</p>
```

And then use the following selector:

```
p {
  color: #000000;
}
h2+p {
  color: #FFFFFF;
}
```

Only the first paragraph will be displayed in white. The second p element is not adjacent to an h2 and therefore its text would be displayed in the black we have specified for p elements in the first rule.

 **Internet Explorer 6 Doesn't Support the Adjacent Selector**

Unfortunately, IE6 fails to support the adjacent selector, therefore if the style is essential to the layout of your page then I'd advise finding another way to target the element.

## Pseudo-class Selectors for Links

The formatting options available for links in HTML—created using the the a, or **anchor** element—are more extensive than those on offer for most other elements. CSS provides a way of setting link styles according to their state—if they've been visited or remain unvisited, if the cursor is hovering over the link, or if the link is being clicked on. Consider the following example:

```css
a:link { color: #0000FF; }
a:visited { color: #FF00FF; }
a:hover { color: #00CCFF; }
a:active { color: #FF0000; }
```

The above code contains four CSS style definitions. Each of the selectors uses what is termed a **pseudo-class** of the a element. A pseudo-class is one of a small collection of labels that can be added to selectors to represent the state of the target elements, and is indicated by the colon (:) at the beginning. Here are the commonly used pseudo-classes for links:

- :link applies to *unvisited* links only, and specifies that they should be blue.
- :visited applies to *visited* links, and makes them magenta.
- :hover overrides the first two definitions by making links light blue when the cursor moves over them, whether they've been visited or not.
- :active makes links red when they're clicked on.

The order in which you specify these pseudo-class selectors in your style sheet is important; because :active appears last, it overrides the first three selectors, so it will take effect regardless of whether the links have been visited or not, or whether the cursor is over them or not.

The :hover and :active states are officially known as **dynamic pseudo-class selectors**, as they only occur when the user interacts in some way with the element, that is, by clicking on the link or holding the cursor over it.

### :hover on Other Elements

The :hover dynamic pseudo-class selector can be used on other elements beside links, so you can create effects such as highlighting a row in a data table as the mouse hovers over it. However Internet Explorer 6 and earlier versions only supports this selector for anchor elements.

## First Child Pseudo-class Selector

Another example of a pseudo-class is the first child pseudo-class, :first-child. Where the adjacent element selector matches an element if it's *next to* another element in the document source, the first child pseudo-class selector matches an element only if it's the first child element of its parent. So this is essentially the same as using a child selector except that only the first instance will be matched:

```
<div class="article">
  <p>
    This is an intro paragraph to be
    displayed with a larger font size.
  </p>
  <p>
    Here is a second paragraph of text
    displayed at normal text size.
  </p>
</div>
```

And then use the following CSS:

```
p {
  font-size: 100%
}
```

```
.article p:first-child {
  font-size: 160%;
}
```

The first paragraph will be displayed in a larger font as it's the first child of the parent div element with a class of article. The second paragraph will be displayed in the font size set for all p elements.

 **Internet Explorer 6 Doesn't Support the First Child Selector**

Again, IE6 is found wanting in supporting the first child selector, therefore if the style is essential to the layout of your page then you may need to find an alternate way to target the element.

# How does the browser know which styles to apply?

So how does the browser understand our intentions? When more than one rule can be applied to the same element, the browser uses **the cascade** to determine which style properties to apply.

Understanding the cascade is important when dealing with CSS, because many CSS development problems are due to styles being unintentionally applied to an element. We've already presented examples in this chapter where we've written a general style rule focused on paragraph elements, and then a more specific rule aimed at one or more particular paragraphs. Both style rules target paragraphs, *but the more specific rule overrides the general rule in the case of matching paragraphs.*

## Solution

There are four factors that the browser uses to make the decision: weight, origin, specificity, and source order.

The **weight** of a particular style declaration is determined by the use of the keyword, !important. When the keyword appears after a property value, that value can't be overridden by the same property in another style rule, except in very specific circumstances. Using !important in your style sheets has a huge negative impact on maintainability and there's often little call for it anyway. For these reasons it should be avoided, as we do in this book. If you'd like to know more you can read about it in the SitePoint CSS Reference.[1]

There are three possible style sheet **origins**: the browser, the author, and the user. In this book we focus on what are called **author style sheets**—style sheets written by the web page creator; that's you. We've mentioned the browser internal style sheet that provides the default styles for all elements, but styles in author style sheets will always override styles in the browser default style sheet. The only other possible origin for style sheets are **user style sheets**—custom styles written by the browser users—and even these are overridden by the author style sheet except in rare circumstances. Again, if you'd like to know more the SitePoint CSS Reference[2] has a whole section about it.

The two parts of the cascade that will affect your daily CSS work the most are specificity and source order.

The rule of **specificity** ensures that the style rule with the most specific selector overrides any others with less specific selectors. To give you an example of how this works, consider this simple snippet of HTML markup:

```
<div id="content">
  <p class="message">
    This is an important message.
  </p>
</div>
```

Now consider the follow style rules that are to be applied to the HTML above:

```
p { color: #000000; }

.message  { color: #CCCCCC; }

p.message  { color: #0000FF; }

#content p.message  { color: #FF0000; }
```

---

[1] http://reference.sitepoint.com/css/importantdeclarations/
[2] http://reference.sitepoint.com/css/cascade/

The four selectors above all match the paragraph element in the example HTML and set the text color. What color will be applied to the paragraph? If you guessed #FF0000 or red, you'd be right. The selectors p (any p element) and .message (any element with class message) have the same amount of specificity; the selector p.message (any p element with class message), has a higher level of specificity; but the selector #content p.message (any p element with class message that is a child of the element with id content) has the highest.

However, longer selectors are not necessarily more specific. An ID selector, for example, will always have a higher specificity than an element type or class selector. It becomes trickier the more complex your selectors are, but you should find the examples in this book simple enough. If you'd like to know the exact formula for measuring specificity, the SitePoint CSS Reference[3] has all the answers.

If, after all of the above have been taken into account, two or more style rules are still applicable to an element, then the *order* in which the rules appear—the **source order**—is used; the last rule to be declared is applied. In the above example the selectors p and .message have the same specificity, so in the absence of any other applicable rules, the last one declared is used—the rule with the selector .message. This is also true if you declare more than one style rule with the same selector, .message for example, in your style sheet; it'll be the second instance of that rule that will be applied to the element. As we'll see in later chapters this behavior is very useful.

# Summary

This chapter has given you a taste of CSS and its usage at the most basic level. We've even touched on the sometimes difficult concept of the cascade. If you're a newbie to CSS but have an understanding of the concepts discussed in this chapter, you should be able to start using the examples in this book.

The examples in the early chapters are simpler than those found near the end, so if you've yet to work with CSS, you might want to begin with the earlier chapters. These will build on the knowledge you gained in this chapter to start you using and, I hope, enjoying CSS.

---

[3] http://reference.sitepoint.com/css/specificity/

# 2

# Text Styling and Other Basics

This chapter explores the applications of CSS for styling text and covers a lot of CSS basics, as well as answering some of the more frequently asked questions about these techniques. If you're new to CSS, these examples will introduce you to a variety of properties and their usages, and will give you a solid foundation from which to start your own experiments. For those who are already familiar with CSS, this chapter will serve as a quick refresher in those moments when you're struggling to remember how to achieve a certain effect.

The examples I've provided here are well supported across a variety of browsers and versions, though, as always, testing your code in different browsers is important. While there may be small inconsistencies or a lack of support for these techniques in older browsers, none of the solutions presented here should cause you any serious problems.

# How do I set my text to display in a certain font?

## Solution

Specify the typeface that your text will adopt using the `font-family` property, like so:

```
p {
  font-family: Verdana;
}
```

## Discussion

As well as specific fonts, such as Verdana or Times, CSS allows the specification of some more generic font families:

- `serif`
- `sans-serif`
- `monospace`
- `cursive`
- `fantasy`

When you specify fonts, it's important to remember that users are unlikely to have the fonts you have on your computer. If you define a font that the user lacks, your text will display according to their browsers' default fonts, regardless of what you'd have preferred.

To avoid this eventuality, you can simply specify generic font names and let users' systems decide which font to apply. For instance, if you want your document to appear in a sans-serif font such as Arial, you could use the following style rule:

```
p {
  font-family: sans-serif;
}
```

Now, you'll probably want to have more control than this over the way your site displays—and you can. It's possible to specify both font names and generic fonts in the same declaration block. Take, for example, the following style rule for the p element:

```
p {
   font-family: Verdana, Geneva, Arial, Helvetica, sans-serif;
}
```

Here, we've specified that if Verdana is installed on the system, it should be used; otherwise, the browser is instructed to see if Geneva is installed; failing that, the computer will look for Arial, then Helvetica. If none of these fonts are available, the browser will then use that system's default sans-serif font.

If a font family name contains spaces then it should be enclosed in quotation marks, like so:

```
p {
   font-family: "Courier New", "Andale Mono", monospace;
}
```

The generic font-family names should always be without quotes and should always appear last in the list.

Fonts that you can feel fairly confident to use are:

**Windows**  Arial, Lucida, Impact, Times New Roman, Courier New, Tahoma, Comic Sans, Verdana, Georgia, Garamond

**Mac**  Helvetica, Futura, Bodoni, Times, Palatino, Courier, Gill Sans, Geneva, Baskerville, Andale Mono

This list reveals the reason why we chose the fonts we specified in our style rule: we begin by specifying our first preference, a common Windows font (Verdana), then list a similar Mac font (Geneva). We then follow up with other fonts that would be usable if neither of these fonts were available.

# Should I use pixels, points, ems, or another unit identifier to set font sizes?

You can size text in CSS using the `font-size` property, like so:

```
font-size: 12px;
```

We've used pixel sizing here, but the `font-size` property can take a variety of other values. Before you can decide which to use, you'll need to know the relative merits of each option.

## Solution

### Sizing Fonts Using Units of Measurement

Table 2.1 identifies the units that you can use to size fonts.

### Table 2.1. Units available for setting font size

| Unit Identifier | Corresponding Units |
|-----------------|---------------------|
| pt | points |
| pc | picas |
| px | pixels |
| em | ems |
| ex | exes |
| % | percentages |

Let's look at each of these units in turn.

### Points and Picas

```
p {
  font-size: 10pt;
}
```

You should avoid using **points** and **picas** to style text for display on screen. This unit is an excellent way to set font sizes for print design, as the point measurement was created for that purpose. A point has a fixed size of 1/72nd of an inch, while a pica is one-sixth of an inch. A printed document whose fonts are specified using these units will appear exactly as you intended—after all, one-sixth of an inch is the same physical measurement whether you're printing on an A4 page or a billboard. However, computers are unable to accurately predict the physical size at which elements will appear on the monitor, so they guess—and guess badly—at the size of a point or pica, with results that vary between platforms.

If you're creating a print style sheet (as we do in "How do I create a print style sheet?" in Chapter 8) or a document that's intended for print—rather than on screen—viewing, points and picas are the units to use. However, a general rule of thumb indicates that we should avoid them when designing for the Web.

### Pixels

```
p {
  font-size: 12px;
}
```

Many designers like to set font sizes in **pixel measurements**, as this unit makes it easy to achieve consistent text displays across various browsers and platforms. However, pixel measurements ignore any preferences users may have set in their own browsers; furthermore, in the case of Internet Explorer, font sizes that the designer has dictated in pixels are unable to be resized by users. This limitation presents a serious accessibility problem for users who need to make text larger in order to read it clearly.

While pixels may seem like the easiest option for setting font sizes, pixel measurements should be avoided if another method can be used, particularly for large blocks of content. If you're creating a document for print or creating a print style sheet, you should avoid pixels entirely. Pixels have no meaning in the world of print and, like the application of points to the on-screen environment, when print applications are provided with a pixel measurement, they will simply try to guess the size at which the font should appear on paper—with erratic results.

### Ems

The **em** is a relative font measurement. The name *em* comes from the world of typography, where it relates to the size of the capital letter M, usually the widest character in a font. In CSS 1em is seen to be equal to the user's default font size, or the font size of the parent element when it is set to a value other than the default.

If you use ems (or any other relative unit) to set all your font sizes, users will be able to resize the text, which will comply with the text size preferences they have set in their browsers. As an example, let's create a declaration that sets the text within a p element to display at a size of 1em:

```
p {
  font-size: 1em;
}
```

A visitor who uses Internet Explorer 8, in which the text size is set to **Medium**, will see the paragraph shown in Figure 2.1 when he or she views the page.

Figure 2.1. Viewing the display when the font-size is set to 1em and text size is **Medium**

If the users have set the text size to **Largest**, the `1em` text will display as shown in Figure 2.2.

Figure 2.2. Viewing the display when the `font-size` is set to `1em` and text size is set to **Largest**

It's true that using ems to size text gives you less control over the way users view the document. However, this approach means that users who need a very large font size, for instance, can read your content—which, presumably, is the reason why you're publishing the text to the page.

Em values can be set using decimal numbers. For example, to display text at a size 10% smaller than the user's default (or the font size of its parent element), you could use this rule:

```
p {
  font-size: 0.9em;
}
```

To display the text 10% larger than the default or inherited size, you'd use this rule:

```
p {
  font-size: 1.1em;
}
```

## Exes

The **ex** is a relative unit measurement that corresponds to the height of the lowercase letter x in the default font size. In theory, if you set the font-size of a paragraph to 1ex, the uppercase letters in the text will display at the height at which the lowercase letter x would have appeared if the font size had been unspecified (and the lowercase letters will be sized relative to those uppercase letters).

Unfortunately, modern browsers are yet to support the typographical features needed to determine the precise size of an ex—they usually make a rough guess for this measurement. For this reason, exes are rarely used at the time of writing.

## Percentages

```
p {
  font-size: 100%;
}
```

As with ems and exes, font sizes that are set in **percentages** will honor users' text size settings and can be resized by the user. Setting the size of a p element to 100% will display your text at users' default font size settings (as will setting the font size to 1em). Decreasing the percentage will make the text smaller:

```
p {
  font-size: 90%;
}
```

Increasing the percentage will make the text larger:

```
p {
  font-size: 150%;
}
```

## Sizing Fonts Using Keywords

As an alternative to using numerical values to set text sizes, you can use absolute and relative keywords.

### Absolute Keywords

We can use any of seven absolute keywords to set text size in CSS:

- `xx-small`
- `x-small`
- `small`
- `medium`
- `large`
- `x-large`
- `xx-large`

These keywords are defined relative to each other, and browsers implement them in different ways. Most browsers display `medium` at the same size as unstyled text, with the other keywords resizing text accordingly, as indicated by their names to varying degrees.

These keyword measurements are considered absolute in that they don't inherit from any parent element. Yet, unlike the absolute values provided for height, such as pixels and points, they do allow the text to be resized in the browser, and will honor the user's browser settings. The main problem with using these keywords is consistency between browsers—`x-small`-sized text may be perfectly readable in one browser, and minuscule in another. Internet Explorer 6 in quirks mode, for example, treats `small` as being the same size as unstyled text. We discuss quirks mode in "What is quirks mode and how do I avoid it?" in Chapter 7.

### Relative Keywords

Text sized using relative keywords—`larger` and `smaller`—takes its size from the parent element in the same way that text sized with `em` and `%` does. Therefore, if you set the size of your `p` element to `small` using absolute keywords, and decide that you want emphasized text to display comparatively larger, you could add the following to the style sheet:

```
                                              chapter02/relative.css
p {
  font-size: small;
}
em {
  font-size: larger;
}
```

The following markup would display as shown in Figure 2.3, because the text between the <em> and </em> tags will display larger than its parent, the p element:

```
                                        chapter02/relative.html (excerpt)
<p>These <em>stuffed peppers</em> are lovely as a starter or as a
    side dish for a Chinese meal. They also go down well as part of
    a buffet, and even children seem to like them.</p>
```

These *stuffed peppers* are lovely as a starter or as a side dish for a Chinese meal. They also go down well as part of a buffet, and even children seem to like them.

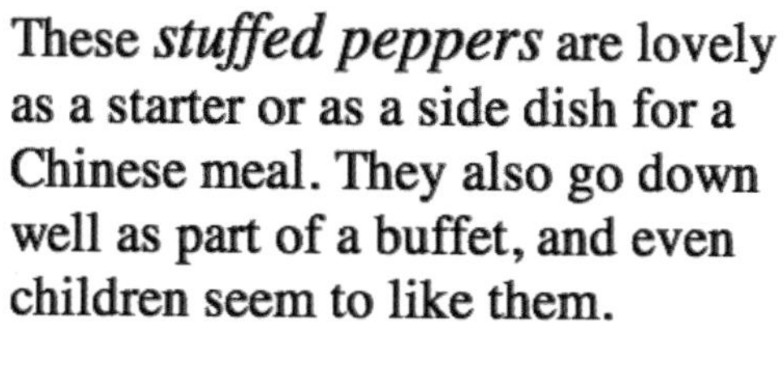

Figure 2.3. The emphasized text displaying larger than its containing paragraph

## Discussion

When you're deciding which method of text sizing to use, it's best to select one that allows all users to resize the text and ensures that the text complies with the settings users have chosen within their browsers. Relative font sizing works well as long as you're careful of the way the elements inherit sizing. However, in order to achieve even a basic level of accessibility, enabling users to set fonts to a comfortable level is necessary.

Designing your layout with resizable text in mind also allows you to avoid an issue that's often seen in browsers that do allow the resizing of pixels, on pages where designers have assumed that setting font sizes in pixels will allow them to fix the heights of containers, or place text on top of a fixed-height image. This approach will work in Internet Explorer, which doesn't resize text whose size is set in pixels; it may, however, result in a complete mess of overflowing text in Firefox (versions prior to 3 or version 3 with **Zoom** set to **zoom text only**), where the heights of boxes containing text is always unknown.

## Relative Sizing and Inheritance

When you use any kind of relative sizing, remember that the element you're considering will inherit its starting size from its parent element, then adjust its size accordingly. Be careful, though, when using a relative font size for the parent element as well—this can become problematic in complex layouts where the parent element is less obvious. Consider the following markup:

chapter02/nesting.html *(excerpt)*

```html
<div>
  <p>
    You'll <em>probably</em> be surprised when using
    <a href="#">a relative <code>font-size</code></a>
    and nested elements.
  </p>
</div>
```

Let's say we wanted to set the `font-size` of the above text to 130% of the default size, and we made the mistake of setting it like so:

chapter02/nesting.css *(excerpt)*

```css
div, p, em, a, code {
  font-size: 130%;
}
```

The effect of the above style rule is to the make the `font-size` of the nested elements progressively bigger—130% of the `font-size` of the parent element, which is already 130% of the `font-size` of *its* parent and so on, as demonstrated in Figure 2.4.

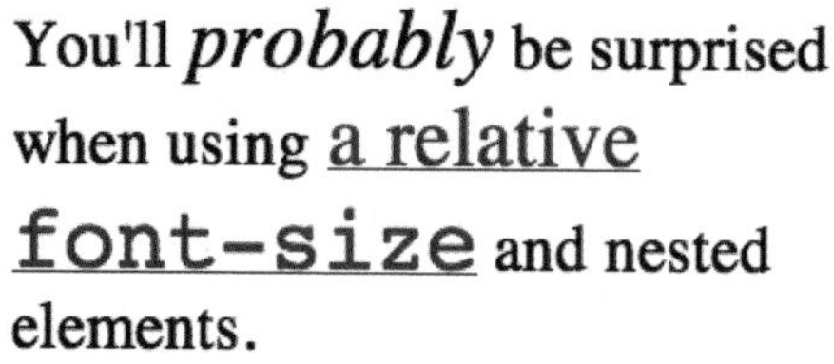

You'll *probably* be surprised when using <u>a relative</u> `font-size` and nested elements.

Figure 2.4. Using relative font sizing within nested elements

# How do I remove underlines from my links?

The widely accepted default visual indicator that text on a web page links to another document is that it's underlined and displays in a different color from the rest of the text. However, there may be instances in which you want to remove that underline.

## Solution

We use the `text-decoration` property to remove the underlines from link text. By default, the browser will set the `text-decoration` property of all `a` elements to underline. To remove the underline, simply set the `text-decoration` property for the link to none:

```
text-decoration: none;
```

The CSS used to create the effect shown in Figure 2.5 is as follows:

**chapter02/textdecoration.css**

```
a:link, a:visited {
  text-decoration: none;
}
```

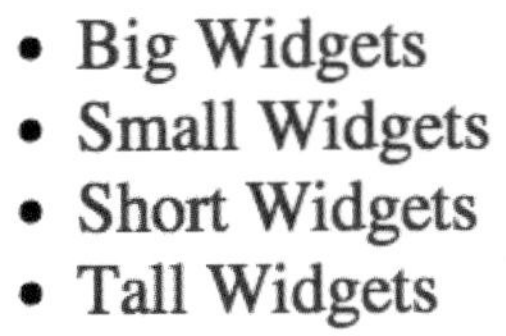

- Big Widgets
- Small Widgets
- Short Widgets
- Tall Widgets

Figure 2.5. Using `text-decoration` to create links without an underline

# Discussion

In addition to `underline` and `none`, there are other values for `text-decoration` that you can try out:

- `overline`
- `line-through`
- `blink`

It is possible to combine these values. For instance, should you wish to have an underline and overline on a particular link—as illustrated in Figure 2.6—you'd use the following style rule:

```
                                                          chapter02/textdecoration2.css
a:link, a:visited {
  text-decoration: underline overline;
}
```

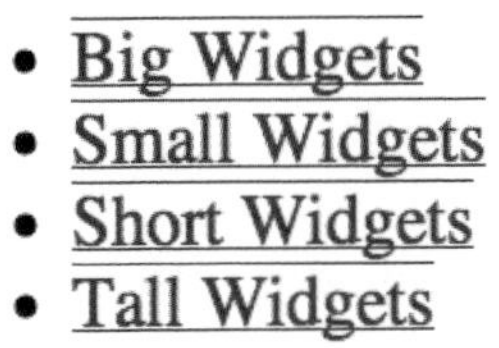

- Big Widgets
- Small Widgets
- Short Widgets
- Tall Widgets

Figure 2.6. Combining `text-decoration` values to create links with underlines and overlines

### Avoid Applying Misleading Lines

You can use the `text-decoration` property to apply underlines to any text, even if it's standard unlinked text, but be wary of doing this. The underlining of links is such a widely accepted convention that users are inclined to think that *any* underlined text is a link to another document.

### When is removing underlines a bad idea?

Underlining links is a standard convention followed by all web browsers and, consequently, users expect to see links underlined. Removing the underline from links that appear within text can make it very difficult for people to realize that these words are in fact links, rather than just highlighted text. I'd advise against removing the underlines from links within text. There are other ways in which you can style links so that they look attractive, and removing the underline is rarely, if ever, necessary.

Links that are used as part of a menu, or appear in some other situation in which the text is quite obviously a link—for instance, where the text is styled with CSS to resemble a graphical button—are a different story. If you wish, you can remove the underline from these kinds of links, because it should be obvious from their context that they're links.

# How do I create a link that changes color when the cursor moves over it?

One attractive link effect changes the color of a link, or otherwise alters its appearance when the cursor is moved across it. This effect can be applied to great advantage on navigation menus created with CSS, but it can also be used on links within regular paragraph text.

## Solution

To create this effect, we need to style the `:hover` and `:active` dynamic pseudo-classes of the anchor element differently from its other pseudo-classes.

Let's look at an example. Here's a typical style rule that applies the same declarations to all of an anchor element's pseudo-classes:

**chapter02/textdecoration3.css**

```
a:link, a:visited, a:hover, a:active {
  text-decoration: underline;
  color: #6A5ACD;
  background-color: transparent;
}
```

When this style sheet is applied, our links will display in the blue color #6A5ACD with an underline, as shown in Figure 2.7.

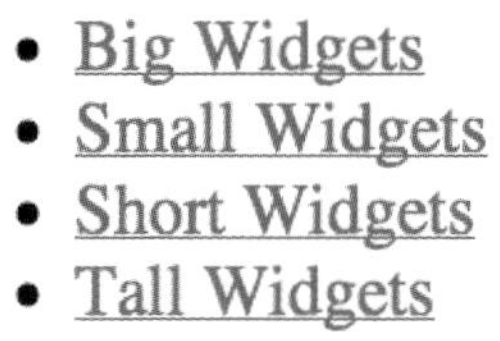

- <u>Big Widgets</u>
- <u>Small Widgets</u>
- <u>Short Widgets</u>
- <u>Tall Widgets</u>

Figure 2.7. Using the same declaration for all of the links' pseudo-classes

To style our `:hover` and `:active` pseudo-classes differently, we need to remove them from the declaration with the other pseudo-classes and give them their own separate declaration. In the CSS below, I decided to apply an overline in addition to the underline. I've also set a background color and made the link's text a darker color; Figure 2.8 shows how these styles display in a browser:

**chapter02/textdecoration4.css**

```
a:link, a:visited {
  text-decoration: underline;
  color: #6A5ACD;
  background-color: transparent;
}
a:hover, a:active {
  text-decoration: underline overline;
  color: #191970;
  background-color: #C9C3ED;
}
```

As you've probably realized, you can style the anchor's other pseudo-classes separately, too. In particular, you might like to apply a different style to links that users have visited. To do so, you'd simply style the :visited pseudo-class separately.

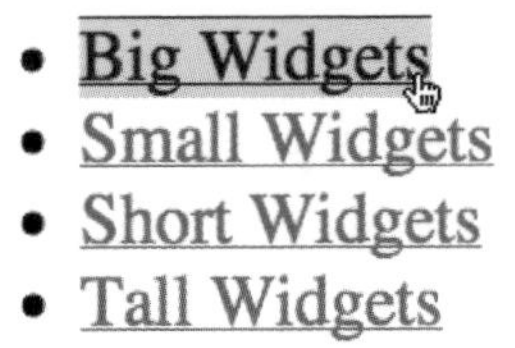

- <u>Big Widgets</u>
- <u>Small Widgets</u>
- <u>Short Widgets</u>
- <u>Tall Widgets</u>

Figure 2.8. Moving the cursor over a link to which a hover style is applied

When styling pseudo-classes, take care that you leave the size or weight (or boldness) of the text unchanged. Otherwise, you'll find that your page appears to jiggle, as the surrounding content has to move to make way for the larger text to display when your cursor hovers over the link.

### Ordering Pseudo-class Declarations

The anchor pseudo-classes should be declared in the following order: :link, :visited, :hover, :active. Otherwise, you may find that they work differently to how you intended. One way to remember this order is the mnemonic: LoVeHAte.

# How do I display two different styles of link on one page?

The previous solution explained how to style the different selectors of the anchor element, but what if you want to use different link styles within the same document? Perhaps you want to display links without underlines in your navigation menu, yet make sure that links within the body content are easily identifiable. Or maybe part of your document has a dark background color, so you need to use a light-colored link style there.

# Solution

To demonstrate how to create multiple styles for links displayed on one page, let's take an example in which we've already styled the regular links:

chapter02/linktypes.css *(excerpt)*

```css
a:link, a:visited {
  text-decoration: underline;
  color: #6A5ACD;
  background-color: transparent;
}

a:hover, a:active {
  text-decoration: underline overline;
  color: #191970;
  background-color: #C9C3ED;
}
```

These should be taken as the default link styles—they reflect the way links will normally be styled within your documents. The first rule makes the link blue, so if an area of our page has a blue background, the links that appear in that space will be unreadable. We need to create a second set of styles for links in that area.

First, let's create a `class` or an `id` for the element that will contain the differently colored links. If the container is already styled with CSS, it may already have a `class` or `id` that we can use. Suppose that our document contains the following markup:

chapter02/linktypes.html *(excerpt)*

```html
<div class="boxout">
  <p>Visit our <a href="store.html">online store</a>, for all your
    widget needs.</p>
</div>
```

We need to create a style rule that affects any link appearing within an element of class boxout:

chapter02/linktypes.css *(excerpt)*

```
.boxout {
  color: #FFFFFF;
  background-color: #6A5ACD;
}
.boxout a:link, .boxout a:visited {
  text-decoration: underline;
  color: #E4E2F6;
  background-color: transparent;
}
.boxout a:hover, .boxout a:active {
  background-color: #C9C3ED;
  color: #191970;
}
```

As you can see in Figure 2.9, this rule will display all links in the document as per the first style *except* those that appear within the div element with the class boxout—these links will be displayed in the lighter color.

Visit our online store, for all your widget needs.

- Big Widgets
- Small Widgets
- Short Widgets
- Tall Widgets

Figure 2.9. Using two different link styles in one document

# How do I style the first item in a list differently from the others?

Frequently, designers find that we need to style the first of a set of items—be they list items or a number of paragraphs within a container—differently from the rest of the set. One way to achieve this would be to assign a `class` to the first item, and style that class differently from other items; however, there's a more elegant way to create this effect in modern browsers using the pseudo-class selector `first-child`.

## Solution

Here's a simple list of items marked up as an unordered list:

chapter02/firstchild.html *(excerpt)*

```
<ul>
  <li>Brie</li>
  <li>Cheddar</li>
  <li>Red Leicester</li>
  <li>Shropshire Blue</li>
</ul>
```

### Using `first-child`

To change the color of the first item in the list without affecting its neighbors, we can use the `first-child` selector. This allows us to target the first element within the `ul` element, as shown in Figure 2.10:

chapter02/firstchild.css *(excerpt)*

```
li:first-child {
  color: red;
}
```

- Brie
- **Cheddar**
- **Red Leicester**
- **Shropshire Blue**

Figure 2.10. Displaying the first list item in red text

Unfortunately `:first-child` is unsupported by Internet Explorer 6. So, if you still need to fully support it, until the number of visitors using this browser to view your site becomes negligible, you'll need to find another method to create this effect. One such method is to use a class selector.

## Using a Class Selector

To create this effect in IE6, we add a `class` or `id` attribute to the element that we wish to style differently. For this example, let's use a `class`:

chapter02/firstchildwithclass.html *(excerpt)*

```
<ul>
  <li class="unusual">Brie</li>
  <li>Cheddar</li>
  <li>Red Leicester</li>
  <li>Shropshire Blue</li>
</ul>
```

Once this in place, we create a style rule to implement the desired effect:

chapter02/firstchildwithclass.css *(excerpt)*

```
li.unusual {
  color: red;
}
```

# How do I add a background color to a heading?

CSS allows us to add a background color to any element, including a heading.

## Solution

Below, I've created a CSS rule for all the level-one headings in a document:

chapter02/headingcolor.css *(excerpt)*

```
h1 {
  background-color: #ADD8E6;
  color: #256579;
```

```
    font: 1.6em Verdana, Geneva, Arial, Helvetica, sans-serif;
    padding: 0.2em;
}
```

The result is shown in Figure 2.11.

## Chinese-style stuffed peppers

**These stuffed peppers are lovely as a starter or as a side dish for a Chinese meal. They also go down well as part of a buffet and even children seem to like them.**

Figure 2.11. Displaying a heading with a background color

**Make Way for Color!**

When you add a background to a heading, you may also want to adjust the padding so that there's space between the heading text and the edge of the colored area, as I've done in this example.

# How do I style headings with underlines?

## Solution

There are two ways in which you can add an underline to your text. The simplest is to use the `text-decoration` property that we encountered earlier in this chapter in "How do I remove underlines from my links?". This method will allow you to apply to text an underline that's the same color as the text itself, as this code and Figure 2.12, show:

chapter02/headingunderline.css *(excerpt)*

```
h1 {
    font: 1.6em Verdana, Geneva, Arial, Helvetica, sans-serif;
    text-decoration: underline;
}
```

## Chinese-style stuffed peppers

These stuffed peppers are lovely as a starter or as a side dish for a Chinese meal. They also go down well as part of a buffet and even children seem to like them.

Figure 2.12. Adding an underline to a heading using `text-decoration`

You can also create an underline effect by adding a bottom border to the heading. This solution, which produces the result shown in Figure 2.13, is more flexible in that it allows you to separate the underline from the heading with the use of padding, and you can change the color of the underline so that it's different from that of the text.

A heading to which this effect is applied is also less likely to be confused with underlined link text than is a heading whose underline is created using the `text-decoration` property. However, this effect may display with slight inconsistencies in different browsers, so you'll need to test it to make sure the effect looks reasonable on the browsers your visitors may use. Here's the style rule you'll need:

**chapter02/headingunderline2.css**

```
h1 {
  font: 1.6em Verdana, Geneva, Arial, Helvetica, sans-serif;
  padding: 0.2em;
  border-bottom: 1px solid #AAAAAA;
}
```

## Chinese-style stuffed peppers

These stuffed peppers are lovely as a starter or as a side dish for a Chinese meal. They also go down well as part of a buffet and even children seem to like them.

Figure 2.13. Creating an underline effect using a bottom border

# How do I remove the large gap between an h1 element and the following paragraph?

By default, browsers render a gap between all heading and paragraph elements. The gap is produced by default top and bottom margins that browsers apply to these elements. The margin on the heading shown in Figure 2.14 reflects the default value. This gap can be removed using CSS.

## Chinese-style stuffed peppers

These stuffed peppers are lovely as a starter or as a side dish for a Chinese meal. They also go down well as part of a buffet and even children seem to like them.

Figure 2.14. The default heading and paragraph spacing

## Solution

To remove all space between a heading and the paragraph that follows it, you must remove the bottom margin from the heading as well as the top margin from the paragraph. In modern browsers—including Internet Explorer 7 and above—we can do this through CSS, using an **adjacent selector**. However, to achieve the same effect in older browsers, we need to revert to other techniques that are better supported.

### Using an Adjacent Selector

An adjacent selector lets you target an element that follows another element, as long as both share the same parent. In fact, you can use adjacent selectors to specify an element that follows several other elements, instead of just one; the element to which the style is applied is always the *last element in the chain*. If you're confused, be reassured that this concept will become a lot clearer once we've seen it in action.

The following style rules remove the top margin from any paragraph that immediately follows a level-one heading. Note that the top margin is actually removed from the paragraph that follows the h1—rather than the level-one heading itself:

chapter02/headingnospace.css *(excerpt)*

```css
h1 {
  font: 1.6em Verdana, Geneva, Arial, Helvetica, sans-serif;
  margin-bottom: 0;
}
h1+p {
  margin-top: 0;
}
```

Figure 2.15 shows the display of the original page once this rule is applied.

## Chinese-style stuffed peppers

These stuffed peppers are lovely as a starter or as a side dish for a Chinese meal. They also go down well as part of a buffet and even children seem to like them.

Figure 2.15. Using an adjacent selector to change the heading display

As you can see, the first paragraph that follows the h1 no longer has a top margin; all subsequent paragraphs, however, retain their top margins.

As I mentioned, adjacent selectors only work with newer browsers—for example, only Internet Explorer version 7 and above include support for the adjacent selector. In some cases, you might decide that it's acceptable for users of older browsers to see a gap between the heading and the text. Alternatively, you may want to remove the margins from the page that's seen by users of older browsers, and if that's what you're after, you have a couple of options.

You can make use of class selectors, as we did in "How do I display two different styles of link on one page?", to apply a margin of 0 to that class. If you've read that solution, you should find it fairly straightforward to implement this approach. Another option is to apply a negative margin to the heading, which I'll explain next.

**Applying a Negative Margin**

In CSS, margins can take either a positive or a negative value. Padding, however, can only take a positive value.

Applying a negative margin to the heading is another way to remove the space between the heading and the first paragraph. The style rule below produces a similar effect to the one we saw in Figure 2.15:

```
h1 {
    font: 1.6em Verdana, Geneva, Arial, Helvetica, sans-serif;
    margin-bottom: -0.6em;
}
```

# How do I highlight text on the page?

A common feature on many web sites is to highlight an important term on a page, such as identifying the search terms visitors have used to locate our web page through a search engine. It's easy to highlight text using CSS.

## Solution

If you wrap the text to be highlighted with <span> tags and add a class attribute, you can easily add a CSS rule for that class. For example, in the following paragraph, we've wrapped a phrase in <span> tags that apply the class hilite:

chapter02/hilite.html *(excerpt)*

```
<p>These <span class="hilite">stuffed peppers</span> are lovely
    as a starter or as a side dish for a Chinese meal. They also
    go down well as part of a buffet, and even children seem to
    like them.</p>
```

The style rule for the hilite class is shown below; the highlighted section will display as shown in Figure 2.16:

chapter02/hilite.css *(excerpt)*

```
.hilite {
  background-color: #FFFFCC;
  color: #B22222;
}
```

# Chinese-style stuffed peppers

**These stuffed peppers are lovely as a starter or as a side dish for a Chinese meal. They also go down well as part of a buffet and even children seem to like them.**

Figure 2.16. Highlighting text with CSS

# How do I alter the line height (leading) on my text?

One of the great advantages that CSS had over earlier web design methods like <font> tags is that it gave you far more control over the way text looks on the page. In this solution, we'll alter the leading of the text in your document.

## Solution

If the default spacing between the lines of text on your page looks a little narrow, you can change it with the line-height property:

chapter02/leading.css

```
p {
  font: 1em Verdana, Geneva, Arial, Helvetica, sans-serif;
  line-height: 2.0;
}
```

The result is shown in Figure 2.17.

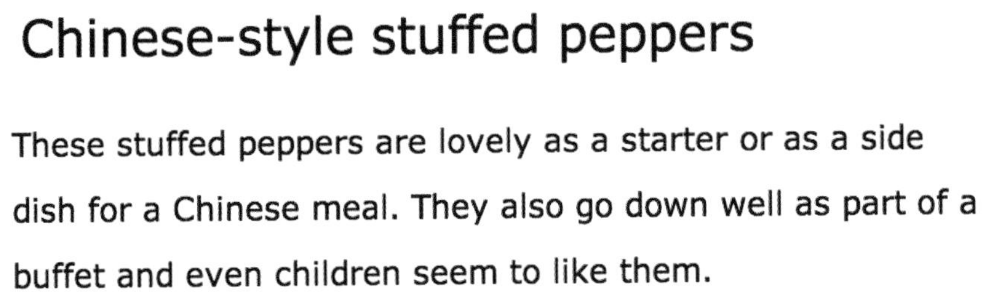

## Chinese-style stuffed peppers

These stuffed peppers are lovely as a starter or as a side dish for a Chinese meal. They also go down well as part of a buffet and even children seem to like them.

Figure 2.17. Altering leading using the `line-height` property

Easy! Just be careful to avoid spacing the text out so much that it becomes difficult to read.

### No Units?

You'll notice that we stopped short of specifying any unit of measurement in this example—the value of 2.0 is a ratio. You *can* specify a value for `line-height` using standard CSS units of measurement, such as ems or pixels, but doing so breaks the link between the line height and the font size for child elements.

For instance, if the example above contained a `span` that set a large `font-size`, the line height would scale up proportionally and maintain the same ratio, because the `line-height` of the paragraph was set to the numerical value `2.0`. If, however, the `line-height` was set to `2em` or `200%`, the `span` would inherit the actual line height instead of the ratio, and the large font size would have no effect on the line height of the span. Depending on the effect you're going for, this may actually be a desirable result.

# How do I justify text?

When you justify text, you alter the spacing between the words so that both the right and left margins are straight. You can create this effect easily using CSS.

## Solution

You can justify paragraph text with the help of the `text-align` property, like so:

```
                                              chapter02/justify.css
p {
  text-align: justify;
  font: 1em Verdana, Geneva, Arial, Helvetica, sans-serif;
  line-height: 2.0;
}
```

Figure 2.18 shows the effect of setting text-align to justify.

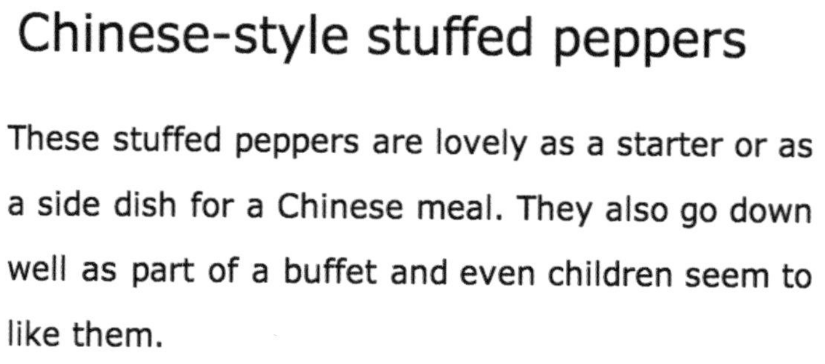

## Chinese-style stuffed peppers

These stuffed peppers are lovely as a starter or as a side dish for a Chinese meal. They also go down well as part of a buffet and even children seem to like them.

Figure 2.18. Justifying text using text-align

## Discussion

The other values for text-align are:

right    aligns the text to the right of the container
left     aligns the text to the left of the container
center   centers the text in the container

# How do I style a horizontal rule?

For markup generally, you should avoid including elements that are purely presentational, such as the horizontal rule (hr). A document that is structured semantically is easier to maintain, loads faster, and is optimized for search engine indexing. Applying borders to existing elements can usually achieve a similar effect produced by the hr element.

However, there are occasions when using an `hr` is either the best way to achieve the desired effect, or is necessary to serve unstyled content to an older browser that fails to support CSS.

## Solution

You can change the color, height, and width of a horizontal rule with CSS. However, you'll need to watch out for some inconsistencies between browsers. For instance, in the example below I've used the same values for `color` and `background-color`; that's because Gecko-based browsers like Firefox color the rule using `background-color`, while Internet Explorer uses `color`:

chapter02/hrstyle.css *(excerpt)*

```
hr {
  border: none;
  background-color: #256579;
  color: #256579;
  height: 2px;
  width: 80%;
}
```

The result of this rule can be seen in Figure 2.19.

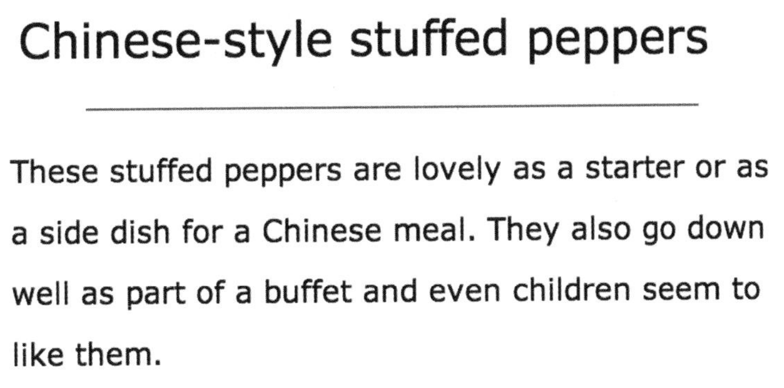

# Chinese-style stuffed peppers

These stuffed peppers are lovely as a starter or as a side dish for a Chinese meal. They also go down well as part of a buffet and even children seem to like them.

Figure 2.19. Changing the color, height, and width of a horizontal rule

# How do I indent text?

## Solution

To indent text, we apply a rule to its container that sets a `padding-left` value, like this:

```html
<h1>Chinese-style stuffed peppers</h1>
<p class="indent">These stuffed peppers …</p>
```

```css
.indent {
  padding-left: 1.5em;
}
```

You can see the indented paragraph in Figure 2.20.

## Chinese-style stuffed peppers

These stuffed peppers are lovely as a starter or as a side dish for a Chinese meal. They also go down well as part of a buffet and even children seem to like them.

Figure 2.20. Indenting text using CSS

## Discussion

You should avoid using the HTML tag `<blockquote>` to indent text, unless the text is actually a quote. This bad habit was a technique encouraged in the past by visual editing environments such as Dreamweaver. If you're currently using an editor that uses `<blockquote>` tags to indent text, then—apart from switching editors— you should resist the temptation to use it for this purpose; instead, set up a CSS rule to indent the appropriate blocks as shown above.

The <blockquote> tag is designed to mark up a quote, and devices such as screen readers used by visually impaired users will read this text in a way that helps them understand that what they're hearing is a quote. If you use <blockquote> to indent regular paragraphs, it will be very confusing for users who hear the content read as a quote.

 **A One-liner**

A related technique enables us to indent just the first line of each paragraph. Simply apply the CSS property text-indent to the paragraph—or to a class that's applied to the paragraphs—that you wish to display in this way:

chapter02/indent2.css

```
p {
    text-indent: 1.5em;
}
```

# How do I center text?

## Solution

You can center text, or any other element, using the text-align property with a value of center:

chapter02/center.html *(excerpt)*

```
<h1>Chinese-style stuffed peppers</h1>
<p class="centered">These stuffed peppers …</p>
```

chapter02/center.css *(excerpt)*

```
.centered {
  text-align: center;
}
```

The result of this rule can be seen in Figure 2.21.

# Chinese-style stuffed peppers

These stuffed peppers are lovely as a starter or
as a side dish for a Chinese meal. They also go
down well as part of a buffet and even children
seem to like them.

Figure 2.21. Centering text using `text-align`

# How do I change text to all capitals using CSS?

## Solution

You can change text to all capitals, and perform other transformations, using the
`text-transform` property:

**chapter02/uppercase.html** *(excerpt)*

```html
<h1>Chinese-style stuffed peppers</h1>
<p class="transform">These stuffed peppers are lovely …</p>
```

**chapter02/uppercase.css** *(excerpt)*

```css
.transform {
  text-transform: uppercase;
}
```

Note the uppercase text in Figure 2.22.

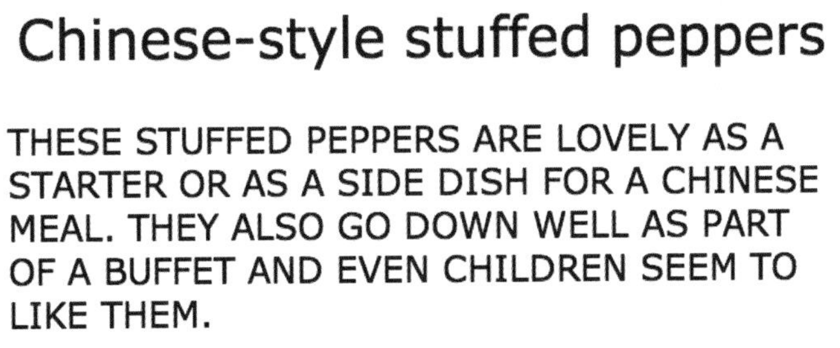

# Chinese-style stuffed peppers

THESE STUFFED PEPPERS ARE LOVELY AS A
STARTER OR AS A SIDE DISH FOR A CHINESE
MEAL. THEY ALSO GO DOWN WELL AS PART
OF A BUFFET AND EVEN CHILDREN SEEM TO
LIKE THEM.

Figure 2.22. Using `text-transform` to display the text in uppercase letters

## Discussion

The `text-transform` property has other useful values. The value `capitalize` will capitalize the first letter of each word, as illustrated in Figure 2.23:

chapter02/capitalize.css *(excerpt)*

```css
.transform {
  text-transform: capitalize;
}
```

The other values that the `text-transform` property can take are:

- `lowercase`
- `none` (the default)

# Chinese-style stuffed peppers

These Stuffed Peppers Are Lovely As A Starter
Or As A Side Dish For A Chinese Meal. They
Also Go Down Well As Part Of A Buffet And
Even Children Seem To Like Them.

Figure 2.23. Applying `text-transform` to capitalize the first letter of every word

# How do I change or remove the bullets on list items?

## Solution

You can change the style of bullets displayed on an unordered list by altering the `list-style-type` property. First, here's the markup for the list:

*chapter02/listtype.html (excerpt)*

```
<ul>
  <li>list item one</li>
  <li>list item two</li>
  <li>list item three</li>
</ul>
```

To display square bullets, like the ones shown in Figure 2.24, set the `list-style-type` property to `square`:

*chapter02/listtype.css*

```
ul {
  list-style-type: square;
}
```

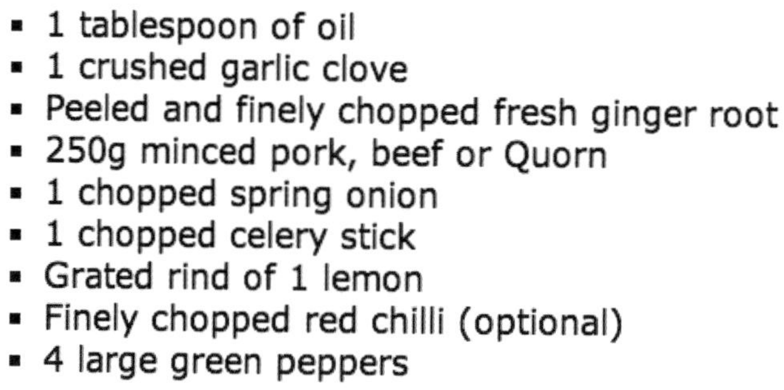

- 1 tablespoon of oil
- 1 crushed garlic clove
- Peeled and finely chopped fresh ginger root
- 250g minced pork, beef or Quorn
- 1 chopped spring onion
- 1 chopped celery stick
- Grated rind of 1 lemon
- Finely chopped red chilli (optional)
- 4 large green peppers

Figure 2.24. Using square bullets for list items

# Discussion

Some of the other values that the `list-style-type` property can take are `disc`, `circle`, `decimal-leading-zero`, `decimal`, `lower-roman`, `upper-roman`, `lower-alpha`, `upper-alpha`, and `none`.

You'll find that some of these values are unsupported by certain browsers; those browsers that lack support for a particular bullet type will display the default type instead. You can see the different types, and check the support your browser provides for them, at the CSS Test Suite for `list-style-type`.[1] Setting `list-style-type` to none will remove bullets from the display, although the list will still be indented as if the bullets were there, as Figure 2.25 shows:

```
ul {
   list-style-type: none;
}
```

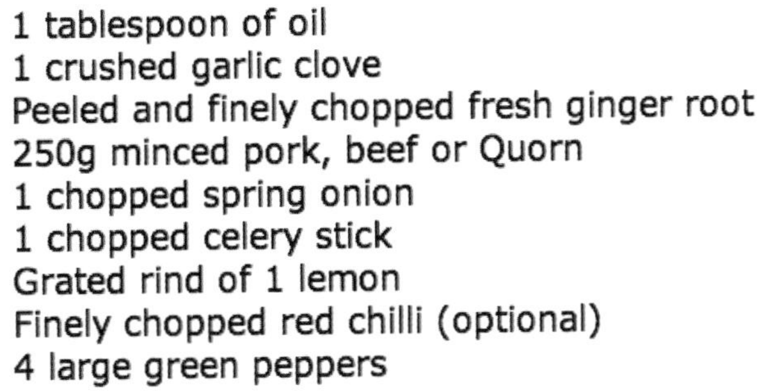

1 tablespoon of oil
1 crushed garlic clove
Peeled and finely chopped fresh ginger root
250g minced pork, beef or Quorn
1 chopped spring onion
1 chopped celery stick
Grated rind of 1 lemon
Finely chopped red chilli (optional)
4 large green peppers

Figure 2.25. Displaying a list without bullets

---

[1] http://www.meyerweb.com/eric/css/tests/css2/sec12-06-02a.htm

# How do I use an image for a list-item bullet?

## Solution

To use an image for a bullet, create your image, then use the `list-style-image` property, instead of `list-style-type` to set your bullets. This property accepts a URL, which can incorporate the path to your image file as a value:

**chapter02/listimage.css**

```
ul {
  list-style-image: url(bullet.gif);
}
```

Figure 2.26 shows how this effect can be used to spruce up a list.

✓ 1 tablespoon of oil
✓ 1 crushed garlic clove
✓ Peeled and finely chopped fresh ginger root
✓ 250g minced pork, beef or Quorn
✓ 1 chopped spring onion
✓ 1 chopped celery stick
✓ Grated rind of 1 lemon
✓ Finely chopped red chilli (optional)
✓ 4 large green peppers

Figure 2.26. Using an image as a list bullet

### Setting Bullets on Individual List Items

The `list-style-image` property actually applies to the list item (`li`) elements in the list. However, if you apply `list-style-image` to the list as a whole (the `ul` or `ol` element), each individual list item will inherit it. You do, however, have the option of setting the property on individual list items (by assigning a `class` or `id` to each), giving individual items their own unique bullet images.

# How do I remove the indented left-hand margin from a list?

If you've set `list-style-type` to `none`, you may also wish to remove or decrease the default left-hand margin that the browser sets on a list.

## Solution

To remove the indentation entirely and have your list left-aligned so that it lines up with, for example, a preceding paragraph as shown in Figure 2.27, use a style rule similar to this:

chapter02/listnomargin.css

```
ul {
  list-style-type: none;
  padding-left: 0;
  margin-left: 0;
}
```

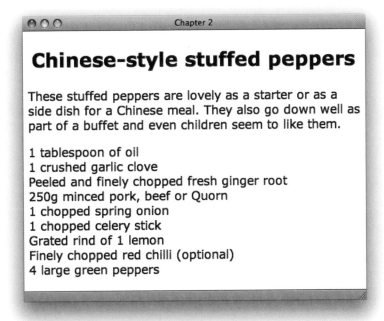

Figure 2.27. A list without indentation or bullets

## Discussion

You can apply new indentation values to the list items if you wish. To indent the content by a few pixels, try this:

chapter02/listsmallmargin.css

```
ul {
  list-style-type: none;
  padding-left: 5px;
  margin-left: 0;
}
```

# How do I display a list horizontally?

By default, list items display as block elements; therefore, each new item will display on a new line. However, there may be times when some content on your page is, structurally speaking, a list, even though you'd prefer to display it in a different way—a collection of navigation links is a good example. How can you display these list items horizontally?

## Solution

You can set a list to display horizontally by altering the `display` property of the `li` element to `inline`, like so:

chapter02/listinline.html *(excerpt)*

```
<ul class="horiz">
  <li><a href="#">Big Widgets</a></li>
  <li><a href="#">Small Widgets</a></li>
  <li><a href="#">Short Widgets</a></li>
  <li><a href="#">Tall Widgets</a></li>
</ul>
```

chapter02/listinline.css

```
ul.horiz li {
  display: inline;
}
```

The result of this style rule is depicted in Figure 2.28.

Big Widgets Small Widgets Short Widgets Tall Widgets

Figure 2.28. Displaying a list horizontally

# How do I remove page margins?

The default styles of most browsers add margin or padding between the browser chrome and the page content; this is so that text in an unstyled page stops short of the edge of the browser window. You'll probably want to remove this gap or dictate the size of it, rather than leave it up to the browser.

## Solution

To remove all margin and padding around your content use the following style rules, which have been defined for the body element:

```
body {
  margin: 0;
  padding: 0;
}
```

The result is shown in Figure 2.29.

Figure 2.29. Removing the default margins and padding from the page body

# How can I remove browsers' default padding and margins from all elements?

The display that you see in a browser when you view an unstyled document is the result of the browser's internal style sheet. Often, the differences that arise in the way various browsers display an unstyled page occur because those browsers have slightly different internal style sheets.

## Solution

One way to solve this problem is to remove the default margins and padding from all elements before you create your styles.

The following rule will set the padding and margins on *all* elements to zero. It will have the effect of causing every element on the page—paragraphs, headings, lists, and more—to display without leaving any space between itself and its neighbors, as Figure 2.30 demonstrates:

chapter02/zeropagemargin.css *(excerpt)*

```
* {
  margin: 0;
  padding: 0
}
```

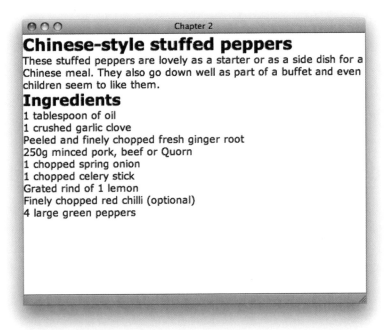

Figure 2.30. Removing the default margins and padding from all elements on a page

## Discussion

This style rule uses the universal selector—*—to remove the margins and padding from *everything*, a technique known as **performing a global whitespace reset.**[2] If

---

[2] http://leftjustified.net/journal/2004/10/19/global-ws-reset/

you're working on a particularly complex design, this may well be the best way to start.

However, once you've done it, you'll need to go back and add margins and padding to every element that you use. This is particularly important for some form elements, which may be rendered unusable by this style rule!

For simpler designs, removing the whitespace from every element is usually overkill, and will simply generate more work; you'll need to go back and add padding and margins to elements such as paragraphs, blockquotes, and lists. A viable alternative is to remove the margins and padding from a select set of elements only. The following style rule shows how this works, removing whitespace from heading and list elements:

```
h1, h2, h3, h4, h5, h6, ul, ol {
    margin: 0;
    padding: 0;
}
```

# How do I add comments to my CSS file?

You can, and should, add comments to your CSS file, though for very simple files with just a few rules for text styling purposes—for instance—they may be unnecessary. However, once you start to use a large number of style rules and multiple style sheets on a site, comments come in very handy! Without them, you can spend a lot of time hunting around for the right classes, pondering which class does what, and trying to find the style sheet in which it lives.

## Solution

CSS supports comments split over multiple lines, just like JavaScript. So, to comment out an area, use the following sequence of characters:

```
/*
  : Many useful comments in here…
*/
```

At the very least, you should add a comment at the top of each style sheet to explain what's in that style sheet, like so:

```
/* This is the default style sheet for all text on the site */
```

## Summary

This chapter has covered some of the more common questions asked by those who are relatively new to CSS—questions that relate to styling and manipulating text on the page. By combining these techniques, you can create attractive effects that will degrade appropriately for browsers that fail to support CSS.

# CSS and Images

The Web is filled with sites featuring beautiful, rich graphic design that take advantage of the power of CSS. To work with images in CSS requires just a few simple skills—once you've learned them, they can be combined to create countless interesting effects. The solutions in this chapter demonstrate the basic concepts of working with images while answering some common questions. We'll be using images more in the other chapters, but, as with most of the solutions in this book, feel free to experiment to see what unique effects you can create.

## How do I add borders to images?

Photographic images, which might be used to illustrate an article or be displayed in a photo album, look neat when they're bordered with a thin line. However, it's a time-consuming process to open each image in a graphics program in order to add borders, and if you ever need to change that border's color or thickness, you'll be required to go through the same arduous process all over again. Fortunately, CSS makes this chore a whole lot easier.

## Solution

Adding a border to an image is a simple procedure using CSS. There are two images in the document displayed in Figure 3.1.

Figure 3.1. Displaying images in a web browser

The following rule adds a single black border to our images:

```
img {
  border-width: 1px;
  border-style: solid;
  border-color: #000000;
}
```

The rule could also be written in shortened form, like this:

**chapter03/borderbasic.css** *(excerpt)*

```
img {
  border: 1px solid #000000;
}
```

Figure 3.2 shows the effect this rule has on the images.

Figure 3.2. Applying a CSS border to make the images look neater

Now, this is all well and good, but your layout probably contains other images to which you *don't* want to apply a permanent black border. The solution is to create a CSS class for the border and apply it to selected images as required:

chapter03/borderclass.css *(excerpt)*

```
.imgborder {
  border: 1px solid #000000;
}
```

chapter03/borderclass.html *(excerpt)*

```
<img src="food1.jpg" alt="food preparation" class="imgborder" />
```

If you're displaying a selection of images—such as a photograph album—on the page, you could set borders on all the images within a particular container, such as an unordered list that has a unique ID:

chapter03/borderalbum.css *(excerpt)*

```
#album img {
  border: 1px solid #000000;
}
```

```
<ul id="album">
  <li><img src="food1.jpg" alt="food preparation" /></li>
  <li><img src="food2.jpg" alt="food preparation" /></li>
</ul>
```

This approach will save you from having to add the class to each individual image within the container.

# How do I use CSS to remove the blue border around my navigation images?

If you use images in your site's navigation links you may notice an ugly blue border, just like the underline on text-based links. So how do you remove it using CSS?

## Solution

Just as you can create a border, so you can remove one. Adding a rule with the border property set to none will remove those borders:

```
img {
  border: none;
}
```

# How do I set a background image for my page using CSS?

The CSS background-image property applied to the body element can be used to set a background image for a web page.

## Solution

This style rule adds the image **background-norepeat.jpg** as a background to any page to which this style sheet is attached:

chapter03/backgrounds.css *(excerpt)*

```
body {
  font: 0.9em Verdana, Geneva, Arial, Helvetica, sans-serif;
  background-color: #D2D7E4;
  color: #000000;
  background-image: url(background-norepeat.jpg);
  background-repeat: no-repeat;
}
```

The effects of this style are shown in Figure 3.3.

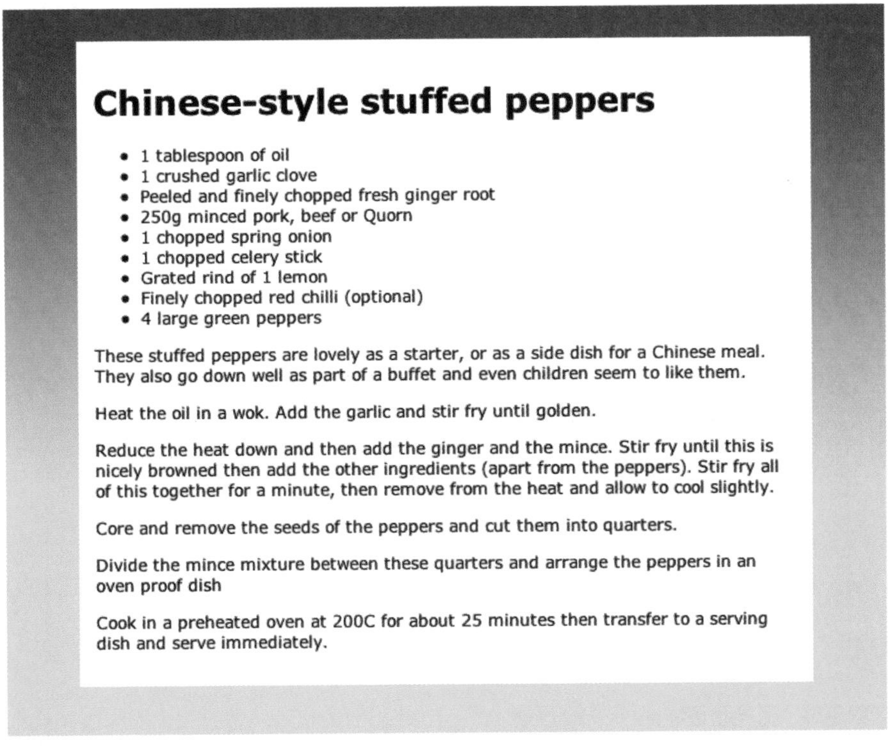

## Chinese-style stuffed peppers

- 1 tablespoon of oil
- 1 crushed garlic clove
- Peeled and finely chopped fresh ginger root
- 250g minced pork, beef or Quorn
- 1 chopped spring onion
- 1 chopped celery stick
- Grated rind of 1 lemon
- Finely chopped red chilli (optional)
- 4 large green peppers

These stuffed peppers are lovely as a starter, or as a side dish for a Chinese meal. They also go down well as part of a buffet and even children seem to like them.

Heat the oil in a wok. Add the garlic and stir fry until golden.

Reduce the heat down and then add the ginger and the mince. Stir fry until this is nicely browned then add the other ingredients (apart from the peppers). Stir fry all of this together for a minute, then remove from the heat and allow to cool slightly.

Core and remove the seeds of the peppers and cut them into quarters.

Divide the mince mixture between these quarters and arrange the peppers in an oven proof dish

Cook in a preheated oven at 200C for about 25 minutes then transfer to a serving dish and serve immediately.

Figure 3.3. Displaying an image as a background image

# Discussion

The CSS property background-image enables you to specify within the style sheet the location of a background image. To apply a background to the entire document, we'd set this property for the body element, but, as we'll see in a solution later in this chapter, a background image can be applied to any element on the page.

By default, the background will tile, repeating both vertically and horizontally to fill the space required for the content. The effect shown in Figure 3.3 was achieved using the image in Figure 3.4, with the background property set to no-repeat.

# How do I control how my background image repeats?

By default, the background will tile, repeating both vertically and horizontally to fill the space required for the content. However, the background-repeat property can be used to control this behavior.

## Solution

The effect shown in Figure 3.3 above was achieved using the image in Figure 3.4, with the background-repeat property set to no-repeat.

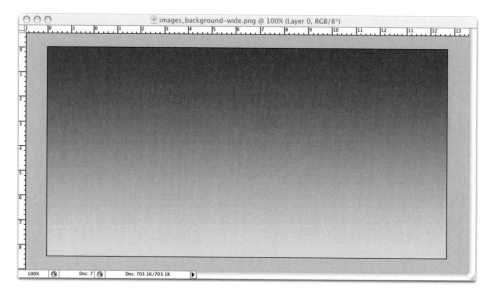

Figure 3.4. Creating a background effect using a rather wide image set to no-repeat

The image is only 400 pixels tall—shorter than a typical web page—so I've given the page a background color that's the same as the bottom row of pixels in the gradient image. In this way, the gradient merges seamlessly into the background color.

There is a better way to achieve this effect, though—using a smaller and faster-loading background image. All we need to do is take a thin slice of our gradient image, like the one shown in Figure 3.5.

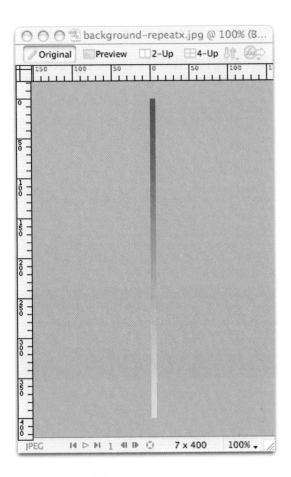

Figure 3.5. A slice of the larger background image

By setting the background-repeat property for this new image to repeat-x, we can achieve exactly the same visual effect that we saw in the first example while using a much smaller image file. Again, we specify a background color that matches the bottom of the gradient image, to ensure that the gradient effect covers the whole of the area exposed in the user's browser.

If the gradient ran from left to right, rather than from top to bottom, we could use the same approach to create the background—we'd simply need to rotate the effect by 90 degrees. Taking a horizontal slice of the image and setting the `background-repeat` to `repeat-y` causes our gradient to repeat *down* the page, as Figure 3.6 shows.

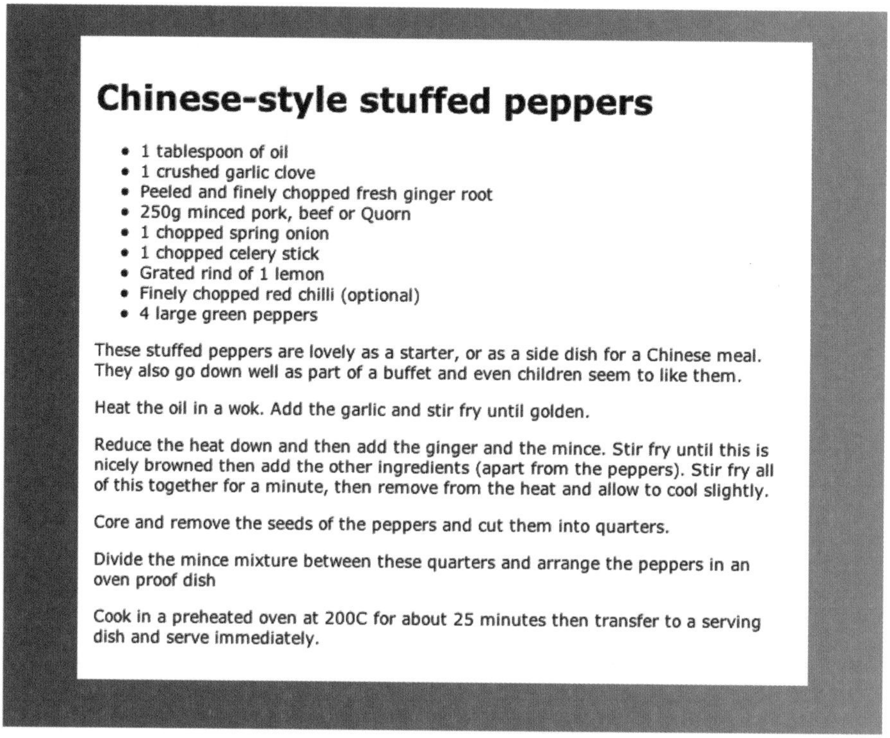

## Chinese-style stuffed peppers

- 1 tablespoon of oil
- 1 crushed garlic clove
- Peeled and finely chopped fresh ginger root
- 250g minced pork, beef or Quorn
- 1 chopped spring onion
- 1 chopped celery stick
- Grated rind of 1 lemon
- Finely chopped red chilli (optional)
- 4 large green peppers

These stuffed peppers are lovely as a starter, or as a side dish for a Chinese meal. They also go down well as part of a buffet and even children seem to like them.

Heat the oil in a wok. Add the garlic and stir fry until golden.

Reduce the heat down and then add the ginger and the mince. Stir fry until this is nicely browned then add the other ingredients (apart from the peppers). Stir fry all of this together for a minute, then remove from the heat and allow to cool slightly.

Core and remove the seeds of the peppers and cut them into quarters.

Divide the mince mixture between these quarters and arrange the peppers in an oven proof dish

Cook in a preheated oven at 200C for about 25 minutes then transfer to a serving dish and serve immediately.

Figure 3.6. A gradient image set to `repeat-y`

# How do I position my background image?

By default, if you add a single, non-repeating background image to the page, it will appear in the top-left corner of the viewport. If you've set the background to tile in any direction, the first image will appear at that location and will tile from that point. However, it's also possible to display the image at other locations on the page.

## Solution

We use the CSS property `background-position` to position the image on the page:

chapter03/backgroundposition.css *(excerpt)*

```
#content {
  margin: 2em 4em 2em 4em;
  background-color: #FFFFFF;
  padding: 1em 1em 40px 1em;
  background-image: url(tick.gif);
  background-repeat: no-repeat;
  background-position: bottom right;
}
```

The above style rule will display a tick graphic at the bottom right of the white content area, as shown in Figure 3.7. To prevent the text in this container from overlapping the image, I've applied some padding to the container.

## Discussion

The `background-position` property can take as its value keywords, percentage values, or values in units, such as pixels.

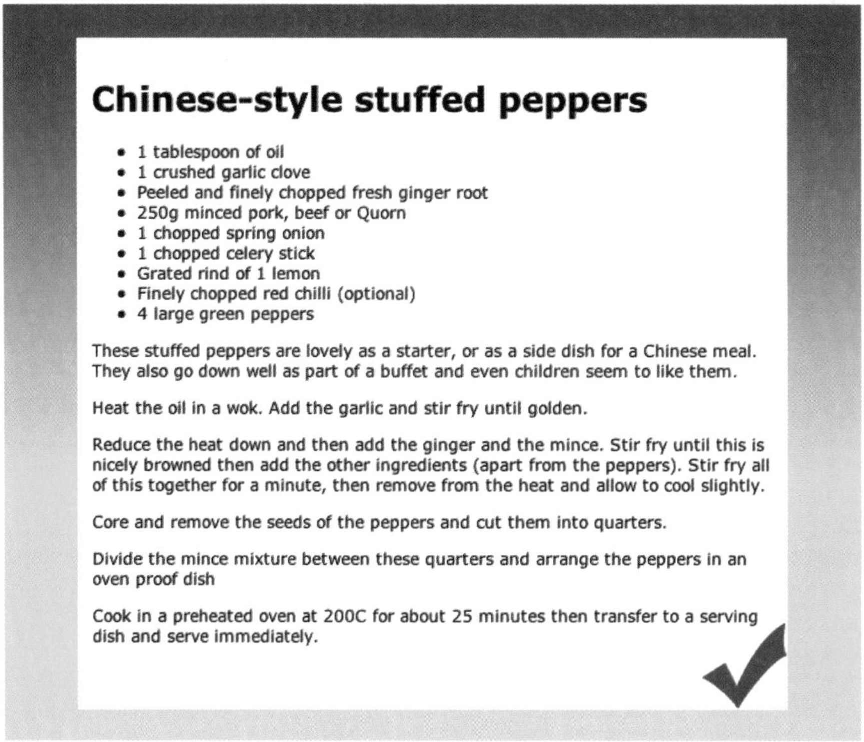

Figure 3.7. Using the background-position property to position the image

## Keywords

In the example above, we used keywords to specify that the background image should be displayed at the bottom right of the content div:

**chapter03/backgroundposition.css** *(excerpt)*

```
background-position: bottom right;
```

You can use any of these keyword combinations:

- top left
- top center
- top right
- center left
- center center

- center right
- bottom left
- bottom center
- bottom right

If you only specify one of the values, the other will default to `center`:

```
background-position: top;
```

So, the style declaration above is the same as:

```
background-position: top center;
```

## Percentage Values

To achieve more accurate image placement, you can specify the values as percentages. This approach is particularly useful in a layout where other page elements are specified in percentages, so that they resize in accordance with the user's screen resolution and dimensions (this is also referred to as a *liquid* layout, as we'll see in Chapter 9):

```
background-position: 30% 80%;
```

The first of the percentages included here refers to the background's horizontal position; the second dictates its vertical position. Percentages are taken from the top-left corner of the display, with `0% 0%` placing the top-left corner of the image against the top-left corner of the browser window, and `100% 100%` placing the bottom-right corner of the image against the bottom-right corner of the window.

As with keywords, a default percentage value comes into play if you only specify one value. That default is `50%`. Take a look at the following declaration:

```
background-position: 30%;
```

The above style declaration creates the same effect as:

```
background-position: 30% 50%;
```

### Unit Values

You can set positioning values using any CSS units, such as pixels or ems:

```
background-position: 20px 20px;
```

As with percentages, the first of the specified values dictates the horizontal position, while the second dictates the vertical. But unlike percentages, the measurements directly control the position of the top-left corner of the background image.

You can mix units with percentages and, if you only specify one value, the second will default to 50%.

# How do I fix my background image in place when the page is scrolled?

You've probably seen sites on which the background image stays static while the content scrolls over it. This effect is achieved using the background-attachment property.

## Solution

We can use the background-attachment property with a value of fixed to fix the background so that it remains stationary while the content moves:

chapter03/backgroundfixed.html *(excerpt)*

```
body {
  font: 0.9em Verdana, Geneva, Arial, Helvetica, sans-serif;
  background-color: #D2D7E4;
  color: #000000;
  background-image: url(background-repeatx.jpg);
  background-repeat: repeat-x;
  background-attachment: fixed;
}
```

This is illustrated in Figure 3.8.

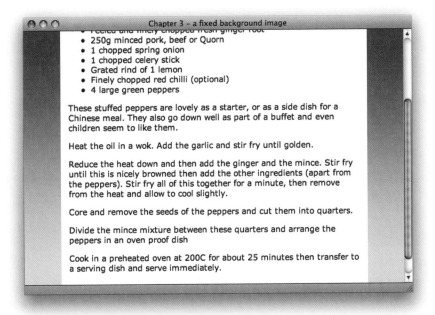

Figure 3.8. A fixed background image stays put when scrolling the content

# Discussion

In this solution, we're using several CSS properties to add our image to the background, position it, and dictate how it behaves when the document is scrolled.

Alternatively, we could use a shorthand method to supply this information—the CSS background property. This property allows you to declare background-color, background-image, background-repeat, background-attachment, and background-position in a single property declaration. Take, for example, the CSS rule shown below:

chapter03/backgroundfixed.css *(excerpt)*

```css
body {
  background-color: #D2D7E4;
  background-image: url(background-repeatx.jpg);
  background-repeat: repeat-x;
```

```
    background-attachment: fixed;
    background-position: 0 0;
}
```

These declarations could be written more succinctly as follows:

```
body {
    background: #D2D7E4 url(background-repeatx.jpg) repeat-x fixed 0 0;
}
```

A final note on background-attachment: fixed. As is often the case with CSS styles, support for this declaration is limited among the Internet Explorer family. From version 7, Internet Explorer implements it correctly, unlike earlier versions of the browser. Though workarounds involving JavaScript are available, they may be more trouble than they're worth.[1] By default, users of older versions of Internet Explorer that lack support for background-attachment: fixed will see a scrolling background image—an outcome that's generally considered an acceptable compromise (and may even entice these users to upgrade their browsers).

# Can I set a background image on any element?

In this chapter, we've already looked at setting background images for the document and for the main content area of the page. However, background images can be used on other elements, too.

## Solution

This style rule creates the effect that displays on the Ingredients box in the recipe featured in Figure 3.9:

chapter03/backgrounds2.css *(excerpt)*

```
#smallbox {
    background-image: url(boxbg.gif);
    background-repeat: repeat-x;
```

---

[1] http://www.howtocreate.co.uk/fixedBackground.html

```
  float: left;
  margin-right: 20px;
  width: 220px;
  border:1px solid #D2D7E4;
}
```

The gradient background on the Ingredients box (shown in Figure 3.9) uses a very similar background image to what I used for the body text's background, except that the Ingredients box coloring graduates from light blue to white. I've also added a border that's the same color as the darkest part of the gradient.

### Chinese-style stuffed peppers

- 1 tablespoon of oil
- 1 crushed garlic clove
- Peeled and finely chopped fresh ginger root
- 250g minced pork, beef or Quorn
- 1 chopped spring onion
- 1 chopped celery stick
- Grated rind of 1 lemon
- Finely chopped red chilli (optional)
- 4 large green peppers

These stuffed peppers are lovely as a starter, or as a side dish for a Chinese meal. They also go down well as part of a buffet and even children seem to like them.

Heat the oil in a wok. Add the garlic and stir fry until golden.

Reduce the heat down and then add the ginger and the mince. Stir fry until this is nicely browned then add the other ingredients (apart from the peppers). Stir fry all of this together for a minute, then remove from the heat and allow to cool slightly.

Core and remove the seeds of the peppers and cut them into quarters.

Divide the mince mixture between these quarters and arrange the peppers in an oven proof dish

Cook in a preheated oven at 200C for about 25 minutes then transfer to a serving dish and serve immediately.

Back to the main menu

Figure 3.9. Using a background image to create a gradient behind the Ingredients box

# Discussion

Background images can be applied to any page element, including headings, as Figure 3.10 shows. You can see I've used a repeated image to display a dotted border beneath the heading. The image is positioned at the bottom left of the heading, and I've given the heading six pixels of bottom padding so that the text avoids appearing as if it's sitting on top of the background image:

chapter03/backgrounds2.html *(excerpt)*

```
<h1>Chinese-style stuffed peppers</h1>
```

chapter03/backgrounds2.css *(excerpt)*

```
h1 {
  background-image: url(dotty.gif);
  background-repeat: repeat-x;
  background-position: bottom left;
  padding: 0 0 6px 0;
  color: #41667F;
  font-size: 160%;
  font-weight: normal;
  background-color: transparent;
}
```

You can even apply backgrounds to links, enabling you the ability to create some interesting effects, as Figure 3.11 shows:

chapter03/backgrounds2.css *(excerpt)*

```
a:link, a:visited {
  color: #41667F;
  background-color: transparent;
  padding-right: 10px;
}
a:hover {
  background-image: url(arrow.gif);
  text-decoration: none;
  background-position: center right;
  background-repeat: no-repeat;
}
```

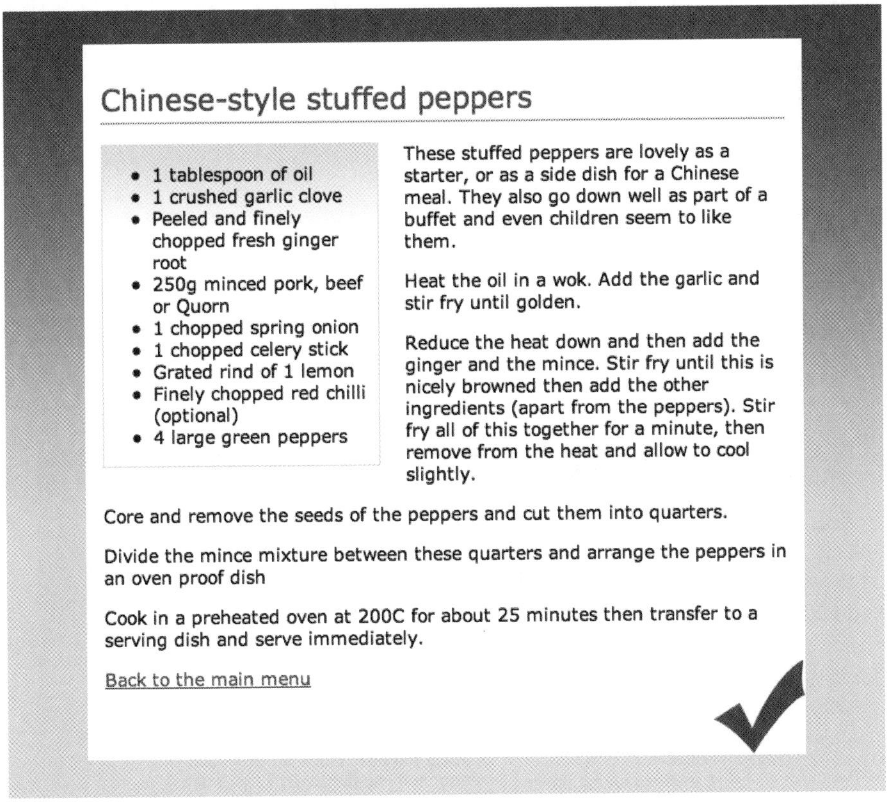

## Chinese-style stuffed peppers

- 1 tablespoon of oil
- 1 crushed garlic clove
- Peeled and finely chopped fresh ginger root
- 250g minced pork, beef or Quorn
- 1 chopped spring onion
- 1 chopped celery stick
- Grated rind of 1 lemon
- Finely chopped red chilli (optional)
- 4 large green peppers

These stuffed peppers are lovely as a starter, or as a side dish for a Chinese meal. They also go down well as part of a buffet and even children seem to like them.

Heat the oil in a wok. Add the garlic and stir fry until golden.

Reduce the heat down and then add the ginger and the mince. Stir fry until this is nicely browned then add the other ingredients (apart from the peppers). Stir fry all of this together for a minute, then remove from the heat and allow to cool slightly.

Core and remove the seeds of the peppers and cut them into quarters.

Divide the mince mixture between these quarters and arrange the peppers in an oven proof dish

Cook in a preheated oven at 200C for about 25 minutes then transfer to a serving dish and serve immediately.

Back to the main menu

Figure 3.10. Applying a background image to the heading to create an underline

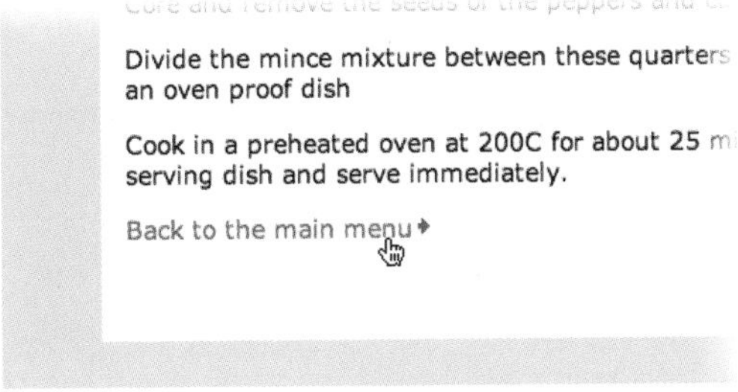

Core and remove the seeds of the peppers and ...

Divide the mince mixture between these quarters an oven proof dish

Cook in a preheated oven at 200C for about 25 m serving dish and serve immediately.

Back to the main menu ➔

Figure 3.11. Applying a background image to the link on hover

# How do I place text on top of an image?

In the bad old pre-CSS days, the only way to overlay text on an image was to add the text via your graphics program! CSS provides far better means to achieve this effect.

## Solution

The easiest way to layer text over of an image is to set the image as a background image. The image that appears beneath the heading on the Ingredients box in Figure 3.12 was added using the following style rule:

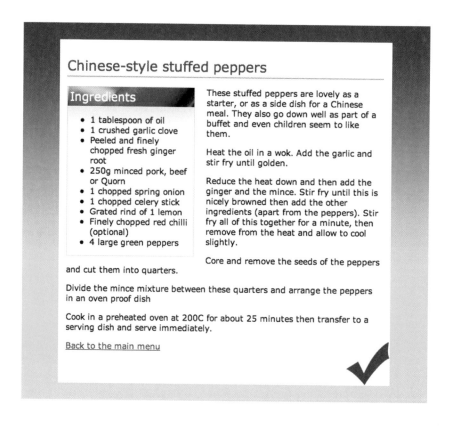

Figure 3.12. Applying a background image to the Ingredients box heading

chapter03/backgrounds3.css *(excerpt)*

```
#smallbox h2 {
  margin: 0;
  padding: 0.2em;
  background-image: url(boxheaderbg.jpg);
  background-repeat: no-repeat;
  color: #FFFFFF;
  background-color: red;
  font-size: 140%;
  font-weight: normal;
}
```

## Discussion

Using CSS to place text on top of an image offers many advantages distinct from simply adding text to the image through a graphics program.

First, it's harder to change text that's part of a graphic; to do so, you need to find the original graphic, re-edit it in a graphics program, and upload it again every time you want to change the text.

Second, text is far more accessible if it's included on the page as text content rather than as part of an image. Browsers that lack support for images will be able to read text that has been added using CSS, and such text can also be resized by the user. Including image text via CSS can also benefit your search engine rankings; though search engines are unable to index text that's part of an image, they can see regular text that has been placed on top of an image, and index it accordingly.

 **Check Your Contrast!**

If you're going to overlay a background image with light-colored text (as I've done in Figure 3.12), be sure also to give the area a dark background color. This way, the text will remain readable against the background if the user has disabled images in the browser, or is browsing on a connection over which the images are slow to load.

# How do I add more than one background image to my document?

Although it's detailed in the CSS2 specification, Apple's Safari browser is currently the only browser in which it's possible to apply more than one background image to your document. So, what should you do if you want to add two images to the document—for example, one that repeats, and one that stands alone?

## Solution

It's possible to give the effect of multiple background images by applying different backgrounds to various nested elements, such as the html and body elements:

chapter03/backgrounds4.css *(excerpt)*

```css
html {
  background-image: url(background-repeatx.jpg);
  background-repeat: repeat-x;
  background-color: #D2D7E4;
}

body {
  font: 0.9em Verdana, Geneva, Arial, Helvetica, sans-serif;
  color: #000000;
  background-image: url(recipes.gif);
  background-repeat: no-repeat;
  background-position: 98% 2%;
  margin: 0;
  padding: 46px 0 0 0;
}
```

The effects of these styles can be seen in Figure 3.13.

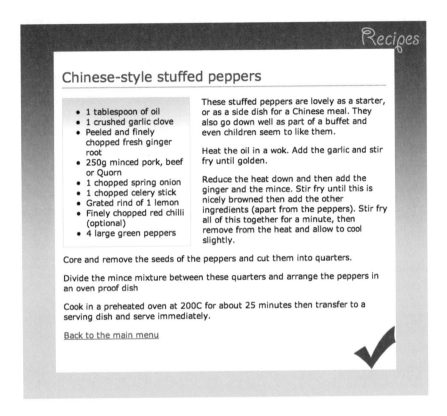

Figure 3.13. Applying background images to the html and body elements

# Discussion

This simple example can form the basis of more complex effects using multiple background images. As you've seen through the examples in this chapter, a background image can be applied to any element on the page. The careful and creative use of images in this way can achieve many interesting visual effects while maintaining the accessibility of the document (as the background images causes no interference with the document's structure).

Many of the entries in the CSS Zen Garden site rely on such careful use of background images to achieve their layouts.[2]

---

[2] http://www.csszengarden.com/

# How can I use transparency in my pages?

Achieving real transparency using images is possible with the PNG image format; by saving your images as a 24-bit PNG, you can achieve opacity and true transparency. While GIF images also support transparency, the format requires us to use a **matte**—a color that's similar to the background upon which the image will be placed—when we save a transparent GIF image.

This technicality means that creating a transparent GIF image that spans differently colored backgrounds is very difficult. It often involves chopping the image in two, saving each part separately, then reassembling the image pieces on the page—a process that reeks of old-school methods, and one we usually try to avoid in CSS-based layouts. Using the GIF format for an image that will scroll over a fixed background results in an ugly "halo effect." While the transparency is effective in Figure 3.14, upon scrolling, the undesirable halo effect is apparent.

Figure 3.14. The ugly "halo effect"

## Solution

The example in Figure 3.15 uses two PNG images. The first replaces the white background of #content with a ten-pixel PNG image. I developed this image in Photoshop by creating a new transparent image, then placing a solid white layer over the top of the transparent background. I then reduced the opacity of this layer to 40% and saved the file as a 24-bit PNG, giving it the name **opaque.png**.

The second image is a replacement for the background image **recipes.gif**; it's a 24-bit PNG with a transparent background. I'd like to fix the image in the top right of the viewport (using background-attachment: fixed), so that it remains in that location when the user scrolls the page. If I were to use a GIF image (with a dark blue as the matte), we'd see the halo effect mentioned above when the background moves and the image appears above the lighter page background.

Here's the CSS that creates the effect shown in Figure 3.15:

```
                                    chapter03/background5.css (excerpt)

body {
  font: 0.9em Verdana, Geneva, Arial, Helvetica, sans-serif;
  color: #000000;
  background-image: url(recipes.png);
  background-repeat: no-repeat;
  background-position:98% 2%;
  background-attachment:fixed;
  margin: 0;
  padding: 46px 0 0 0;
}

#content {
  margin: 0 4em 2em 4em;
  background-image: url(opaque.png);
  padding: 1em 50px 40px 1em;
}
```

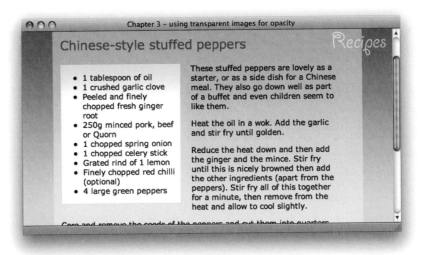

Figure 3.15. Displaying an opaque background without the halo effect on the Recipes image

# Discussion

PNG images can be used to create unique and attractive effects. Unfortunately Internet Explorer 6 lacks the level of support required to render transparent PNGs.

However, as long as you think through your layout carefully, it's often possible to include this kind of effect in your pages for visitors using other modern browsers, such as Firefox, Safari, Opera, and Internet Explorer version 7 and up. Another alternative is to use JavaScript to work around this limitation of Internet Explorer 6 and earlier. I'll outline a method for doing this in Chapter 7.

# Can I create more complex image borders, such as a double border?

If you want to display photographs to best effect then you may want to add more than the simple borders that we explored earlier in this chapter. We can combine background images and borders to create some stunning effects, all using CSS. Once again, this will save you needing to process images in Photoshop to add the border effects.

## Solution

In Figure 3.16 we have a photograph displayed as a feature element on a page, or as part of an album. The simplest double border effect combines adding a background color and some padding to our image; the color of the background becomes the first *border* and the actual border the second one:

chapter03/doubleborder.css *(excerpt)*

```
img.doubleborder {
  border: 1px solid #333;
  padding: 5px;
  background-color: #EEEEEE;
}
```

Figure 3.16. A simple double border effect using only CSS

We can create more complex effects by including a background image. The following CSS uses a small background tile repeated behind the photo to create the effect shown in Figure 3.17:

**chapter03/doubleborder-bg.css** *(excerpt)*

```
img.doubleborder {
  border: 5px solid #8E787B;
  padding: 20px;
  background-image: url(doubleborder-bg.gif);
}
```

Figure 3.17. A double border effect using a background image

## Discussion

Both of the above effects work by creating padding around the image. This creates space between the edge of the image and the border. The padding will be the color of the background or show the background image, and we can use this to create attractive double border effects without needing to wrap the image in another element.

# Summary

This chapter has explained the answers to some common image-related questions. We've concentrated mainly on background images, as these really are the building blocks with which we create image-rich design in CSS. Keeping images in the background enables you to more easily offer alternative style sheets and change the look of your pages, as well as to create interesting effects.

There will, of course, be image-related questions all through this book. In particular, Chapter 9 will explore the positioning of images along with other elements on the page, and the use of images in more complex layouts than the ones we've seen in this chapter.

# Navigation

Unless you limit yourself to one-page web sites, you'll need to design navigation. In fact, navigation is among the most important parts of any web design, and requires a great deal of thought if visitors are to move around your site easily.

Making site navigation easy is one area in which CSS really comes into its own. Older methods of creating navigation tended to rely on lots of images, nested tables, and JavaScript—all of which can seriously affect the usability and accessibility of a site. If your site cannot be navigated using a device that lacks JavaScript support, for example, you risk blocking users who have turned JavaScript off, as well as locking out text-only devices such as screen readers and search engine robots—they'll never penetrate past your home page to index the content of your site. If your design clients seem unconcerned about accessibility, tell them their clunky menu is stopping them from achieving a decent search engine ranking!

CSS allows you to create attractive navigation that, in reality, is no more than text—text that can be marked up in such a way as to ensure that it's both accessible and understandable by all those who are unable to physically see your design, but still want to access your content. In this chapter, we'll look at a variety of solutions for creating CSS-based navigation. Some are suited to implementation on an existing site, to make it load more quickly and boost its accessibility by replacing an old-fashioned, image-based navigation. Others are more suited to incorporation within a pure CSS layout.

# How do I style a structural list as a navigation menu?

Navigation is essentially a list of places to visit on your site, so marking up navigation menus as lists makes sense semantically and we can hook our CSS styles to the list elements themselves. However, we want to avoid our navigation looking like a standard bulleted list as rendered by the browser's internal style sheet.

## Solution

The navigation in Figure 4.1 is marked up as a list and styled using CSS, as you can see here.

Figure 4.1. Creating navigation by styling a list

Here's the markup required to create the navigation list:

```
                                          chapter04/listnav1.html
<!DOCTYPE html PUBLIC "-//W3C//DTD XHTML 1.0 Strict//EN"
    "http://www.w3.org/TR/xhtml1/DTD/xhtml1-strict.dtd">
<html xmlns="http://www.w3.org/1999/xhtml" lang="en-US">
  <head>
    <title>Lists as navigation</title>
    <meta http-equiv="content-type" content="text/html;
```

```
          charset=utf-8" />
    <link rel="stylesheet" type="text/css" href="listnav1.css" />
  </head>
  <body>
    <div id="navigation">
      <ul>
        <li><a href="#">Recipes</a></li>
        <li><a href="#">Contact Us</a></li>
        <li><a href="#">Articles</a></li>
        <li><a href="#">Buy Online</a></li>
      </ul>
    </div>
  </body>
</html>
```

Here's the complete CSS that transforms our dull unordered list into an attractive menu:

chapter04/listnav1.css

```css
#navigation {
  width: 200px;
}
#navigation ul {
  list-style: none;
  margin: 0;
  padding: 0;
}
#navigation li {
  border-bottom: 1px solid #ED9F9F;
}
#navigation li a:link, #navigation li a:visited  {
  font-size: 90%;
  display: block;
  padding: 0.4em 0 0.4em 0.5em;
  border-left: 12px solid #711515;
  border-right: 1px solid #711515;
  background-color: #B51032;
  color: #FFFFFF;
  text-decoration: none;
}
```

# Discussion

To create navigation based on an unordered list—first create your list, placing each navigation link inside a li element:

chapter04/listnav1.html *(excerpt)*

```
<ul>
  <li><a href="#">Recipes</a></li>
  <li><a href="#">Contact Us</a></li>
  <li><a href="#">Articles</a></li>
  <li><a href="#">Buy Online</a></li>
</ul>
```

Next, wrap the list in a div with an appropriate ID:

chapter04/listnav1.html *(excerpt)*

```
<div id="navigation">
  <ul>
    <li><a href="#">Recipes</a></li>
    <li><a href="#">Contact Us</a></li>
    <li><a href="#">Articles</a></li>
    <li><a href="#">Buy Online</a></li>
  </ul>
</div>
```

As Figure 4.2 shows, this markup looks fairly ordinary with the browser's default styles applied.

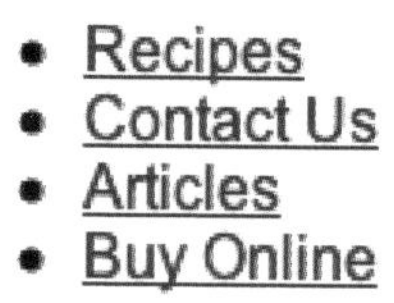

- Recipes
- Contact Us
- Articles
- Buy Online

Figure 4.2. A very basic, unstyled list

The first job we need to do is style the container in which the navigation sits—in this case, navigation:

```
                                          chapter04/listnav1.css (excerpt)

#navigation {
  width: 200px;
}
```

I've given `navigation` a width. If this navigation system were part of a CSS page layout, I'd probably add some positioning information to this ID as well.

Next, we style the list:

```
                                          chapter04/listnav1.css (excerpt)

#navigation ul {
  list-style: none;
  margin: 0;
  padding: 0;
}
```

As Figure 4.3 illustrates, the above rule removes list bullets and the indented margin that browsers apply, by default, when displaying a list.

<u>Recipes</u>
<u>Contact Us</u>
<u>Articles</u>
<u>Buy Online</u>

Figure 4.3. Viewing the list after indentation and bullets are removed

The next step is to style the `li` elements within `navigation`, to give them a bottom border:

```
                                          chapter04/listnav1.css (excerpt)

#navigation li {
  border-bottom: 1px solid #ED9F9F;
}
```

Finally, we style the link itself:

```
#navigation li a:link, #navigation li a:visited  {
  font-size: 90%;
  display: block;
  padding: 0.4em 0 0.4em 0.5em;
  border-left: 12px solid #711515;
  border-right: 1px solid #711515;
  background-color: #B51032;
  color: #FFFFFF;
  text-decoration: none;
}
```

Most of the work is done here, creating CSS rules to add left and right borders, removing the underline, and so on. The first property declaration in this rule sets the display property to block. This causes the link to display as a block element, meaning that the whole area of each navigation "button" is active when you move the cursor over it—the same effect you'd see if you used an image for the navigation.

# How do I use CSS to create rollover navigation without images or JavaScript?

Site navigation often features a **rollover effect**: when a user holds the cursor over a menu button, a new button image displays, creating a highlighting effect. To achieve this effect using image-based navigation, you need to use two images and JavaScript.

## Solution

Using CSS to build your navigation makes the creation of attractive rollover effects far simpler than it would be if you used images. The CSS rollover is created using the :hover pseudo-class selector—the same selector you'd use to style a hover state for your links.

Let's take the above list navigation example and add the following rule to create a rollover effect:

```
chapter04/listnav2.css (excerpt)
#navigation li a:hover {
  background-color: #711515;
  color: #FFFFFF;
}
```

Figure 4.4 shows what the menu looks like when the cursor is positioned over the first menu item.

Figure 4.4. The CSS navigation showing a rollover effect

## Discussion

The CSS we've used to create this effect is very simple. You can create hover states for heavily styled links just as you can for standard links. In this example, I simply changed the background color to make it the same as the left-hand border; however, you could alter the background, text, and border color to create interesting effects for the navigation.

**Hover Here? Hover There!**

In modern browsers, including Internet Explorer 7, you can apply the `:hover` pseudo-selector to *any* element you like, but in Internet Explorer 6 and below, you can apply it only to links.

Older versions of Internet Explorer allow only the anchor text to be made clickable, because the link fails to expand to fill its container (in this case, the list item). This means that the user is forced to click on the *text*, rather than the red background, to select the menu item.

One way to rectify this issue is to use a CSS hack that expands the width of the link—but only in Internet Explorer version 6 and earlier. Here's the rule that does just that:

```
* html #navigation li a {
  width: 100%;
}
```

Of course, you may decide that leaving the links as is and avoiding the hack is an acceptable compromise. We'll cover cross-browser techniques in more detail in Chapter 7.

# Can I use CSS and lists to create a navigation system with subnavigation?

The examples we've seen so far in this chapter have assumed that you only have one navigation level to display. Sometimes, more than one level is necessary—but is it possible to create multi-leveled navigation using styled lists in CSS?

## Solution

The perfect way to display subnavigation within a navigation system is to create a sublist within a list. The two levels of navigation will be easy to understand when they're marked up in this way—even in browsers that lack support for CSS.

To produce multilevel navigation, we can edit the example we saw in Figure 4.4, adding a nested list and styling the colors, borders, and link properties of the new list's items:

chapter04/listnav_sub.html

```
<!DOCTYPE html PUBLIC "-//W3C//DTD XHTML 1.0 Strict//EN"
    "http://www.w3.org/TR/xhtml1/DTD/xhtml1-strict.dtd">
<html xmlns="http://www.w3.org/1999/xhtml" lang="en-US">
<head>
<title>Lists as navigation</title>
<meta http-equiv="content-type"
    content="text/html; charset=utf-8" />
<link rel="stylesheet" type="text/css" href="listnav_sub.css" />
</head>
<body>
<div id="navigation">
  <ul>
    <li><a href="#">Recipes</a>
      <ul>
        <li><a href="#">Starters</a></li>
        <li><a href="#">Main Courses</a></li>
        <li><a href="#">Desserts</a></li>
      </ul>
    </li>
    <li><a href="#">Contact Us</a></li>
    <li><a href="#">Articles</a></li>
    <li><a href="#">Buy Online</a></li>
  </ul>
</div>
</body>
</html>
```

```
#navigation {
  width: 200px;
}
#navigation ul {
  list-style: none;
  margin: 0;
  padding: 0;
}
#navigation li {
  border-bottom: 1px solid #ED9F9F;
}
#navigation li a:link, #navigation li a:visited  {
  font-size: 90%;
  display: block;
  padding: 0.4em 0 0.4em 0.5em;
  border-left: 12px solid #711515;
  border-right: 1px solid #711515;
  background-color: #B51032;
  color: #FFFFFF;
  text-decoration: none;
}
#navigation li a:hover {
  background-color: #711515;
  color: #FFFFFF;
}
#navigation ul ul {
  margin-left: 12px;
}
#navigation ul ul li {
  border-bottom: 1px solid #711515;
  margin:0;
}
#navigation ul ul a:link, #navigation ul ul a:visited {
  background-color: #ED9F9F;
  color: #711515;
}
#navigation ul ul a:hover {
  background-color: #711515;
  color: #FFFFFF;
}
```

The result of these additions is shown in Figure 4.5.

Recipes
Starters
Main Courses
Desserts
Contact Us
Articles
Buy Online

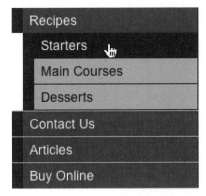

Figure 4.5. The CSS list navigation containing subnavigation

## Discussion

Nested lists are a perfect way to describe the navigation system that we're working with here. The first list contains the main sections of the site, while the sublist under **Recipes** shows the subsections within the **Recipes** category. Even without any CSS styling, the structure of the list is still clear and comprehensible, as you can see in Figure 4.6.

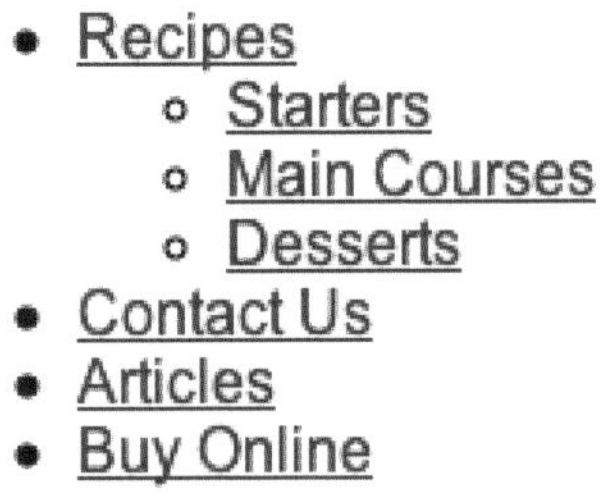

Recipes
Starters
Main Courses
Desserts
Contact Us
Articles
Buy Online

Figure 4.6. The navigation remaining logical without the CSS

The HTML that we use to mark up this list simply nests the sublist inside the `li` element of the appropriate main item:

```
                                          chapter04/listnav_sub.html
<div id="navigation">
  <ul>
    <li><a href="#">Recipes</a>
      <ul>
        <li><a href="#">Starters</a></li>
        <li><a href="#">Main Courses</a></li>
        <li><a href="#">Desserts</a></li>
      </ul>
    </li>
    <li><a href="#">Contact Us</a></li>
    <li><a href="#">Articles</a></li>
    <li><a href="#">Buy Online</a></li>
  </ul>
</div>
```

With this HTML, and without any changes to the CSS, the menu will display as shown in Figure 4.7 on the left, where the li elements inherit the styles of the main menu.

Let's add a style rule for the nested list to communicate visually that it's a submenu, distinct from the main navigation:

```
                                      chapter04/listnav_sub.css (excerpt)
#navigation ul ul {
  margin-left: 12px;
}
```

This rule will indent the nested list so that it's in line with the right edge of the border for the main menu, as demonstrated in Figure 4.7 on the right.

Figure 4.7. The sublist taking on the styles of the main navigation and the indented version

Let's add some simple styles to the `li` and `a` elements within the nested list to complete the effect:

```
                                          chapter04/listnav_sub.css (excerpt)

#navigation ul ul li {
  border-bottom: 1px solid #711515;
  margin: 0;
}
#navigation ul ul a:link, #navigation ul ul a:visited {
  background-color: #ED9F9F;
  color: #711515;
}
#navigation ul ul a:hover {
  background-color: #711515;
  color: #FFFFFF;
}
```

# How do I make a horizontal menu using CSS and lists?

All the examples we've seen in this chapter have dealt with vertical navigation—the kind of navigation that will most likely be found in a column to the left or right of a site's main content area. However, site navigation is also commonly found as a horizontal menu close to the top of the document.

# Solution

As Figure 4.8 shows, this type of menu can be created using styled lists in CSS. The li elements must be set to display inline to avoid that line break between list items.

Figure 4.8. Using CSS to create horizontal list navigation

Here's the HTML and CSS that creates this display:

```
                                        chapter04/listnav_horiz.html
<!DOCTYPE html PUBLIC "-//W3C//DTD XHTML 1.0 Strict//EN"
    "http://www.w3.org/TR/xhtml1/DTD/xhtml1-strict.dtd">
<html xmlns="http://www.w3.org/1999/xhtml" lang="en-US">
<head>
<title>Lists as navigation</title>
<meta http-equiv="content-type"
    content="text/html; charset=utf-8" />
<link rel="stylesheet" type="text/css" href="listnav_horiz.css" />
</head>
<body>
<div id="navigation">
  <ul>
    <li><a href="#">Recipes</a></li>
    <li><a href="#">Contact Us</a></li>
    <li><a href="#">Articles</a></li>
    <li><a href="#">Buy Online</a></li>
  </ul>
</div>
</body>
</html>
```

```
                                        chapter04/listnav_horiz.css
body {
  padding: 1em;
}
```

```
#navigation {
  font-size: 90%;
}
#navigation ul {
  list-style: none;
  margin: 0;
  padding: 0;
  padding-top: 1em;
}
#navigation li {
  display: inline;
}
#navigation a:link, #navigation a:visited {
  padding: 0.4em 1em 0.4em 1em;
  color: #FFFFFF;
  background-color: #B51032;
  text-decoration: none;
  border: 1px solid #711515;
}
#navigation a:hover {
  color: #FFFFFF;
  background-color: #711515;
}
```

## Discussion

To create the horizontal navigation, we start with a list that's identical to the one we created for our vertical list menu:

**chapter04/listnav_horiz.html** *(excerpt)*

```
<div id="navigation">
  <ul>
    <li><a href="#">Recipes</a></li>
    <li><a href="#">Contact Us</a></li>
    <li><a href="#">Articles</a></li>
    <li><a href="#">Buy Online</a></li>
  </ul>
</div>
```

We style the #navigation container to apply some basic font information, as we did with the vertical navigation. In a CSS layout, this ID would probably also contain some additional styles that determine the navigation's position on the page:

chapter04/listnav_horiz.css *(excerpt)*

```
#navigation {
  font-size: 90%;
}
```

In styling the ul element, we remove the list bullets and default indentation applied to the list by the browser:

chapter04/listnav_horiz.css *(excerpt)*

```
#navigation ul {
  list-style: none;
  margin: 0;
  padding: 0;
  padding-top: 1em;
}
```

The property that transforms our list from a vertical to a horizontal display is applied to the li element. After we set the display property to inline, the list looks like Figure 4.9:

chapter04/listnav_horiz.css *(excerpt)*

```
#navigation li {
  display: inline;
}
```

Recipes Contact Us Articles Buy Online

Figure 4.9. Displaying the list menu horizontally

All that's left for us to do is to style the links for our navigation:

chapter04/listnav_horiz.css *(excerpt)*

```
#navigation a:link, #navigation a:visited {
  padding: 0.4em 1em 0.4em 1em;
  color: #FFFFFF;
  background-color: #B51032;
  text-decoration: none;
  border: 1px solid #711515;
}
#navigation a:hover {
  color: #FFFFFF;
  background-color: #711515;
}
```

If you're creating boxes around each link—as I have here—remember that, in order to make more space between the text and the edge of its container, you'll need to add more left and right padding to the links. To create more space between the navigation items, add left and right margins to the links.

# How do I create button-like navigation using CSS?

Navigation that appears to be composed of clickable buttons is a feature of many web sites. This kind of navigation is often created using images to which effects are applied to make the edges look beveled and button-like. Often, some JavaScript code is used to swap in another image, so the button appears to depress when the user holds the cursor over it or clicks on the image.

This brings up the question: Is it possible to create such button-like navigation systems using only CSS? Absolutely!

## Solution

Creating a button effect like that shown in Figure 4.10 is possible, and fairly straightforward, using CSS. The effect's success hinges on your use of the CSS border properties.

Figure 4.10. Building button-like navigation with CSS

Here's the code you'll need:

chapter04/listnav_button.html

```
<!DOCTYPE html PUBLIC "-//W3C//DTD XHTML 1.0 Strict//EN"
    "http://www.w3.org/TR/xhtml1/DTD/xhtml1-strict.dtd">
<html xmlns="http://www.w3.org/1999/xhtml" lang="en-US">
<head>
<title>Lists as navigation</title>
<meta http-equiv="content-type"
    content="text/html; charset=utf-8" />
<link rel="stylesheet" type="text/css" href="listnav_button.css"
    />
</head>
<body>
<div id="navigation">
  <ul>
    <li><a href="#">Recipes</a></li>
    <li><a href="#">Contact Us</a></li>
    <li><a href="#">Articles</a></li>
    <li><a href="#">Buy Online</a></li>
  </ul>
</div>
</body>
</html>
```

chapter04/listnav_button.css

```
#navigation {
  font-size:90%
}
#navigation ul {
  list-style: none;
  margin: 0;
  padding: 0;
  padding-top: 1em;
```

```
}
#navigation li {
  display: inline;
}
#navigation a:link, #navigation a:visited {
  margin-right: 0.2em;
  padding: 0.2em 0.6em 0.2em 0.6em;
  color: #A62020;
  background-color: #FCE6EA;
  text-decoration: none;
  border-top: 1px solid #FFFFFF;
  border-left: 1px solid #FFFFFF;
  border-bottom: 1px solid #717171;
  border-right: 1px solid #717171;
}
#navigation a:hover {
  border-top: 1px solid #717171;
  border-left: 1px solid #717171;
  border-bottom: 1px solid #FFFFFF;
  border-right: 1px solid #FFFFFF;
}
```

## Discussion

To create this effect, we'll use the horizontal list navigation described in "How do I make a horizontal menu using CSS and lists?". However, to create the button look, we'll use different colored borders at the top and left than we use for the bottom and right sides of each button. By giving the top and left edges of the button a lighter colored border than we assign to the button's bottom and right edges, we create a slightly beveled effect:

chapter04/listnav_button.css *(excerpt)*

```
#navigation a:link, #navigation a:visited {
  margin-right: 0.2em;
  padding: 0.2em 0.6em 0.2em 0.6em;
  color: #A62020;
  background-color: #FCE6EA;
  text-decoration: none;
  border-top: 1px solid #FFFFFF;
  border-left: 1px solid #FFFFFF;
  border-bottom: 1px solid #717171;
  border-right: 1px solid #717171;
}
```

We reverse the border colors for the hover state, which creates the effect of the button being pressed:

chapter04/listnav_button.css *(excerpt)*

```
#navigation a:hover {
  border-top: 1px solid #717171;
  border-left: 1px solid #717171;
  border-bottom: 1px solid #FFFFFF;
  border-right: 1px solid #FFFFFF;
}
```

Try using heavier borders and changing the background images on the links, to create effects that suit your design.

# How do I create tabbed navigation with CSS?

Navigation that appears as tabs across the top of the page is a popular navigation choice. Many sites create tabs using images. However, this can be less accessible and also problematic if your navigation is created using a Content Management System, with users of that system being able to add tabs or change the text in the tabs. However, it's possible to create a tab effect by combining background images and text styled with CSS.

# Solution

The tabbed navigation shown in Figure 4.11 can be created by styling a horizontal list.

Figure 4.11. Using CSS to create tabbed navigation

Here's the HTML and CSS that creates this effect:

**chapter04/tabs.html**

```
<!DOCTYPE html PUBLIC "-//W3C//DTD XHTML 1.0 Strict//EN"
    "http://www.w3.org/TR/xhtml1/DTD/xhtml1-strict.dtd">
<html xmlns="http://www.w3.org/1999/xhtml" lang="en-US">
<head>
<title>Lists as navigation</title>
<meta http-equiv="content-type"
    content="text/html; charset=utf-8" />
<link rel="stylesheet" type="text/css" href="tabs.css" />
</head>
<body id="recipes">
<div id="header">
<ul>
  <li class="recipes"><a href="#">Recipes</a></li>
  <li class="contact"><a href="#">Contact Us</a></li>
  <li class="articles"><a href="#">Articles</a></li>
  <li class="buy"><a href="#">Buy Online</a></li>
</ul>
</div>
<div id="content">
<h1>Recipes</h1>
<p>Lorem ipsum dolor sit amet, … </p>
</div>
</body>
</html>
```

```css
body {
  font: .8em/1.8em verdana, arial, sans-serif;
  background-color: #FFFFFF;
  color: #000000;
  margin: 0 10% 0 10%;
}

#header {
  float: left;
  width: 100%;
  border-bottom: 1px solid #8DA5FF;
  margin-bottom: 2em;
}

#header ul {
  margin: 0;
  padding: 2em 0 0 0;
  list-style: none;
}

#header li {
  float: left;
  background-image: url("images/tab_left.gif");
  background-repeat: no-repeat;
  margin: 0 1px 0 0;
  padding: 0 0 0 8px;
}

#header a {
  float: left;
  display: block;
  background-image: url("images/tab_right.gif");
  background-repeat: no-repeat;
  background-position: right top;
  padding: 0.2em 10px 0.2em 0;
  text-decoration: none;
  font-weight: bold;
  color: #333366;
}

#recipes #header li.recipes,
#contact #header li.contact,
```

```
#articles #header li.articles,
#buy #header li.buy {
  background-image: url("images/tab_active_left.gif");
}

#recipes #header li.recipes a,
#contact #header li.contact a,
#articles #header li.articles a,
#buy #header li.buy a {
  background-image: url("images/tab_active_right.gif");
  background-color: transparent;
  color:#FFFFFF;
}
```

## Discussion

The tabbed navigation approach I've used here is a basic version of Douglas Bowman's Sliding Doors of CSS method, which is a tried and tested technique for creating a tabbed interface.[1] The structure that I've given to the navigation menu is the same kind of simple unordered list that we've worked with throughout this chapter, except that each list item is assigned a class attribute that describes the link it contains. We've also wrapped the entire list in a div with an id of header. The technique takes its name from the two images used to implement it—one overlaps the other, and the images slide apart as the text size increases.

You'll need four images to create this effect: two to create the regular tab color, and two to use when the tab is the currently selected (highlighted) tab. The images I've used in this example are shown in Figure 4.12. As you can see, they're far wider and taller than would generally be necessary for a tab—this provides plenty of space for the tab to *grow* if the user's browser is configured to display text at a very large size.

[1] http://www.alistapart.com/articles/slidingdoors/

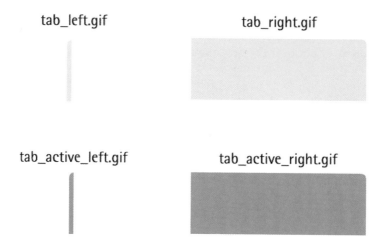

Figure 4.12. The image files used to create the tabs

Here's the basic list of navigation items:

```
                                         chapter04/tabs.html (excerpt)

<div id="header">
<ul>
  <li class="recipes"><a href="#">Recipes</a></li>
  <li class="contact"><a href="#">Contact Us</a></li>
  <li class="articles"><a href="#">Articles</a></li>
  <li class="buy"><a href="#">Buy Online</a></li>
</ul>
</div>
```

The first step is to style the container that surrounds the navigation. We're going to give our header a simple bottom border for the purposes of this exercise, but on a real, live web site this container may hold other elements in addition to our tabs (such as a logo or search field):

```
#header {
  float: left;
  width: 100%;
  border-bottom: 1px solid #8DA5FF;
  margin-bottom: 2em;
}
```

As you'll have noticed, we float the header to the left. We'll also float the individual list items; floating the container that houses them ensures that they remain contained once they're floated, and that the border will display below them.

Next, we create a style rule for the `ul` element inside the header:

**chapter04/tabs.css** ***(excerpt)***

```
#header ul {
  margin: 0;
  padding: 2em 0 0 0;
  list-style: none;
}
```

This rule removes the bullets and alters the margin and padding on our list—we've added two ems of padding to the top of the `ul` element. Figure 4.13 shows the results of our work so far.

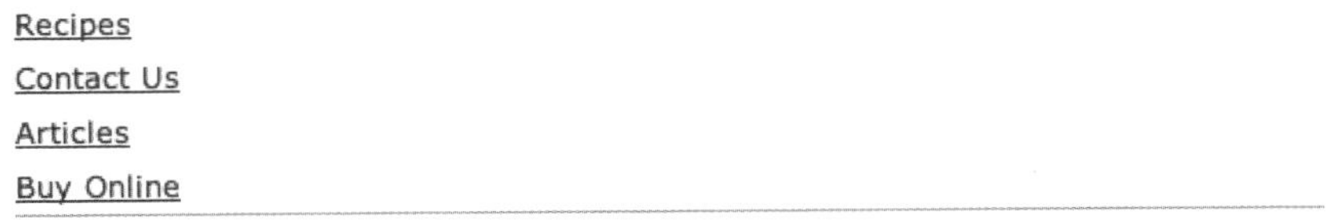
Recipes
Contact Us
Articles
Buy Online

Figure 4.13. Displaying the navigation after styling the `ul` element

Now we need to style the list items:

**chapter04/tabs.css** ***(excerpt)***

```
#header li {
  float: left;
  background-image: url("images/tab_left.gif");
  background-repeat: no-repeat;
  margin: 0 1px 0 0;
  padding: 0 0 0 8px;
}
```

This rule uses the `float` property to position the list items horizontally while maintaining the block-level status of each. We then add the first of our *sliding door* images—the thin left-hand side of the tab—as a background image. A single-pixel right margin on the list item creates a gap between one tab and the next. Figure 4.14 shows that the left-hand tab image now appears for each tab.

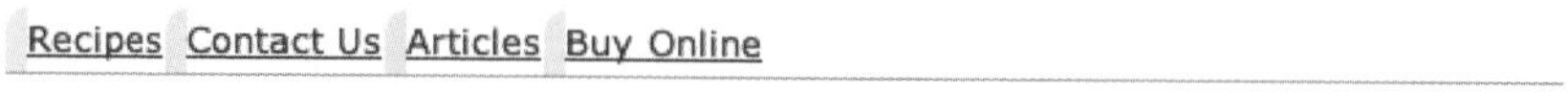

Recipes
Contact Us
Articles
Buy Online

Figure 4.14. The navigation tabs reflecting the new styles

Next, we style the links, completing the look of our tabs in their unselected state. The image that forms the right-hand side of the tab is applied to each link, completing the tab effect:

**chapter04/tabs.css** ***(excerpt)***

```
#header a {
  float: left;
  display: block;
  background-image: url("images/tab_right.gif");
  background-repeat: no-repeat;
  background-position: right top;
  padding: 0.2em 10px 0.2em 0;
  text-decoration: none;
  font-weight: bold;
  color: #333366;
}
```

The results are shown in Figure 4.15.

Recipes
Contact Us
Articles
Buy Online

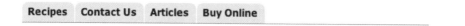

Figure 4.15. Styling the navigation links

If you increase the text size in the browser, you can see that the tabs neatly increase in size too. In fact, they do so without overlapping and without the text protruding out of the tab—this is because we have used images that allow plenty of room for growth.

To complete the tab navigation, we need to highlight the tab that corresponds to the currently displayed page. You'll recall that each list item has been assigned a unique class name. If we assign to the body element an ID that has a value equal to the value of each list item class, CSS can do the rest of the work:

chapter04/tabs.html *(excerpt)*

```
<body id="recipes">
```

Although it looks like a lot of code, the CSS code that styles the tab matching the body ID is relatively straightforward. The images I've used are exact copies of the left and right images that we applied to the tabs, but they're a different color, which produces the effect of one tab appearing to be highlighted.

Here's the CSS:

chapter04/tabs.css *(excerpt)*

```
#recipes #header li.recipes,
#contact #header li.contact,
#articles #header li.articles,
#buy #header li.buy {
  background-image: url("images/tab_active_left.gif");
}

#recipes #header li.recipes a,
#contact #header li.contact a,
#articles #header li.articles a,
#buy #header li.buy a {
  background-image: url("images/tab_active_right.gif");
  background-color: transparent;
  color: #FFFFFF;
}
```

With these rules in place, specifying an ID of recipes to our body will cause the **Recipes** tab to be highlighted, specifying contact will cause the **Contact Us** tab to be highlighted, and so on. The results of this work are shown in Figure 4.16.

### Identifying a Useful Technique

The technique of adding an ID to the body element can be very useful. For example, you may have various color schemes for different sections of your site to help the user identify which section they're using. You can simply add the section name to the body element and make use of it within the style sheet, as we did in this example.

Recipes  Contact Us  Articles  Buy Online

Figure 4.16. Highlighting the **Contact Us** tab by specifying `contact` as the ID of the body element

# How can I visually indicate which links are external to my site?

When linking to other content it's a nice touch to visually demonstrate to users when a link is to another site. We can do this using CSS without needing to add anything to our markup.

## Solution

We can use a CSS3 selector that's supported in many modern browsers to select the external links. The first link in the paragraph below is to a page on our own site, the second to an external web site (Google):

```
                                          chapter04/external_links.html
<!DOCTYPE html PUBLIC "-//W3C//DTD XHTML 1.0 Strict//EN"
"http://www.w3.org/TR/xhtml1/DTD/xhtml1-strict.dtd">
<html xmlns="http://www.w3.org/1999/xhtml" lang="en-US">
  <head>
    <title>Chapter 4 - Show external links</title>
    <meta http-equiv="content-type" content="text/html;
        charset=utf-8" />
    <link rel="stylesheet" type="text/css"
        href="external_links.css" />
```

```
    </head>
    <body>
    <p>Lorem ipsum dolor sit amet, <a href="page2.html">consectetur
        adipiscing elit</a>. Aenean porta. Donec eget quam. Morbi
        libero.Curabitur ut justo vehicula elit feugiat lacinia. Morbi
        ac quam. <a href="http://www.google.com">Sed venenatis</a>,
        lectus quis porta viverra, lectus sapien tempus odio, ac
        volutpat mi dolor ac elit.</p>
    </body>
</html>
```

We can use a CSS3 selector to target the link that starts with `http:` and add an icon
to it:

```
                                                        chapter04/external_links.css

a[href ^="http:"] {
  padding-left: 20px;
  background-image: url(link_icon_external.gif);
  background-repeat: no-repeat;
}
```

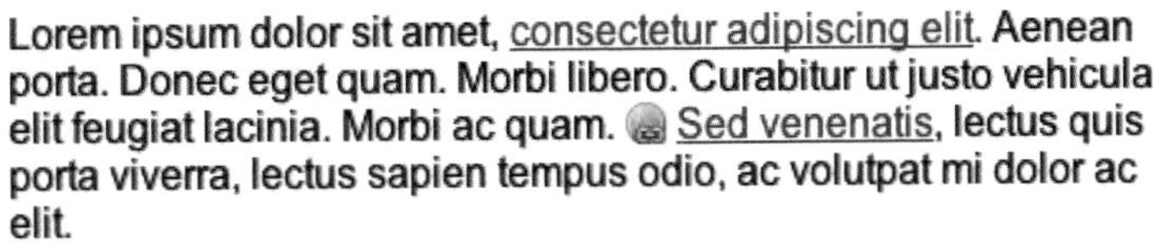

Lorem ipsum dolor sit amet, consectetur adipiscing elit. Aenean
porta. Donec eget quam. Morbi libero. Curabitur ut justo vehicula
elit feugiat lacinia. Morbi ac quam. Sed venenatis, lectus quis
porta viverra, lectus sapien tempus odio, ac volutpat mi dolor ac
elit.

Figure 4.17. The external link displays with an icon

Any links on our page that start with `http:` (which should be external as it is unnecessary to link to pages on our own site like that) will display with the world icon.

## Discussion

This CSS3 attribute selector is widely supported in modern browsers, although it
will be ignored in Internet Explorer 6. In browsers that lack support for this selector
the link will just display as normal; so, it's a nice enhancement for browsers with
support but leaves the experience unchanged for those with older browsers.

Let's take a closer look at that selector: a[href ^="http:"].

The attribute that we're selecting is the href attribute, and we want our selector to match when it finds the text http: at the beginning of the attribute value. The ^= operator means "begins with". You could use a similar selector to match all email links, for example, a[href ^="mailto:"].

Another useful attribute selector is to select on the file extension of a link. This means you can add a small icon to show that a document is a PDF or other document type, depending on the extension. The selector a[href $=".pdf"] will match any link that has a file extension of **.pdf**. The $= operator means "ends with", so this selector will match when an href attribute value ends with **.pdf**. The example below shows all three types in action:

*chapter04/external_links.html*

```
<ul class="links">
  <li><a href="http://www.google.com">Go somewhere else</a></li>
  <li><a href="/files/example.pdf">Download a PDF</a></li>
  <li><a href="mailto:info@example.com">Email someone</a></li>
</ul>
```

*chapter04/external_links.css*

```
a[href ^="http:"] {
  padding-left: 20px;
  background-image: url(link_icon_external.gif);
  background-repeat: no-repeat;
}

a[href ^="mailto:"] {
  padding-left: 20px;
  background-image: url(link_icon_email.gif);
  background-repeat: no-repeat;
}

a[href $=".pdf"] {
  padding-left: 20px;
  background-image: url(link_icon_pdf.gif);
  background-repeat: no-repeat;
}
```

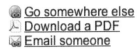

Figure 4.18. Links with icons for external and email links, and PDF files[2]

Attribute selectors are a very useful part of CSS and you can safely use them in this kind of situation where you're just adding an enhancement to your design.

# How do I change the cursor type?

It's common for the cursor to change to a hand icon when the cursor's moved over a link on any part of the page. Occasionally—perhaps to fit in with a particular interface—you might want to change the cursor to represent a different action.

## Solution

We change the cursor using the CSS `cursor` property. For example, if we wanted to change the cursor on anchor elements that link to help documentation we can specify the style like so:

```
a.help {
  cursor: help;
}
```

Table 4.1 identifies the properties that are available in CSS 2.1, and how they appear in Internet Explorer 8.

---

[2] The icons you can see in Figure 4.18 are from http://www.famfamfam.com/lab/icons/silk/.

## Table 4.1. The CSS 2.1 Standard Cursors in IE8

| | | |
|:---:|:---:|:---:|
| pointer | default | crosshair |
| text | help | move |
| n-resize | ne-resize | nw-resize |
| s-resize | se-resize | sw-resize |
| e-resize | w-resize | wait |
| progress | browser-determined <br> auto | custom image <br> url("*url*") |

# Discussion

The cursor property can take a range of values. Changing the cursor display can be a useful way for web applications with friendly interfaces to provide valuable user feedback. For example, you might decide to use a question mark cursor for indicating help text.

**Changing the Cursor Can Cause Confusion!**

You should use this effect with care, and keep in mind that people are generally used to standard browser behavior. For instance, users are familiar with the cursor representing a pointing hand icon when hovered over a link.

Table 4.1 lists the various properties that are available in the CSS standard; these are supported by most modern browsers, including Internet Explorer 6 and above, Safari, Opera, Firefox, and Chrome. Browser support for the complete range of values varies so make sure to test.

CSS3 increases the range of cursor values available, as shown in Table 4.2, but browser support for these values varies. They're well supported by Safari, Firefox, and Chrome, and IE8 supports most of them; however, Opera, as of the time of writing, only supports CSS 2.1 cursor values.

## Table 4.2. New CSS3 Cursors

| cursor value | Appearance (as in IE8) |
| --- | --- |
| `copy` | unsupported |
| `alias` | unsupported |
| `cell` | unsupported |
| `all-scroll` | ✥ |
| `no-drop` | 🖑⊘ |
| `not-allowed` | ⊘ |
| `col-resize` | ╫ |
| `row-resize` | ╪ |
| `vertical-text` | ⊢⊣ |

# How do I create rollover images in my navigation without using JavaScript?

CSS-based navigation can provide some really interesting effects, but there are still some effects that require the use of images. Is it possible to enjoy the advantages of text-based navigation and still use images?

## Solution

It is possible to combine images and CSS to create JavaScript-free rollovers. This solution is based on a technique described at WellStyled.com.[3] Here's the code you'll need:

chapter04/images.html

```
<!DOCTYPE html PUBLIC "-//W3C//DTD XHTML 1.0 Strict//EN"
    "http://www.w3.org/TR/xhtml1/DTD/xhtml1-strict.dtd">
<html xmlns="http://www.w3.org/1999/xhtml" lang="en-US">
<head>
<title>Lists as navigation</title>
<meta http-equiv="content-type"
    content="text/html; charset=utf-8" />
<link rel="stylesheet" type="text/css" href="images.css" />
</head>
<body>
<ul id="nav">
  <li><a href="#">Recipes</a></li>
  <li><a href="#">Contact Us</a></li>
  <li><a href="#">Articles</a></li>
  <li><a href="#">Buy Online</a></li>
</ul>
</body>
</html>
```

chapter04/images.css

```
ul#nav {
  list-style-type: none;
  padding: 0;
```

---

[3] http://wellstyled.com/css-nopreload-rollovers.html

```
  margin: 0;
}
#nav a:link, #nav a:visited {
  display: block;
  width: 150px;
  padding: 10px 0 16px 32px;
  font: bold 80% Arial, Helvetica, sans-serif;
  color: #FF9900;
  background: url("peppers.gif") top left no-repeat;
  text-decoration: none;
}
#nav a:hover {
  background-position: 0 -69px;
  color: #B51032;
}
#nav a:active {
  background-position: 0 -138px;
  color: #006E01;
}
```

The results can be seen in Figure 4.19, but to enjoy the full effect I suggest you try it for yourself. Remember to click on a link or two!

Figure 4.19. Using images to advantage in the completed menu

# Discussion

This solution offers a means of using images in your navigation without having to resort to preloading lots of separate files.

The navigation has three states, but there's no need to use three separate images to depict these states. Instead, we use one large image that contains the graphics for all three states, as shown in Figure 4.20.

Figure 4.20. All three rollover states

The navigation is marked up as a simple list:

```
                                    chapter04/images.html (excerpt)

<ul id="nav">
  <li><a href="#">Recipes</a></li>
  <li><a href="#">Contact Us</a></li>
  <li><a href="#">Articles</a></li>
  <li><a href="#">Buy Online</a></li>
</ul>
```

We control the display of the background image within the declaration block for the navigation links. However, because the image is far bigger than the area required for this element, we only see the yellow pepper at first:

```
                                    chapter04/images.css (excerpt)

#nav a:link, #nav a:visited {
  display: block;
  width: 150px;
  padding: 10px 0 16px 32px;
  font: bold 80% Arial, Helvetica, sans-serif;
  color: #FF9900;
  background: url("peppers.gif") top left no-repeat;
  text-decoration: none;
}
```

When the :hover state is activated, the background image moves up the exact number of pixels required to reveal the red pepper. In this example, I had to move it by 69 pixels, but this figure will vary depending on the image that you use. You could probably work it out mathematically, or you could do as I do and simply increment the background position a few pixels at a time, until it appears in the right location on hover:

chapter04/images.css *(excerpt)*

```
#nav a:hover {
  background-position: 0 -69px;
  color: #B51032;
}
```

When the `:active` state is activated, the background image shifts again, this time to display the green pepper when the link is clicked:

chapter04/images.css *(excerpt)*

```
#nav a:active {
  background-position: 0 -138px;
  color: #006E01;
}
```

That's all there is to it! The effect can fall apart if the user resizes the text in the browser to a larger font, which allows the edges of the hidden images to display. You can anticipate this to some degree by leaving quite a large space between each of the three images—keep this in mind when preparing your images.

### Image Flickering in Internet Explorer

This technique sometimes causes the navigation to flicker in Internet Explorer. In my tests, this only tends to be a problem when the image is larger than the ones we've used here; however, if your navigation items flicker, a well-documented remedy is available.[4]

---

[4] http://wellstyled.com/css-nopreload-rollovers.html

# How should I style a site map?

A site map is a helpful page on your web site that lists all pages in the site. It can help those who are unable to find what they're looking for through the navigation—as well as providing a quick way to see what's available at a glance and go to it with one click.

## Solution

A site map is really a list of all of the destinations available on your site and so is ideally marked up as a set of nested lists. The first list is your main navigation, with the internal navigation nested within each main navigation point. A list works even if your site structure has many levels and should be easy to generate from your content management system. Figure 4.21 displays the results of the following code:

```
chapter04/sitemap.html (excerpt)

<ul id="sitemap">
  <li><a href="/about">About us</a>
  <ul>
    <li><a href="/about/team">The team</a></li>
    <li><a href="/about/history">Our history</a></li>
  </ul>
  </li>
  <li><a href="/products">Our products</a></li>
  <li><a href="/order">Ordering information</a>
  <ul>
    <li><a href="/order/shops">Our shops</a></li>
    <li><a href="/order/stockists">Other stockists</a></li>
    <li><a href="/order/onlinestockists">Online stockists</a></li>
  </ul>
  </li>
  <li><a href="/contact">Contact us</a></li>
</ul>
```

chapter04/sitemap.css *(excerpt)*

```css
ul#sitemap {
  margin: 0;
  padding: 0;
  list-style: none;
}

ul#sitemap ul {
  padding-left: 1em;
  list-style: none;
}

ul#sitemap li {
  border-bottom: 2px solid #FFFFFF;
}

ul#sitemap li a:link, ul#sitemap li a:visited{
  background-color: #CCCCCC;
  display: block;
  padding: 0.4em;
  text-decoration: none;
  color: #057FAC;
}

ul#sitemap li a:hover {
  background-color: #999999;
  color: #FFFFFF;
}

ul#sitemap li li a:link, ul#sitemap li li a:visited{
  background-color: #FFFFFF;
  display: block;
  padding: 0.4em;
}

ul#sitemap li li a:hover {
  background-color: #FFFFFF;
  color: #057FAC;
}
```

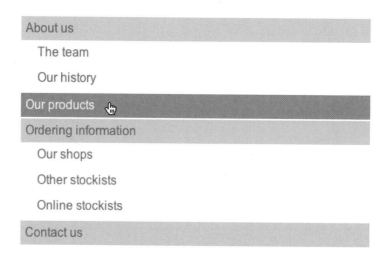

Figure 4.21. The styled sitemap

## Discussion

The sitemap starts life as a list for the main navigation elements with the submenus nested inside—in the same way as the list with subnavigation discussed earlier in this chapter. The difference with the sitemap is that all menus will display their subnavigation. If the sitemap becomes deeper (with further levels), you just continue nesting in the same way, with subpages being a sublist of their parent page.

Take care to nest the list items properly. The submenu needs to go before the closing `</li>` of the parent list. Without CSS the sitemap displays as in Figure 4.22. We can then style the parent list and sublists. I'm taking the margins and padding off the main list, but giving nested lists a left padding of 1em to indent them and make it clear that they're nested inside their parent list item:

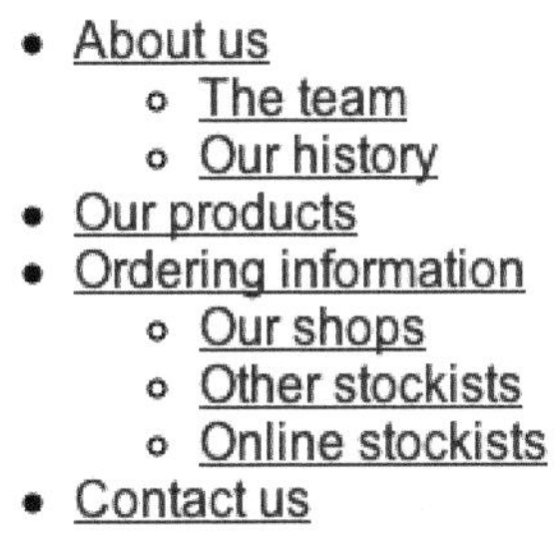

- About us
  - The team
  - Our history
- Our products
- Ordering information
  - Our shops
  - Other stockists
  - Online stockists
- Contact us

Figure 4.22. The marked up sitemap without CSS

**chapter04/sitemap.css** *(excerpt)*

```
ul#sitemap {
  margin: 0;
  padding: 0;
  list-style: none;
}

ul#sitemap ul {
  padding-left: 1em;
  list-style: none;
}
```

I then want to give the main list items a strong style to show that they represent the main sections of my site. As with the navigation, I put most of the styling onto the a element and set the `display` property to `block`, so as to make the full width of the item clickable, as opposed to just the link text itself:

**chapter04/sitemap.css** *(excerpt)*

```
ul#sitemap li {
  border-bottom: 2px solid #FFFFFF;
}

ul#sitemap li a:link, ul#sitemap li a:visited{
  background-color: #CCCCCC;
  display: block;
  padding: 0.4em;
  text-decoration: none;
```

```
  color: #057FAC;
}

ul#sitemap li a:hover {
  background-color: #999999;
  color: #FFFFFF;
}
```

As we're selecting elements within the sitemap list, we'll also select the nested a elements which should have no gray background color. So to finish off we need to deal with these elements with a more specific selector:

chapter04/sitemap.css *(excerpt)*

```
ul#sitemap li li a:link, ul#sitemap li li a:visited{
  background-color: #FFFFFF;
  display: block;
  padding: 0.4em;
}

ul#sitemap li li a:hover {
  background-color: #FFFFFF;
  color: #057FAC;
}
```

That's all there is to styling a sitemap using CSS. Just as with site navigation you can develop all kinds of creative effects working from this simple idea.

# Can I create a drop-down menu using only CSS?

A previous edition of this book included a CSS-only drop-down menu that I have removed in this edition.

When this book was originally written, I—like many other web developers—was really looking forward to a utopia where we would just use CSS for everything, managing without JavaScript to create effects like drop-down menus. As we've learned more about these technologies and also about the ways in which people use the Web, I've come to the opinion that in this circumstance, JavaScript is a far better choice.

It is possible to create a drop-down navigation using only CSS. However, the techniques used to do this can actually be less accessible in practice than a well-thought through JavaScript-driven, drop-down menu would be. It's possible to make JavaScript menus navigable with the keyboard, for example, and to ensure that links are unhidden using `display: none;`, which renders them hidden for screen readers as well as those viewing the site on screen. If you really need a drop-down menu I'd advise taking a look at the excellent UDM4 menu,[5] which can be styled using CSS but provides a good experience for all of your visitors.

# How can I use CSS to keep image-based navigation clean and accessible?

While there are many benefits to using text-based navigation styled with CSS rather than images, it's likely that sometimes you'll need to use images to gain a particular effect or to use a certain font. When this happens, you can use all you know about CSS to ensure that the images are used in a way that is as problem-free as possible. This solution pulls together several different techniques to create a slick image-based navigation.

## Solution

This solution starts with text-based navigation and replaces it, using CSS and a single image, with image-based navigation. Figure 4.23 shows us the final product, and here's the code:

*chapter04/image_nav.html (excerpt)*

```
<ul id="nav">
  <li class="recipes"><a href="#"><span>Recipes</span></a></li>
  <li class="contact"><a href="#"><span>Contact Us</span></a></li>
  <li class="articles"><a href="#"><span>Articles</span></a></li>
  <li class="buy"><a href="#"><span>Buy Online</span></a></li>
</ul>
```

[5] http://www.udm4.com/

chapter04/image_nav.css *(excerpt)*

```css
ul#nav {
  width: 360px;
  height: 30px;
  overflow:hidden;
  margin: 0;
  padding: 0;
  list-style: none;
}

ul#nav li {
  float: left;
}

ul#nav li a span {
  margin-left: -5000px;
}

ul#nav li a {
  background-image: url(reflectonav.gif);
  background-repeat: no-repeat;
  display: block;
  width: 75px;
  overflow:hidden;
}

ul#nav li.recipes a {
  background-position: 0 0;
}

ul#nav li.recipes a:hover {
  background-position: 0 -42px;
}

ul#nav li.contact a {
  background-position: -75px 0;
  width: 105px;
}

ul#nav li.contact a:hover {
  background-position: -75px -42px;
}
```

```
ul#nav li.articles a {
  background-position: -180px 0;
  width: 85px;
}

ul#nav li.articles a:hover {
  background-position: -180px -42px;
}

ul#nav li.buy a {
  background-position: -265px 0;
  width: 85px;
}

ul#nav li.buy a:hover {
  background-position: -265px -42px;
}
```

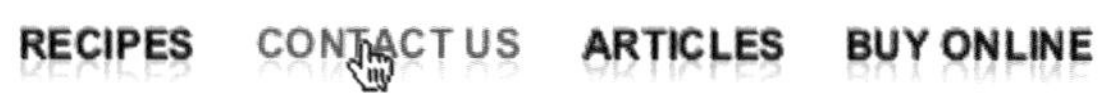

RECIPES    CONTACT US    ARTICLES    BUY ONLINE

Figure 4.23. The completed navigation

# Discussion

In this solution we want to ensure that any text-only devices such as screen readers and search engines still understand our navigation, even though we're using images. Therefore, we start out as usual by creating an unordered list of navigation items. The only addition is a span element wrapped around the text inside the element:

*chapter04/image_nav.html (excerpt)*

```
<ul id="nav">
  <li class="recipes"><a href="#"><span>Recipes</span></a></li>
  <li class="contact"><a href="#"><span>Contact Us</span></a></li>
  <li class="articles"><a href="#"><span>Articles</span></a></li>
  <li class="buy"><a href="#"><span>Buy Online</span></a></li>
</ul>
```

Our navigation is now just a structured list. Next, we need to create our images for the navigation. As with the rollover navigation image above we're going to use a composite image with several image states in it—in this case all of the navigation images and their rollover states in one image, as shown in Figure 4.24.

RECIPES    CONTACT US    ARTICLES    BUY ONLINE

RECIPES    CONTACT US    ARTICLES    BUY ONLINE

Figure 4.24. The background image used in this example

Using one image saves making multiple requests to the server, and the file size for our one large image will be less that it would be if we had eight images chopped up. Now that we have our markup and image we can start to style the navigation using CSS. First, we remove the default browser styling on the `ul` element and float our list items left to make a horizontal navigation bar.

We also give the navigation width and height values. As the navigation is made up of images, we know how tall it will be and specifying the height ensures that there are no parts of the background showing through:

```
                                        chapter04/image_nav.css (excerpt)
ul#nav {
  width: 360px;
  height: 30px;
  overflow:hidden;
  margin: 0;
  padding: 0;
  list-style: none;
}

ul#nav li {
  float: left;
}
```

We now want to hide the text from browsers that support images and CSS. We do this by setting a large negative margin on the span within the list items, throwing them off the left side of the screen:

chapter04/image_nav.css *(excerpt)*

```
ul#nav li a span {
  margin-left: -5000px;
}
```

We can now replace the text with the background image. Create a rule for the element in which `display` is set to `block` so it takes up the full area of the `li`, then add the background image:

chapter04/image_nav.css *(excerpt)*

```
ul#nav li a {
  display: block;
  background-image: url(reflectonav.gif);
  background-repeat: no-repeat;
  width: 75px;
  overflow:hidden;
}
```

If you look at your navigation in a browser after adding the above rules you'll see that it shows the "Recipes" item 4 times. This is because you've added the background image to each link in the navigation bar and the image displayed is positioned at the top left of that item, as Figure 4.25 shows.

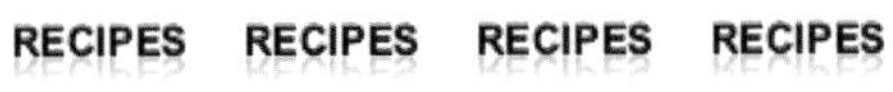

RECIPES    RECIPES    RECIPES    RECIPES

Figure 4.25. After adding the background image to the element

To correct this situation we need to position the background image differently for each navigation item. As with the rollover images above, it's often simplest just to tweak the position pixel by pixel until it appears in the right place. The following CSS shows how we position the background for each link, and Figure 4.26 shows the results:

```
ul#nav li.recipes a {
  background-position: 0 0;
}

ul#nav li.contact a {
  background-position: -75px 0;
  width: 105px;
}

ul#nav li.articles a {
  background-position: -180px 0;
  width: 85px;
}

ul#nav li.buy a {
  background-position: -265px 0;
  width: 85px;
}
```

RECIPES    CONTACT US    ARTICLES    BUY ONLINE

Figure 4.26. After positioning the background image

The final task we need to do is add our hover state. This is created in much the same way as the rollover background images in the earlier example. Using CSS, we can move the background image on hover so that the rollover state comes into view:

chapter04/image_nav.css *(excerpt)*

```
ul#nav li.recipes a:hover {
  background-position: 0 -42px;
}

ul#nav li.contact a:hover {
  background-position: -75px -42px;
}

ul#nav li.articles a:hover {
  background-position: -180px -42px;
}

ul#nav li.buy a:hover {
  background-position: -265px -42px;
}
```

# Summary

This chapter has discussed a range of different ways in which we can create navigation using structurally sound markup, as well as provided examples that can be used as starting points for your own experiments.

On existing sites where a full redesign is unfeasible, introducing a CSS-based navigation system can be a good way to improve the site's accessibility and performance without affecting its look and feel in a big way.

# Chapter 5

# Tabular Data

You've probably heard the mantra "tables are for tabula data, not layout." Originally designed to display tabular data correctly in HTML documents, they were soon misappropriated as a way to lay out web pages. Back then, understanding how to create complex layouts using nested tables was a part of the standard skill set of every web designer. However, using tables in this way requires large amounts of markup, and can cause real problems for users who are trying to access content using screen readers or other text-only devices. Since then, the Web Standards movement has pushed for the replacement of tabular layouts with CSS, which is designed for the job and is, ultimately, far more flexible, as we'll discover in Chapter 9.

But, far from being evil, tables can (and should) still be used for their true purpose—that of displaying tabular data. This chapter will illustrate some common, correct uses of tables, incorporating elements and attributes that, though used infrequently, help to make your tables accessible. We'll also look at how CSS can make these tables more attractive and usable for those viewing them in a web browser.

# How do I lay out spreadsheet data using CSS?

## Solution

The quick answer is, you don't! Spreadsheet data is tabular by nature and, therefore, should be displayed in an HTML table. However, we can still spruce them up using CSS, as we'll see later in this chapter. And we should still be concerned about the accessibility of our tables, even when we're using them to display the right kind of content.

## Discussion

**Tabular data** is information that's displayed in a table, and which may logically be arranged into columns and rows.

Your accounts, when stored in spreadsheet format, are a good example of tabular data. If you needed to mark up the annual accounts of an organization for which you were building a site, you might be given a spreadsheet that looked like Figure 5.1.

| | A | B | C | D | E | F |
|---|---|---|---|---|---|---|
| 1 | | 1999 | 2000 | 2001 | 2002 | |
| 2 | Grants | 11,980 | 12,650 | 9,700 | 10,600 | |
| 3 | Donations | 4,780 | 4,989 | 6,700 | 6,590 | |
| 4 | Investments | 8,000 | 8,100 | 8,760 | 8,490 | |
| 5 | Fundraising | 3,200 | 3,120 | 3,700 | 4,210 | |
| 6 | Sales | 28,400 | 27,100 | 27,950 | 29,050 | |
| 7 | Miscellaneous | 2,100 | 1,900 | 1,300 | 1,760 | |
| 8 | Total | 58,460 | 57,859 | 58,110 | 60,700 | |

Figure 5.1. Displaying the accounts information as tabular data in Excel

Obviously, this is tabular data. We see column and row headings to which the data in each cell relates. Ideally, we'd display this data in a table, as shown in Figure 5.2, complete with table headings to ensure that the data is structured logically.

Yearly Income 1999 - 2002

| | 1999 | 2000 | 2001 | 2002 |
|---|---|---|---|---|
| **Grants** | 11,980 | 12,650 | 9,700 | 10,600 |
| **Donations** | 4,780 | 4,989 | 6,700 | 6,590 |
| **Investments** | 8,000 | 8,100 | 8,760 | 8,490 |
| **Fundraising** | 3,200 | 3,120 | 3,700 | 4,210 |
| **Sales** | 28,400 | 27,100 | 27,950 | 29,050 |
| **Miscellaneous** | 2,100 | 1,900 | 1,300 | 1,760 |
| **Total** | 58,460 | 57,859 | 58,110 | 60,700 |

Figure 5.2. The accounts data formatted as an HTML table

# How do I ensure that my tabular data is accessible as well as attractive?

## Solution

The HTML table specification includes elements and attributes that go beyond the basics required to achieve a certain look for tabular data. These extra parts of the table can be used to ensure that the content of the table is clear when it's read out to visually impaired users who are unable to see the layout for themselves. They're also easy to implement, though they're often omitted by web developers. Take a look at this example:

*chapter05/table.html (excerpt)*

```
<table summary="This table shows the yearly income for years 1999
    through 2002">
  <caption>Yearly Income 1999 - 2002</caption>
  <tr>
    <th></th>
    <th scope="col">1999</th>
    <th scope="col">2000</th>
    <th scope="col">2001</th>
    <th scope="col">2002</th>
  </tr>
  <tr>
```

```
  <th scope="row">Grants</th>
  <td>11,980</td>
  <td>12,650</td>
  <td>9,700</td>
  <td>10,600</td>
</tr>
<tr>
  <th scope="row">Donations</th>
  <td>4,780</td>
  <td>4,989</td>
  <td>6,700</td>
  <td>6,590</td>
</tr>
<tr>
  <th scope="row">Investments</th>
  <td>8,000</td>
  <td>8,100</td>
  <td>8,760</td>
  <td>8,490</td>
</tr>
<tr>
  <th scope="row">Fundraising</th>
  <td>3,200</td>
  <td>3,120</td>
  <td>3,700</td>
  <td>4,210</td>
</tr>
<tr>
  <th scope="row">Sales</th>
  <td>28,400</td>
  <td>27,100</td>
  <td>27,950</td>
  <td>29,050</td>
</tr>
<tr>
  <th scope="row">Miscellaneous</th>
  <td>2,100</td>
  <td>1,900</td>
  <td>1,300</td>
  <td>1,760</td>
</tr>
<tr>
  <th scope="row">Total</th>
  <td>58,460</td>
```

```
    <td>57,859</td>
    <td>58,110</td>
    <td>60,700</td>
  </tr>
</table>
```

# Discussion

The above markup creates a table that uses elements and attributes to clearly explain the contents of each cell. Let's discuss the value that each of these elements and attributes adds.

## The summary Attribute of the table Element

chapter05/table.html *(excerpt)*

```
<table summary="This table shows the yearly income for years 1999
    through 2002">
```

A table's summary will be unseen by browser users, but will be read out to visitors with screen readers. We use the summary attribute to make sure that screen reader users understand the purpose and context of the table—information that, while apparent to the sighted user with a standard browser, might be less apparent when the text is being read in a linear manner by the screen reader.

## The caption Element

chapter05/table.html *(excerpt)*

```
<caption>Yearly Income 1999 - 2002</caption>
```

The caption element adds a caption to the table. By default, browsers generally display the caption above the table; however, you can manually set the position of the caption in relation to the table using the caption-side CSS property.

```
table {
  caption-side: bottom;
}
```

Why might you want to use a caption, instead of just adding a heading or paragraph text for display with the table? By using a caption, you can ensure that the text is tied to the table, and that it's recognized as the table's caption—there's no chance that the screen reader could interpret it as a separate element. If you want your table captions to display as paragraph text or level three headings in a graphical browser, no problem! You can create CSS rules for captions just as you would for any other element.

## The th Element

```
<th scope="col">2000</th>
```

The th element identifies data that's a row or column heading. The example markup contains both row and column headings and, to ensure that this is clear, we use the scope attribute of the <th> tag. The scope attribute shows whether a given heading is applied to the column (col) or row (row).

Before you begin to style your tables to complement the look and feel of the site, it's good practice to ensure the accessibility of those tables to users of devices such as screen readers. Accessibility is one of those concerns that many developers brush off, saying, "I'll check it when I'm finished." However, if you leave accessibility checks until the end of development, you may never actually deal with them; if you do, the problems they identify may well require time-consuming fixes, particularly in complex applications. Once you make a habit of keeping accessibility in mind as you design, you'll find that it becomes second nature and adds very little to a project's development time.

CSS attributes make the styling of data tables simple and quick. For instance, when I begin a new site on which I know I'll have to use a lot of data tables, I create a style rule with the class selector .datatable; this contains the basic styles that I want to affect all data tables, and can easily be applied to the <table> tag of each. I then create style rules for .datatable th (the heading cells), .datatable td (the regular cells), and .datatable caption (the table captions).

From that point, adding a new table is easy. All the styles are there—I just need to apply the datatable class. If I decide to change the styles after I've created all the tables in my site, I simply edit my style sheet.

# How do I add a border to a table without using the HTML **border** attribute?

## Solution

The HTML border attribute creates fairly ordinary-looking borders for tables, and its use is discouraged. You can replace it with a CSS border, which will give you far more flexibility in terms of design. Here's how we set a border:

chapter05/table.css *(excerpt)*

```
.datatable {
  border: 1px solid #338BA6;
}
```

This style rule will display a one-pixel, light-blue border around your table, as in Figure 5.3.

You can also add borders to individual cells:

chapter05/table.css *(excerpt)*

```
.datatable td, .datatable th {
  border: 1px solid #73C0D4;
}
```

This style rule renders a slightly lighter border around td and th table cells that have a class of datatable, as Figure 5.4 shows.

Yearly Income 1999 - 2002

| | 1999 | 2000 | 2001 | 2002 |
|---|---|---|---|---|
| Grants | 11,980 | 12,650 | 9,700 | 10,600 |
| Donations | 4,780 | 4,989 | 6,700 | 6,590 |
| Investments | 8,000 | 8,100 | 8,760 | 8,490 |
| Fundraising | 3,200 | 3,120 | 3,700 | 4,210 |
| Sales | 28,400 | 27,100 | 27,950 | 29,050 |
| Miscellaneous | 2,100 | 1,900 | 1,300 | 1,760 |
| Total | 58,460 | 57,859 | 58,110 | 60,700 |

Figure 5.3. Applying a CSS border to the table as a whole

Yearly Income 1999 - 2002

| | 1999 | 2000 | 2001 | 2002 |
|---|---|---|---|---|
| Grants | 11,980 | 12,650 | 9,700 | 10,600 |
| Donations | 4,780 | 4,989 | 6,700 | 6,590 |
| Investments | 8,000 | 8,100 | 8,760 | 8,490 |
| Fundraising | 3,200 | 3,120 | 3,700 | 4,210 |
| Sales | 28,400 | 27,100 | 27,950 | 29,050 |
| Miscellaneous | 2,100 | 1,900 | 1,300 | 1,760 |
| Total | 58,460 | 57,859 | 58,110 | 60,700 |

Figure 5.4. Applying a CSS border to individual table cells

# Discussion

By experimenting with CSS borders on your tables, you can create countless appealing effects—even if the data contained within is dull! You can use differently colored borders for table headings and table cells, and apply various thicknesses and styles of border to table cells. You might even try out such tricks as using one shade for top and left borders, and another for bottom and right borders, to create an indented effect.

We can apply a range of different values to the CSS `border-style` property. We've already met `solid`, which displays a solid line as the border, and this is shown along with the other available options in Table 5.1.

Table 5.1. CSS `border-style` Values

| | | |
|---|---|---|
| double | groove | inset |
| double | groove | inset |
| outset | ridge | solid |
| outset | ridge | solid |
| dashed | dotted | none |
| dashed | dotted[a] | none, or hidden |

[a] Internet Explorer 6 displays some quirky behavior: a one-pixel dotted border will actually appear dashed.

# How do I stop spaces appearing between the cells of my table when I've added borders using CSS?

If you've ever tried to eliminate the spaces between table cells, you might have used the `table` attribute `cellspacing="0"`. This would have left you with a two-pixel border, though, because borders touch without overlapping. This solution explains how to create a neat, single-pixel border around all cells.

## Solution

You can remove the spaces that appear between cells by setting the CSS `border-collapse` property for the table to `collapse`:

```
                                                      chapter05/table.css
.datatable {
  border: 1px solid #338BA6;
  border-collapse: collapse;
}

.datatable td, .datatable th {
  border: 1px solid #73C0D4;
}
```

Figure 5.4 shows a table before the `border-collapse` property is applied; Figure 5.5 shows the effect of this property on the display.

| Yearly Income 1999 - 2002 | 1999 | 2000 | 2001 | 2002 |
|---|---|---|---|---|
| Grants | 11,980 | 12,650 | 9,700 | 10,600 |
| Donations | 4,780 | 4,989 | 6,700 | 6,590 |
| Investments | 8,000 | 8,100 | 8,760 | 8,490 |
| Fundraising | 3,200 | 3,120 | 3,700 | 4,210 |
| Sales | 28,400 | 27,100 | 27,950 | 29,050 |
| Miscellaneous | 2,100 | 1,900 | 1,300 | 1,760 |
| Total | 58,460 | 57,859 | 58,110 | 60,700 |

Figure 5.5. Collapsing the table's borders

# How do I display spreadsheet data in an attractive and usable way?

## Solution

The HTML table is the best way to structure spreadsheet data, even though its default appearance is unattractive. Luckily, we can style the table using CSS, which keeps markup to a minimum and allows us to control our data table's appearance from the style sheet.

| Yearly Income 1999 - 2002 | 1999 | 2000 | 2001 | 2002 |
|---|---|---|---|---|
| Grants | 11,980 | 12,650 | 9,700 | 10,600 |
| Donations | 4,780 | 4,989 | 6,700 | 6,590 |
| Investments | 8,000 | 8,100 | 8,760 | 8,490 |
| Fundraising | 3,200 | 3,120 | 3,700 | 4,210 |
| Sales | 28,400 | 27,100 | 27,950 | 29,050 |
| Miscellaneous | 2,100 | 1,900 | 1,300 | 1,760 |
| Total | 58,460 | 57,859 | 58,110 | 60,700 |

Figure 5.6. Unformatted, unattractive tabular data

The data we saw displayed as an HTML table earlier in this chapter is an example of spreadsheet data. That markup, which is shown unstyled in Figure 5.6, forms the basis for the following example.

Let's apply the following style sheet to that table:

chapter05/spreadsheet.css

```css
body {
  font: 0.8em Verdana, Geneva, Arial, Helvetica, sans-serif;
}

.datatable {
  border: 1px solid #D6DDE6;
  border-collapse: collapse;
}
.datatable td, .datatable th {
  border: 1px solid #D6DDE6;
  text-align: right;
  padding: 0.2em;
}
.datatable th {
  border: 1px solid #828282;
  background-color: #BCBCBC;
  font-weight: bold;
  text-align: left;
  padding: 0.2em;
}

.datatable caption {
  font: bold 120% "Times New Roman", Times, serif;
  background-color: #B0C4DE;
  color: #33517A;
  padding: 0.4em 0 0.3em 0;
  border: 1px solid #789AC6;
}
```

Figure 5.7 shows the result, which is quite attractive, if I do say so myself!

| Yearly Income 1999 - 2002 | | | | |
|---|---|---|---|---|
| | **1999** | **2000** | **2001** | **2002** |
| **Grants** | 11,980 | 12,650 | 9,700 | 10,600 |
| **Donations** | 4,780 | 4,989 | 6,700 | 6,590 |
| **Investments** | 8,000 | 8,100 | 8,760 | 8,490 |
| **Fundraising** | 3,200 | 3,120 | 3,700 | 4,210 |
| **Sales** | 28,400 | 27,100 | 27,950 | 29,050 |
| **Miscellaneous** | 2,100 | 1,900 | 1,300 | 1,760 |
| **Total** | 58,460 | 57,859 | 58,110 | 60,700 |

Figure 5.7. A more attractive table formatted with CSS

# Discussion

In this solution, I aimed to display the table in a way that's similar to the appearance of a desktop spreadsheet. First, I provided a basic rule for the body—this is the kind of rule that's likely to appear in the style sheet of any CSS-styled site:

*chapter05/spreadsheet.css (excerpt)*

```
body {
  font: 0.8em Verdana, Geneva, Arial, Helvetica, sans-serif;
}
```

Next, I styled the table as a whole:

*chapter05/spreadsheet.css (excerpt)*

```
.datatable {
  border: 1px solid #D6DDE6;
  border-collapse: collapse;
}
```

As we've already seen, border displays a border around the outside of the table, while border-collapse removes spaces between the table's cells.

Next, I turned my attention to the table cells:

chapter05/spreadsheet.css *(excerpt)*

```
.datatable td {
  border: 1px solid #D6DDE6;
  text-align: right;
  padding: 0.2em
}
```

Here, I added a border to the table cells and used `text-align` to right-align their contents for that *spreadsheety* look. If you preview the document at this point, you'll see a border around each cell in the table, except the header cells, as shown in Figure 5.8.

| Yearly Income 1999 - 2002 | | | | |
|---|---|---|---|---|
| | **1999** | **2000** | **2001** | **2002** |
| **Grants** | 11,980 | 12,650 | 9,700 | 10,600 |
| **Donations** | 4,780 | 4,989 | 6,700 | 6,590 |
| **Investments** | 8,000 | 8,100 | 8,760 | 8,490 |
| **Fundraising** | 3,200 | 3,120 | 3,700 | 4,210 |
| **Sales** | 28,400 | 27,100 | 27,950 | 29,050 |
| **Miscellaneous** | 2,100 | 1,900 | 1,300 | 1,760 |
| **Total** | 58,460 | 57,859 | 58,110 | 60,700 |

Figure 5.8. Applying the `border` property to the `table` and `td` elements

Next, I added a border to the `th` (heading) cells. I used a darker color for this border, because I also added a background color to these cells to highlight that they're headings, rather than regular cells:

chapter05/spreadsheet.css *(excerpt)*

```
.datatable th {
  border: 1px solid #828282;
  background-color: #BCBCBC;
  font-weight: bold;
  text-align: left;
  padding: 0.2em;
}
```

To complete the table, I styled the caption to make it look like part of the table:

chapter05/spreadsheet.css (excerpt)

```
.datatable caption {
  font: bold 0.9em "Times New Roman", Times, serif;
  background-color: #B0C4DE;
  color: #33517A;
  padding: 0.4em 0 0.3em 0;
  border: 1px solid #789AC6;
}
```

# How do I display table rows in alternating colors?

## Solution

It can be difficult to stay on a particular row as your eyes work across a large table of data. Displaying table rows in alternating colors is a common way to help users stay focused on the row they're on. Whether you're adding rows by hand, or you're displaying the data from a database, you can use CSS classes to create this effect.

Here's the table markup you'll need:

chapter05/alternate.html (excerpt)

```
<table summary="List of new students 2003" class="datatable">
  <caption>Student List</caption>
  <tr>
    <th scope="col">Student Name</th>
    <th scope="col">Date of Birth</th>
    <th scope="col">Class</th>
    <th scope="col">ID</th>
  </tr>
  <tr>
    <td>Joe Bloggs</td>
    <td>27/08/1997</td>
    <td>Mrs Jones</td>
    <td>12009</td>
  </tr>
  <tr class="altrow">
    <td>William Smith</td>
    <td>20/07/1997</td>
```

```
      <td>Mrs Jones</td>
      <td>12010</td>
    </tr>
    <tr>
      <td>Jane Toad</td>
      <td>21/07/1997</td>
      <td>Mrs Jones</td>
      <td>12030</td>
    </tr>
    <tr class="altrow">
      <td>Amanda Williams</td>
      <td>19/03/1997</td>
      <td>Mrs Edwards</td>
      <td>12021</td>
    </tr>
    <tr>
      <td>Kylie Jameson</td>
      <td>18/05/1997</td>
      <td>Mrs Jones</td>
      <td>12022</td>
    </tr>
    <tr class="altrow">
      <td>Louise Smith</td>
      <td>17/07/1997</td>
      <td>Mrs Edwards</td>
      <td>12019</td>
    </tr>
    <tr>
      <td>James Jones</td>
      <td>04/04/1997</td>
      <td>Mrs Edwards</td>
      <td>12007</td>
    </tr>
</table>
```

Here's the CSS to style it:

chapter05/alternate.css *(excerpt)*

```
body {
  font: 0.8em Arial, Helvetica, sans-serif;
}
.datatable {
  border: 1px solid #D6DDE6;
```

```
      border-collapse: collapse;
      width: 80%;
}
.datatable td {
      border: 1px solid #D6DDE6;
      padding: 0.3em;
}
.datatable th {
      border: 1px solid #828282;
      background-color: #BCBCBC;
      font-weight: bold;
      text-align: left;
      padding-left: 0.3em;
}
.datatable caption {
      font: bold 110% Arial, Helvetica, sans-serif;
      color: #33517A;
      text-align: left;
      padding: 0.4em 0 0.8em 0;
}
.datatable tr.altrow {
      background-color: #DFE7F2;
      color: #000000;
}
```

The result can be seen in Figure 5.9.

**Student List**

| Student Name | Date of Birth | Class | ID |
|---|---|---|---|
| Joe Bloggs | 27/08/1997 | Mrs Jones | 12009 |
| William Smith | 20/07/1997 | Mrs Jones | 12010 |
| Jane Toad | 21/07/1997 | Mrs Jones | 12030 |
| Amanda Williams | 19/03/1997 | Mrs Edwards | 12021 |
| Kylie Jameson | 18/05/1997 | Mrs Jones | 12022 |
| Louise Smith | 17/07/1997 | Mrs Edwards | 12019 |
| James Jones | 04/04/1997 | Mrs Edwards | 12007 |

Figure 5.9. Using alternating row colors to assist people using large tables of data

# Discussion

I applied the `altrow` class to every second row of the HTML table above:

chapter05/alternate.html *(excerpt)*

```
<tr class="altrow">
```

In the CSS, I styled the table using properties that will be familiar if you've looked at the previous solutions in this chapter. I also added the following class:

chapter05/alternate.css *(excerpt)*

```
.datatable tr.altrow {
  background-color: #DFE7F2;
  color: #000000;
}
```

This class will be applied to all `tr` elements with a class of `altrow` that appear within a table that has a class of `datatable`.

If you're creating your table dynamically—for instance, using ASP, PHP, or a similar technology to pull data from a database—then, to create the alternating row effect, you must write this class out for every second row that you display.

# The Way of the Future

Adding all of these classes to rows is a nuisance, and you would be right in thinking that there ought to be a better way to achieve striped rows. After all, the striping is a presentational effect that would be better achieved purely in the CSS. Using a CSS3 selector, the **:nth-child pseudo-class**, we can target all odd or even rows in our table without needing to add anything to our markup. Once it has full browser support it'll make our lives as CSS developers much easier. The `:nth-child` pseudo-class is a fairly complicated one to grasp, so if you'd like to know more the SitePoint CSS Reference has an excellent explanation.[1] It allows you to select elements based on the number of siblings before it.

---

[1] http://reference.sitepoint.com/css/understandingnthchildexpressions/

If we take our original table, before adding the class name to the rows, we can target the even rows in the table using the following CSS:

```css
.datatable tr:nth-child(2n) {
  background-color: #DFE7F2;
  color: #000000;
}
```

To target all odd rows use the following:

```css
.datatable tr:nth-child(2n+1) {
  background-color: #DFE7F2;
  color: #000000;
}
```

The number expressions in the selectors above are a little tricky but, thankfully, selecting odd- and even-numbered rows is such a common task, the CSS3 specification has an easier syntax. You can substitute the number expressions in the selectors above with the following to have the same effect:

```css
.datatable tr:nth-child(even) {
  ⋮
}
.datatable tr:nth-child(odd) {
  ⋮
}
```

As at the time of writing, these examples are supported in the latest versions of Safari and Opera, but until more browsers start to offer support, using this technique widely is still a little way away.

 **Use JavaScript to Add Selector Support**

The JavaScript library jQuery has support for CSS3 selectors,[2] which means that you can use it to stripe the rows for you. For an effect like this—an enhancement to the look and feel—you might consider using JavaScript to create this effect and avoid adding classes to the markup.

---

[2] http://docs.jquery.com/Selectors

# How do I change a row's background color when the cursor hovers over it?

## Solution

One way to boost the readability of tabular data is to change the color of the rows as users move the cursor over them, to highlight the row they're reading. This can be seen in Figure 5.10.

**Student List**

| Student Name | Date of Birth | Class | ID |
|---|---|---|---|
| Joe Bloggs | 27/08/1997 | Mrs Jones | 12009 |
| William Smith | 20/07/1997 | Mrs Jones | 12010 |
| Jane Toad | 21/07/1997 | Mrs Jones | 12030 |
| Amanda Williams | 19/03/1997 | Mrs Edwards | 12021 |
| Kylie Jameson | 18/05/1997 | Mrs Jones | 12022 |
| Louise Smith | 17/07/1997 | Mrs Edwards | 12019 |
| James Jones | 04/04/1997 | Mrs Edwards | 12007 |

Figure 5.10. Highlighting a row on mouse over

This can be a very simple solution; all you need to do to create this effect is add the following rule to your CSS:

chapter05/alternate.css *(excerpt)*

```
.datatable tr:hover {
  background-color: #DFE7F2;
  color: #000000;
}
```

Job done!

## Discussion

This solution will work in all modern browsers, including Internet Explorer 7—but it will fail to work in Internet Explorer 6. However, as long as your tables are clear without this highlighting effect in place, the highlight feature could be regarded as a "nice to have," rather than a necessary tool without which the site will be unusable.

If you *must* make this feature work for Internet Explorer 6 users, you can use some simple JavaScript to implement the effect. To change a row's background color when the cursor moves over it in Internet Explorer 6 and earlier, you must first apply the desired style properties to a CSS class, which I've named `hilite` in this example:

*chapter05/hiliterow.css (excerpt)*

```css
.datatable tr:hover, .datatable tr.hilite {
  background-color: #DFE7F2;
  color: #000000;
}
```

Then, add the following JavaScript code to your page after the table:

*chapter05/hiliterow.html (excerpt)*

```javascript
<script type="text/javascript">
var rows = document.getElementsByTagName('tr');
for (var i = 0; i < rows.length; i++) {
  rows[i].onmouseover = function() {
    this.className += ' hilite';
  }
  rows[i].onmouseout = function() {
    this.className = this.className.replace('hilite', '');
  }
}
</script>
```

This code locates all the `<tr>` tags in the document and assigns a `mouseover` and `mouseout` event handler to each. These event handlers apply the CSS `hilite` class to the rows when the cursor moves over them, and removes it when the cursor moves away. As you can see in Figure 5.11, this combination of CSS and HTML produces the desired effect.

**Student List**

| Student Name | Date of Birth | Class | ID |
|---|---|---|---|
| Joe Bloggs | 27/08/1997 | Mrs Jones | 12009 |
| William Smith | 20/07/1997 | Mrs Jones | 12010 |
| Jane Toad | 21/07/1997 | Mrs Jones | 12030 |
| Amanda Williams | 19/03/1997 | Mrs Edwards | 12021 |
| Kylie Jameson | 18/05/1997 | Mrs Jones | 12022 |
| Louise Smith | 17/07/1997 | Mrs Edwards | 12019 |
| James Jones | 04/04/1997 | Mrs Edwards | 12007 |

Figure 5.11. Highlighting a row in Internet Explorer 6 with the help of JavaScript

The JavaScript code works by setting a tag's CSS class dynamically. In this case, we add the `hilite` class to a `<tr>` tag when the `mouseover` event is triggered, as captured by the `onmouseover` property:

chapter05/hiliterow.html *(excerpt)*

```
rows[i].onmouseover = function() {
  this.className += ' hilite';
}
```

We then remove the class when the `mouseout` event is fired:

chapter05/hiliterow.html *(excerpt)*

```
rows[i].onmouseout = function() {
  this.className = this.className.replace('hilite', '');
}
```

You can create very attractive, subtle effects by changing the class of elements in response to user actions using JavaScript. Another way in which you could use this technique would be to highlight a content area by changing the class applied to a `div` when the `mouseover` event for that element is triggered.

**Unobtrusive JavaScript**

You may have noticed that there was no JavaScript added to the table itself; instead, we did our work within the `script` element only. This technique is called **unobtrusive JavaScript**; it aims to keep JavaScript separate from your document in the same way that we keep the presentation of CSS separate from the markup.

The JavaScript needs to run after the table has loaded, because until that point, there are no rows for the JavaScript to work on. Another approach would be to write a function that runs when the page has completed loading—this would mean that you could keep the JavaScript in a separate file that's linked to from your page. You may also consider using conditional comments so that the JavaScript is only loaded when the page is viewed in IE6, but more about that in the section called "How can I specify different styles for Internet Explorer 6 and 7?" in Chapter 7.

As with the previous example, libraries such as jQuery that have support for more advanced selectors can be a great way to plug the gaps where older browsers lack support.

# How do I display table columns in alternating colors?

While alternate row colors are quite a common feature of data tables, we see alternately colored columns less frequently. However, they can be a helpful way to show groupings of data.

## Solution

If we use the `col` element to describe our table's columns, we can employ CSS to add a background to those columns. You can see the `col` elements I've added—one for each column—in the table markup below. I've also added classes to them in much the same way that we added a `class` to the table's rows in "How do I display table rows in alternating colors?":

```
<table class="datatable">
  <col class="odd" />
  <col class="even" />
  <col class="odd" />
  <col class="even" />

  <tr>
    <th>Pool A</th>
    <th>Pool B</th>
    <th>Pool C</th>
    <th>Pool D</th>
  </tr>
  <tr>
    <td>England</td>
    <td>Australia</td>
    <td>New Zealand</td>
    <td>France</td>
  </tr>
  <tr class="even">
    <td>South Africa</td>
    <td>Wales</td>
    <td>Scotland</td>
    <td>Ireland</td>
  </tr>
  <tr>
    <td>Samoa</td>
    <td>Fiji</td>
    <td>Italy</td>
    <td>Argentina</td>
  </tr>
  <tr class="even">
    <td>USA</td>
    <td>Canada</td>
    <td>Romania</td>
    <td>Europe 3</td>
  </tr>
  <tr>
    <td>Repechage 2</td>
    <td>Asia</td>
    <td>Repechage 1</td>
```

```
    <td>Namibia</td>
  </tr>
</table>
```

We can add style rules for the classes we applied to our `col` elements; as shown here; the result is depicted in Figure 5.12:

chapter05/columns.css *(excerpt)*

```css
body {
  font: 0.8em Arial, Helvetica, sans-serif;
}
.datatable {
  border: 1px solid #D6DDE6;
  border-collapse: collapse;
  width: 80%;
}

.datatable col.odd {
  background-color: #80C9FF;
  color: #000000;
}

.datatable col.even {
  background-color: #BFE4FF;
  color: #000000;
}

.datatable td {
  border:2px solid #ffffff;
  padding: 0.3em;
}

.datatable th {
  border:2px solid #ffffff;
  background-color: #00487D;
  color: #FFFFFF;
  font-weight: bold;
  text-align: left;
  padding: 0.3em;
}
```

| Pool A | Pool B | Pool C | Pool D |
|---|---|---|---|
| England | Australia | New Zealand | France |
| South Africa | Wales | Scotland | Ireland |
| Samoa | Fiji | Italy | Argentina |
| USA | Canada | Romania | Europe 3 |
| Repechage 2 | Asia | Repechage 1 | Namibia |

Figure 5.12. Creating alternately striped columns by styling the col element

# Discussion

The col element provides us with further flexibility for styling a table's columns to ensure that they're visually distinct, thus making our table attractive and easier to understand. It's also possible to nest col elements within a colgroup element, which allows us to control the appearance of columns by applying style rules to the parent colgroup element. If a colgroup element is absent, the browser assumes that your table contains one single colgroup that houses all of your col elements.

Here's an example of nested col elements:

**chapter05/colgroups.html** *(excerpt)*

```
<table class="datatable">
<colgroup class="odd">
  <col />
  <col />
</colgroup>
<colgroup class="even">
  <col />
  <col />
</colgroup>
...
```

Here are the style rules that are applied to the colgroup element, rather than to col:

chapter05/colgroups.css *(excerpt)*

```css
.datatable colgroup.odd {
  background-color: #80C9FF;
  color: #000000;
}

.datatable colgroup.even {
  background-color: #BFE4FF;
  color: #000000;
}
```

The result of this change is a table with two columns of one color, and two of another, as shown in Figure 5.13.

| Pool A | Pool B | Pool C | Pool D |
|---|---|---|---|
| England | Australia | New Zealand | France |
| South Africa | Wales | Scotland | Ireland |
| Samoa | Fiji | Italy | Argentina |
| USA | Canada | Romania | Europe 3 |
| Repechage 2 | Asia | Repechage 1 | Namibia |

Figure 5.13. Styling columns using `colgroup`

# How do I display a calendar using CSS?

Calendars, such as the example from a desktop application shown in Figure 5.14, also involve tabular data. The days of the week along the top of the calendar represent the headings of the columns. Therefore, a calendar's display constitutes the legitimate use of a table, but you can keep markup to a minimum by using CSS to control the look and feel.

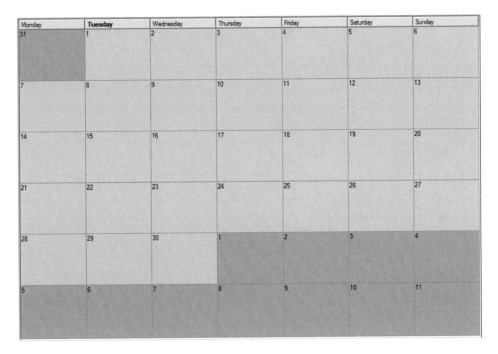

Figure 5.14. A calendar from a desktop application

## Solution

Our solution uses an accessible, simple table that leverages CSS styles to create the attractive calendar shown in Figure 5.15. Given its simple structure, it's ideal for use in a database-driven application in which the table is created via server-side code:

```
                                           chapter05/cal.html (excerpt)

<!DOCTYPE html PUBLIC "-//W3C//DTD XHTML 1.0 Strict//EN"
    "http://www.w3.org/TR/xhtml1/DTD/xhtml1-strict.dtd">
<html xmlns="http://www.w3.org/1999/xhtml" lang="en-US">
<head>
<title>Calendar</title>
<meta http-equiv="content-type"
    content="text/html; charset=utf-8" />
<link rel="stylesheet" type="text/css" href="cal.css" />
</head>
<body>
<table class="clmonth" summary="Calendar for June 2009">
```

```
<caption>June 2009</caption>
<tr>
  <th scope="col">Monday</th>
  <th scope="col">Tuesday</th>
  <th scope="col">Wednesday</th>
  <th scope="col">Thursday</th>
  <th scope="col">Friday</th>
  <th scope="col">Saturday</th>
  <th scope="col">Sunday</th>
</tr>
<tr>
  <td class="previous">31</td>
  <td class="active">1
    <ul>
      <li>New pupils' open day</li>
      <li>Year 8 theater trip</li>
    </ul></td>
  <td>2</td>
  <td>3</td>
  <td>4</td>
  <td>5</td>
  <td>6</td>
</tr>
<tr>
  <td class="active">7
    <ul>
      <li>Year 7 English exam</li>
    </ul></td>
  <td>8</td>
  <td>9</td>
  <td>10</td>
  <td>11</td>
  <td>12</td>
  <td>13</td>
</tr>
<tr>
  <td>14</td>
  <td>15</td>
  <td>16</td>
  <td class="active">17
    <ul>
      <li>Sports Day</li>
    </ul></td>
  <td class="active">18
```

```
    <ul>
      <li>Year 7 parents' evening</li>
      <li>Prizegiving</li>
    </ul></td>
    <td>19</td>
    <td>20</td>
  </tr>
  <tr>
    <td>21</td>
    <td>22</td>
    <td>23</td>
    <td class="active">24
      <ul>
        <li>Year 8 parents' evening</li>
      </ul></td>
    <td>25</td>
    <td>26</td>
    <td>27</td>
  </tr>
  <tr>
    <td>28</td>
    <td>29</td>
    <td class="active">30
      <ul>
        <li>First night of school play</li>
      </ul></td>
    <td class="next">1</td>
    <td class="next">2</td>
    <td class="next">3</td>
    <td class="next">4</td>
  </tr>
</table>
</body>
</html>
```

chapter05/cal.css

```
body {
  background-color: #FFFFFF;
  color: #000000;
  font-size: 90%;
}
.clmonth {
  border-collapse: collapse;
```

```css
  width: 780px;
}
.clmonth caption {
  text-align: left;
  font: bold 110% Georgia, "Times New Roman", Times, serif;
  padding-bottom: 0.4em;
}
.clmonth th {
  border: 1px solid #AAAAAA;
  border-bottom: none;
  padding: 0.2em 0.6em 0.2em 0.6em;
  background-color: #CCCCCC;
  color: #3F3F3F;
  font: 80% Verdana, Geneva, Arial, Helvetica, sans-serif;
  width: 110px;
}
.clmonth td {
  border: 1px solid #EAEAEA;
  font: 80% Verdana, Geneva, Arial, Helvetica, sans-serif;
  padding: 0.2em 0.6em 0.2em 0.6em;
  vertical-align: top;
}
.clmonth td.previous, .clmonth td.next {
  background-color: #F6F6F6;
  color: #C6C6C6;
}
.clmonth td.active {
  background-color: #B1CBE1;
  color: #2B5070;
  border: 2px solid #4682B4;
}
.clmonth ul {
  list-style-type: none;
  margin: 0;
  padding-left: 1em;
  padding-right: 0.6em;
}
.clmonth li {
  margin-bottom: 1em;
}
```

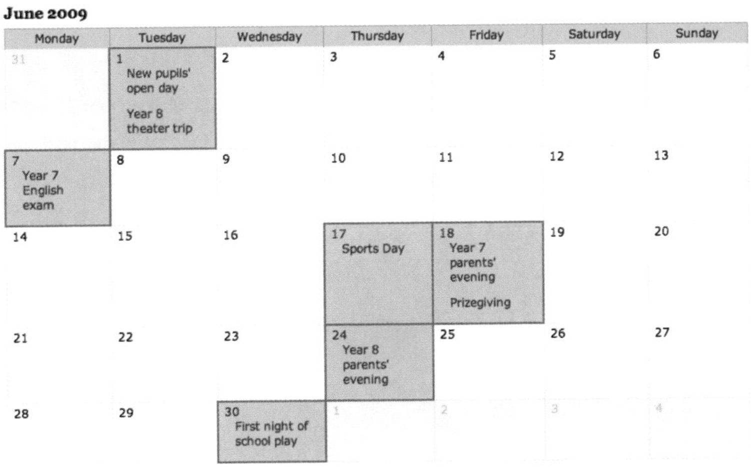

Figure 5.15. The completed calendar styled with CSS

## Discussion

This example starts out as a very simple table. It has a caption, which is the month we're working with, and I've marked up the days of the week as table headers using the <th> tag:

```
                                              chapter05/cal.html (excerpt)
<table class="clmonth" summary="Calendar for June 2009">
  <caption>June 2009</caption>
  <tr>
    <th scope="col">Monday</th>
    <th scope="col">Tuesday</th>
    <th scope="col">Wednesday</th>
    <th scope="col">Thursday</th>
    <th scope="col">Friday</th>
    <th scope="col">Saturday</th>
    <th scope="col">Sunday</th>
  </tr>
```

The table has a class of clmonth. I've used a class rather than an ID because, in some situations, you might want to display more than one month on the page. If you then found that you needed to give the table an ID—perhaps to allow you to show and hide the table using JavaScript—you could add an ID as well as the class.

The days are held within individual table cells, and the events for each day are marked up as a list within the appropriate table cell.

In the markup below, you can see that I've added classes to two of the table cells. Class previous is applied to cells containing days that fall within the preceding month (we'll use next later for days in the following month); class active is applied to cells that contain event information, so that we may highlight them:

chapter05/cal.html *(excerpt)*

```
<tr>
  <td class="previous">31</td>
  <td class="active">1
    <ul>
      <li>New pupils' open day</li>
      <li>Year 8 theater trip</li>
    </ul></td>
  <td>2</td>
  <td>3</td>
  <td>4</td>
  <td>5</td>
  <td>6</td>
</tr>
```

The table, without CSS, displays as shown in Figure 5.16.

Now that we have the structural markup in place, we can style the calendar. I set a basic style for the body, including a base font size. Then I set a style for the class clmonth for the borders to collapse, leaving no space between cells and set a width for the table:

chapter05/cal.css *(excerpt)*

```
body {
  background-color: #FFFFFF;
  color: #000000;
  font-size: 90%;
}
.clmonth {
  border-collapse: collapse;
  width: 780px;
}
```

| | Monday | Tuesday | Wednesday | June 2009 | Thursday | Friday | Saturday | Sunday |
|---|---|---|---|---|---|---|---|---|
| | | 1 | | | | | | |
| 31 | | • New pupils' open day  2<br>• Year 8 theater trip | | 3 | 4 | | 5 | 6 |
| 7 | | | | | | | | |
| | • Year 7 English exam  8 | | 9 | | 10 | 11 | 12 | 13 |
| | | | | 17 | | 18 | | |
| 14 | | 15 | 16 | | • Sports Day | • Year 7 parents' evening<br>• Prizegiving | 19 | 20 |
| | | | | 24 | | | | |
| 21 | | 22 | 23 | | • Year 8 parents' evening  25 | | 26 | 27 |
| | | | | 30 | | | | |
| 28 | | 29 | | • First night of school  1 play | 2 | | 3 | 4 |

Figure 5.16. Displaying the calendar without CSS

I styled the caption within the class clmonth, then created styles for the table headers (th) and table cells (td):

```
                                            chapter05/cal.css (excerpt)

.clmonth caption {
  text-align: left;
  font: bold 110% Georgia, "Times New Roman", Times, serif;
  padding-bottom: 0.4em;
}
.clmonth th {
  border: 1px solid #AAAAAA;
  border-bottom: none;
  padding: 0.2em 0.6em 0.2em 0.6em;
  background-color: #CCCCCC;
  color: #3F3F3F;
  font: 80% Verdana, Geneva, Arial, Helvetica, sans-serif;
  width: 110px;
}
.clmonth td {
  border: 1px solid #EAEAEA;
  font: 80% Verdana, Geneva, Arial, Helvetica, sans-serif;
  padding: 0.2em 0.6em 0.2em 0.6em;
  vertical-align: top;
}
```

As you can see in Figure 5.17, our calendar is beginning to take shape.

**June 2009**

| Monday | Tuesday | Wednesday | Thursday | Friday | Saturday | Sunday |
|---|---|---|---|---|---|---|
| 31 | 1 | 2 | 3 | 4 | 5 | 6 |
| | • New pupils' open day<br>• Year 8 theater trip | | | | | |
| 7 | 8 | 9 | 10 | 11 | 12 | 13 |
| • Year 7 English exam | | | | | | |
| 14 | 15 | 16 | 17 | 18 | 19 | 20 |
| | | | • Sports Day | • Year 7 parents' evening<br>• Prizegiving | | |
| 21 | 22 | 23 | 24 | 25 | 26 | 27 |
| | | | • Year 8 parents' evening | | | |
| 28 | 29 | 30 | 1 | 2 | 3 | 4 |
| | | • First night of school play | | | | |

Figure 5.17. Styling the `caption`, `th`, and `td` elements to make the calendar more user-friendly

We can now style the lists of events within each table cell, removing the bullet and adding space between list items:

chapter05/cal.css *(excerpt)*

```css
.clmonth ul {
  list-style-type: none;
  margin: 0;
  padding-left: 1em;
  padding-right: 0.6em;
}
.clmonth li {
  margin-bottom: 1em;
}
```

Finally, we add styles for the `previous` and `next` classes, which give the effect of graying out those days that are not part of the current month. We also style the `active` class, which highlights those days on which events will take place:

chapter05/cal.css (excerpt)

```
.clmonth td.previous, .clmonth td.next {
  background-color: #F6F6F6;
  color: #C6C6C6;
}
.clmonth td.active {
  background-color: #B1CBE1;
  color: #2B5070;
  border: 2px solid #4682B4;
}
```

This is just one of many ways to create a calendar. Online calendars are commonly used on blogs, where they have clickable days where visitors can view entries made that month. By removing the events from our HTML markup, representing the day names with single letters—M for Monday, and so on—and making a few simple changes to our CSS, we can create a simple mini-calendar that's suitable for this purpose, like the one shown in Figure 5.18.

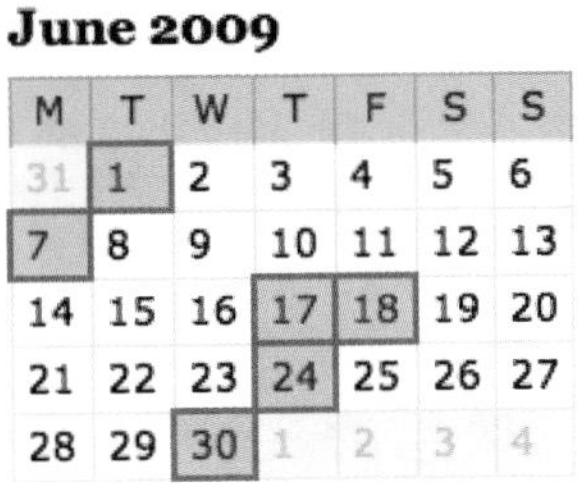

**June 2009**

| M | T | W | T | F | S | S |
|---|---|---|---|---|---|---|
| 31 | 1 | 2 | 3 | 4 | 5 | 6 |
| 7 | 8 | 9 | 10 | 11 | 12 | 13 |
| 14 | 15 | 16 | 17 | 18 | 19 | 20 |
| 21 | 22 | 23 | 24 | 25 | 26 | 27 |
| 28 | 29 | 30 | 1 | 2 | 3 | 4 |

Figure 5.18. Creating a mini-calendar

Here's the HTML and CSS you'll need for this version of the calendar:

chapter05/cal_mini.html *(excerpt)*

```html
<table class="clmonth" summary="Calendar for June 2009">
  <caption>June 2009</caption>
  <tr>
    <th scope="col">M</th>
    <th scope="col">T</th>
    <th scope="col">W</th>
    <th scope="col">T</th>
    <th scope="col">F</th>
    <th scope="col">S</th>
    <th scope="col">S</th>
  </tr>
  <tr>
    <td class="previous">31</td>
    <td class="active">1</td>
    <td>2</td>
    <td>3</td>
    <td>4</td>
    <td>5</td>
    <td>6</td>
  </tr>
  <tr>
    <td class="active">7</td>
    <td>8</td>
    <td>9</td>
    <td>10</td>
    <td>11</td>
    <td>12</td>
    <td>13</td>
  </tr>
  <tr>
    <td>14</td>
    <td>15</td>
    <td>16</td>
    <td class="active">17</td>
    <td class="active">18</td>
    <td>19</td>
    <td>20</td>
  </tr>
  <tr>
    <td>21</td>
```

```
    <td>22</td>
    <td>23</td>
    <td class="active">24</td>
    <td>25</td>
    <td>26</td>
    <td>27</td>
  </tr>
  <tr>
    <td>28</td>
    <td>29</td>
    <td class="active">30</td>
    <td class="next">1</td>
    <td class="next">2</td>
    <td class="next">3</td>
    <td class="next">4</td>
  </tr>
</table>
```

chapter05/cal_mini.css

```
body {
  background-color: #FFFFFF;
  color: #000000;
  font-size: 90%;
}
.clmonth {
  border-collapse: collapse;
}
.clmonth caption {
  text-align: left;
  font: bold 110% Georgia, "Times New Roman", Times, serif;
  padding-bottom: 0.4em;
}
.clmonth th {
  border: 1px solid #AAAAAA;
  border-bottom: none;
  padding: 0.2em 0.4em 0.2em 0.4em;
  background-color: #CCCCCC;
  color: #3F3F3F;
  font: 80% Verdana, Geneva, Arial, Helvetica, sans-serif;
}
.clmonth td {
  border: 1px solid #EAEAEA;
  font: 80% Verdana, Geneva, Arial, Helvetica, sans-serif;
```

```
    padding: 0.2em 0.4em 0.2em 0.4em;
    vertical-align: top;
}
.clmonth td.previous, .clmonth td.next {
    background-color: #F6F6F6;
    color: #C6C6C6;
}
.clmonth td.active {
    background-color: #B1CBE1;
    color: #2B5070;
    border: 2px solid #4682B4;
}
```

## Summary

In this chapter, we've discovered that tables are alive and well—when used for their original purpose of displaying tabular data, that is! CSS gives you the ability to turn data tables into really attractive interface items, without negatively impacting their accessibility. So, please, embrace tables and use them to display tabular data—that's their job!

# Chapter 6

# Forms and User Interfaces

Forms are an inescapable part of web design and development. We use them to capture personal data from our users, to post information to message boards, to add items to shopping carts, and to update our blogs—to name just a few!

Despite the necessity of forms on the Web, HTML makes virtually no styling options available to the designer, so forms have traditionally been rendered in the default style of the browser. CSS has brought with it many ways to address form elements, so this chapter will consider what can be styled in a form and why you might want to do so. That said, this chapter will also cover some of the less-common HTML form tags and attributes whose application can boost the accessibility and usability of our forms, as well as providing additional elements to which we can apply CSS.

In the following pages, we'll consider forms laid out using CSS positioning as well as their table-based counterparts. Debate rages as to whether it's appropriate to lay out a form using a table; my take is that, if a form is tabular in nature—for instance, like the one in the spreadsheet example we'll encounter in this chapter—a table is the most logical way to structure the fields. Otherwise, your form is likely to be more accessible if it's laid out using CSS.

As we work with forms, it's especially important to consider the usability of the forms themselves. Forms are designed to accept user input, but they'll fail in that task if site visitors are unsure how to use them, regardless of how beautiful they look. In most cases I would suggest that you avoid styling forms too heavily, as doing so may confuse visitors. Also be aware that browsers differ in how much control over form elements you have; you'll need to accept the differences and be sure to test your CSS in as many browsers and platforms as possible.

# How do I style form elements using CSS?

Unstyled form elements will display according to browser and operating system defaults. However, you can use CSS to create forms that correspond to your site's visual design.

## Solution

Styles can be created for form elements just as they can for any other HTML element.

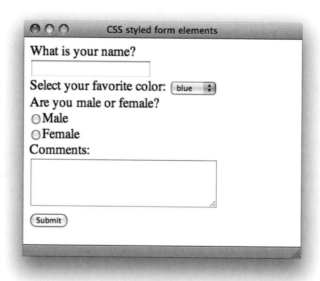

Figure 6.1. The basic appearance of an unstyled form, according to Safari's default styles

The form shown above in Figure 6.1 is unstyled; it's displayed according to Safari's default styles on Mac OS X, and its appearance will change on different browsers and operating systems. Here's a typical form:

chapter06/elements.html *(excerpt)*

```
<!DOCTYPE html PUBLIC "-//W3C//DTD XHTML 1.0 Strict//EN"
    "http://www.w3.org/TR/xhtml1/DTD/xhtml1-strict.dtd">
<html xmlns="http://www.w3.org/1999/xhtml" lang="en-US">
<head>
  <title>CSS styled form elements</title>
  <meta http-equiv="content-type"
    content="text/html; charset=utf-8" />
  <link rel="stylesheet" type="text/css" href="elements.css" />
</head>
<body>
  <form method="post" action="example1.html" id="form1">
    <div><label for="name">What is your name?</label><br/>
    <input type="text" name="name" id="name" /></div>
    <div><label for="color">Select your favorite color:</label>
      <select name="color" id="color">
        <option value="blue">blue</option>
        <option value="red">red</option>
        <option value="green">green</option>
        <option value="yellow">yellow</option>
      </select>
    </div>
    <div><label for="sex">Are you male or female?</label><br/>
      <input type="radio" name="sex" id="male"
          value="male" />Male<br/>
      <input type="radio" name="sex" id="female"
          value="female" />Female
    </div>
    <div>
      <label for="comments">Comments:</label><br/>
      <textarea name="comments" id="comments" cols="30"
          rows="4"></textarea>
    </div>
    <div>
      <input type="submit" name="btnSubmit" id="btnSubmit"
          value="Submit" />
    </div>
  </form>
</body>
</html>
```

We can change the look of this form by creating CSS rules for the form, input, textarea, and select elements:

```
form {
  border: 1px dotted #AAAAAA;
  padding: 0.5em;
}
input {
  color: #00008B;
  background-color: #ADD8E6;
  border: 1px solid #00008B;
}
select {
  width: 100px;
  color: #00008B;
  background-color: #ADD8E6;
  border: 1px solid #00008B;
}
textarea {
  width: 200px;
  height: 40px;
  color: #00008B;
  background-color: #ADD8E6;
  border: 1px solid #00008B;
}
```

The new look is depicted in Figure 6.2.

## Discussion

As you'd expect, the definition of rules for the HTML elements form, input, textarea, and select will affect any instances of these elements in a page to which your style sheet is attached. You can use a variety of CSS properties to change the appearance of a form's fields. For example, CSS allows you to change almost every aspect of an <input type="text"> field:

```
<input type="text" name="name" id="name" />
```

```
input {
  color: #00008B;
  background-color: #ADD8E6;
  border: 1px solid #00008B;
  font: 0.9em Arial, Helvetica, sans-serif;
```

```
  padding: 0.2em;
  width: 200px;
}
```

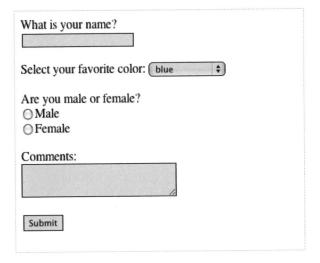

Figure 6.2. The same form displaying differently following the application of CSS

### Forms and Background Colors

Some users of your site are unable to easily distinguish colors, while others may be using a speaking browser. For these reasons you should never rely on colors for functionality on your site—for instance, instructions like, "The yellow fields are required" would be a big no-no.

Let's break down these styles:

**color**               changes the color of the text that's typed inside the field

**background-color**    defines the field's background

**border**              affects the border around the field; any of the other border styles here can be used

**font**                changes the font size and typeface of the text within the field

**padding**             moves the text typed within a field away from the edges of the box

**width**               allows the creation of form fields of the appropriate width for the data you expect users to enter (for example, a short field for a user's first initial)

# How do I apply different styles to fields in a single form?

The input element has many different types, and the styles that you need for a text field are unlikely to be the same as those you want to use for your buttons or checkboxes. How can you create specific styles for different form fields?

## Solution

You can use CSS classes to specify the exact styles that individual fields will use. The form in the following example has two input elements, one of which displays a text field, while the other displays a **Submit** button. Appropriate classes are applied to each:

chapter06/fields.html *(excerpt)*

```
<form method="post" action="fields.html">
<div>
  <label for="name">What is your name?</label><br />
  <input type="text" name="name" id="name" class="txt" />
</div>
```

```
<input type="submit" name="btnSubmit" id="btnSubmit"
    value="Submit" class="btn" />
</form>
```

chapter06/fields.css

```
form {
  border: 1px dotted #AAAAAA;
  padding: 3px 6px 3px 6px;
}
input.txt {
  color: #00008B;
  background-color: #ADD8E6;
  border: 1px inset #00008B;
  width: 200px;
}
input.btn {
  color: #00008B;
  background-color: #ADD8E6;
  border: 1px outset #00008B;
  padding: 2px 4px 2px 4px;
}
```

Figure 6.3 shows the result.

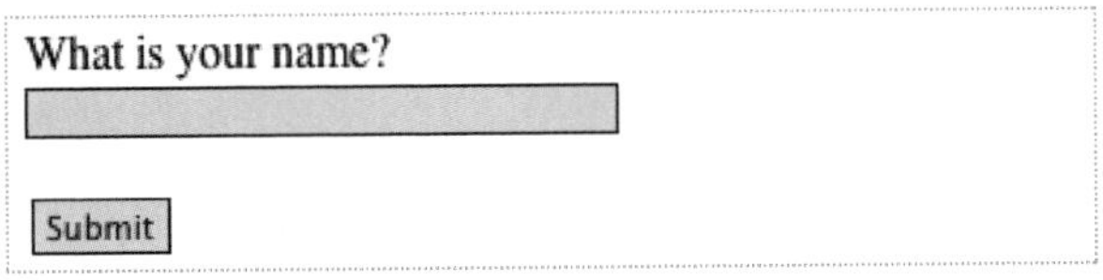


Figure 6.3. Applying different classes to each of the input fields

## Discussion

As we've seen, the `input` element can have several different types, and these types may require different styles in order to display appropriately. In the example above, we used classes to differentiate between an `input` element with a type of `text` and an `input` element with a type of `submit`. Had we simply created one set of styles for input, we might have ended up with the following (having set a width and used an inset border on the text field):

```
input {
    color: #00008B;
    background-color: #ADD8E6;
    border: 1px inset #00008B;
    width: 200px;
}
```

Applied to the form above, these styles would have displayed as shown in Figure 6.4.

Figure 6.4. Applying the same styles to both input fields

The **Submit** button now looks rather like a text field, certainly more so than a button!

Using various classes allows us to style each element exactly as we want it to display. The forms in any application will likely need to cater for a variety of data types. Some text fields may only require the user to enter two characters; others may need to accept a name or other short word; others must take an entire sentence. By creating CSS classes for small, medium, and large text fields, you can choose the field that's appropriate to the data you expect the user to enter. This, in turn, helps users feel confident that they're entering the correct information.

### Style Early, Style Often

When I begin work on a site that includes a lot of forms, one of my first steps is to create within the style sheet a number of classes for standard forms. It's of no concern if the style needs to change at a later date—that just involves tweaking the style sheet values. The important point is that classes are applied from the outset, so that any changes affect all the forms on the site.

**Using Attribute Selectors to Identify Different Form Elements**

You can also use attribute selectors to identify the different form elements rather than adding a class. I introduced attribute selectors back in the section called "How can I visually indicate which links are external to my site?" in Chapter 4. To target the text field in the above example we could use the selector:

```
input[type="text"] {
    ⋮
}
```

To target the submit button we'd use the following selector:

```
input[type="submit"] {
    ⋮
}
```

It would then be unnecessary to add any additional classes to the markup. However Internet Explorer 6 lacks support for this type of selector, so you risk having your forms look strange or be unusable in that browser. If you still need to support IE6 users you'll have to use classes.

# How do I stop my form from creating additional whitespace and line breaks?

A form is a block-level element and, like a paragraph, will display on a new line by default. This is usually the behavior you'd want to implement, but on some occasions you may wish to add a small form within the flow of a document—for instance, placing a small search box alongside other header elements.

## Solution

You can use the `display` property with a value of `inline` to display a form as an inline element:

chapter06/inline.html *(excerpt)*

```
Your email address:
<form method="post" action="inline.html">
  <div><input type="text" name="name" id="name" class="txt" />
  <input type="submit" name="btnSubmit" id="btnSubmit"
      value="Submit" class="btn" /></div>
</form>
```

chapter06/inline.css

```
form {
  display: inline;
}
input.txt {
  color: #00008B;
  background-color: #E3F2F7;
  border: 1px inset #00008B;
  width: 200px;
}
input.btn {
  color: #00008B;
  background-color: #ADD8E6;
  border: 1px outset #00008B;
}
```

As you can see in Figure 6.5, this CSS causes the form to join the document flow and sit inline with the text that surrounds it.

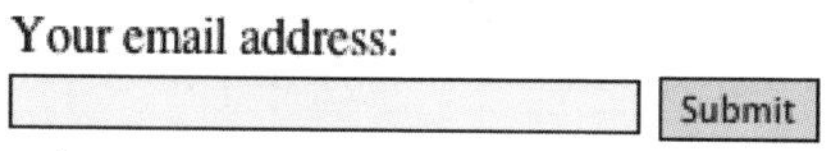

**Your email address:**
[                              ] Submit

Figure 6.5. Displaying a form inline

# How do I make a Submit button look like text?

It's generally a good idea to make buttons look like buttons if you expect people to click on them. However, on occasion, you might want to have your form's **Submit** button look more like plain text.

## Solution

Take a look at this style rule:

```
                                              chapter06/textbutton.css (excerpt)

.btn {
  background-color: transparent;
  border: 0;
  padding: 0;
}
```

The text **Next** » that appears on the second line in Figure 6.6 is actually a button!

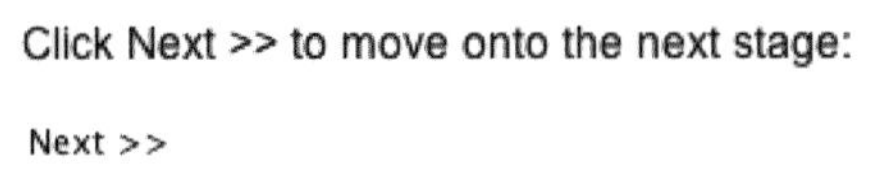

Click Next >> to move onto the next stage:

Next >>

Figure 6.6. Making a button look like text

# How do I ensure that users with text-only devices understand how to complete my form?

It's good to create an attractive and usable form for visitors who have standard web browsers, but bear in mind that many users will have a text-only view of your site. Before you use CSS to style your form, ensure that it's structured in a way that makes completing the form easy for text-only users.

# Solution

One of the most important ways to make your form more accessible is to ensure that all users understand which label belongs with each form field. If a visually impaired visitor is using a text-only device or screen reader—which reads the form aloud—it may be difficult for the visitor to determine which details to enter into each field, unless your form is well planned and created.

The label element ties a label to a specific form field—it's the ideal solution to this particular problem. Like other elements on the page, the label element is easily styled with CSS rules:

*chapter06/textonly.html (excerpt)*

```
<form method="post" action="textonly.html">
  <table>
    <tr>
      <td><label for="fullname">Name:</label></td>
      <td><input type="text" name="fullname" id="fullname"
          class="txt" /></td>
    </tr>
    <tr>
      <td><label for="email">Email Address:</label></td>
      <td><input type="text" name="email" id="email" class="txt"
          /></td>
    </tr>
    <tr>
      <td><label for="password1">Password:</label></td>
      <td><input type="password" name="password1" id="password1"
          class="txt" /></td>
    </tr>
    <tr>
      <td><label for="password2">Confirm Password:</label></td>
      <td><input type="password" name="password2" id="password2"
          class="txt" /></td>
    </tr>
    <tr>
      <td><label for="level">Membership Level:</label></td>
      <td><select name="level">
          <option value="silver">silver</option>
          <option value="gold">gold</option>
        </select></td>
    </tr>
```

```
  </table>
  <p>
    <input type="submit" name="btnSubmit" id="btnSubmit"
        value="Sign Up!" class="btn" />
  </p>
</form>
```

chapter06/textonly.css

```css
h1 {
  font: 1.2em Arial, Helvetica, sans-serif;
}
input.txt {
  color: #00008B;
  background-color: #E3F2F7;
  border: 1px inset #00008B;
  width: 200px;
}
input.btn {
  color: #00008B;
  background-color: #ADD8E6;
  border: 1px outset #00008B;
}
label {
  font : bold 0.9em  Arial, Helvetica, sans-serif;
}
```

The results of these styles can be seen in Figure 6.7—though keep in mind that the benefits of these styles for visually impaired users are less obvious in a printed book! That said, as well as improving the form's usability for text-only browsers and screen readers, these styles will cause visual browsers to place the cursor in the corresponding field when the user clicks on one of the labels. When you add a label, everybody wins!

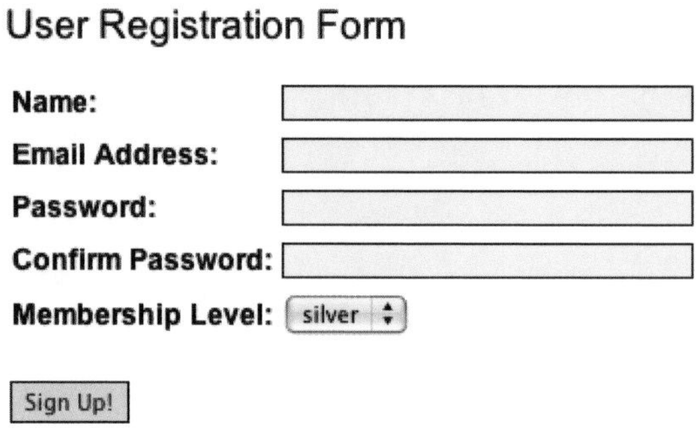

## User Registration Form

Name:

Email Address:

Password:

Confirm Password:

Membership Level: [ silver ↕ ]

[ Sign Up! ]

Figure 6.7. Displaying the form in the browser

# Discussion

The label element makes it possible to indicate clearly what information users need to enter into a field. As we've discussed, forms that may be read out to users by their screen readers need to make the purpose of each field immediately obvious. With a layout such as the one provided in this example, which uses a table to display the label in one cell and the field in another, it's especially important that we include a label element. (In the solution that follows, I'll demonstrate how to achieve the same form layout without using a table.)

The connection between the label and the relevant form element is created with the `<label>` tag's for attribute; you insert the ID of the field that the label describes:

```
chapter06/textonly.html (excerpt)

<tr>
  <td><label for="fullname">Name:</label></td>
  <td><input type="text" name="fullname" id="fullname"
       class="txt" /></td>
</tr>
```

Once you have your label element in place, you'll have made an important step towards ensuring that those using screen readers will understand how to complete your form. Keep in mind that you can also use CSS to style the label element itself:

chapter06/textonly.css *(excerpt)*

```
label {
  font: bold 0.9em  Arial, Helvetica, sans-serif;
}
```

 **Use of Implicit Labels**

An alternative way of using the `label` element is as an **implicit label**. This is where the form element is nested within the label element (thus implying the connection) without using the `for` attribute, like so:

```
<label Name: <input type="text" name="fullname" id="fullname"
    class="txt" /></label>
```

While perfectly valid, this usage is discouraged because some assistive technology software programs handle implicit labels incorrectly.[1] To be safe, always use the `for` attribute.

# How do I lay out a two-column form using CSS instead of a table?

Forms can be tricky to lay out without tables, but the task is still possible. Figure 6.8 shows a form layout that looks remarkably table-like, but if you examine the HTML code that follows, you'll find there's no table in sight:

---

[1] http://www.w3.org/TR/WCAG20-GENERAL/H44.html

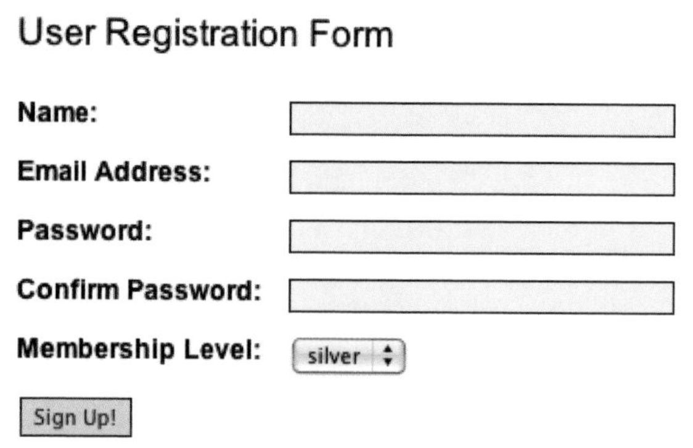

## User Registration Form

**Name:**

**Email Address:**

**Password:**

**Confirm Password:**

**Membership Level:** silver ⇕

Sign Up!

Figure 6.8. A two-column form laid out using CSS

chapter06/tablefree.html

```
<!DOCTYPE html PUBLIC "-//W3C//DTD XHTML 1.0 Strict//EN"
    "http://www.w3.org/TR/xhtml1/DTD/xhtml1-strict.dtd">
<html xmlns="http://www.w3.org/1999/xhtml" lang="en-US">
<head>
<title>Table-free form layout</title>
<meta http-equiv="content-type"
    content="text/html; charset=utf-8" />
<link rel="stylesheet" type="text/css" href="tablefree.css" />
</head>
<body>
<h1>User Registration Form</h1>
<form method="post" action="tablefree.html">
  <div>
    <label for="fullname">Name:</label>
    <input type="text" name="fullname" id="fullname"
        class="txt" />
  </div>
  <div>
    <label for="email">Email Address:</label>
    <input type="text" name="email" id="email" class="txt" />
  </div>
  <div>
    <label for="password1">Password:</label>
    <input type="password" name="password1" id="password1"
        class="txt" />
  </div>
```

```
  <div>
    <label for="password2">Confirm Password:</label>
    <input type="password" name="password2" id="password2"
       class="txt" />
  </div>
  <div>
    <label for="level">Membership Level:</label>
    <select name="level">
      <option value="silver">silver</option>
      <option value="gold">gold</option>
    </select>
  </div>
  <div>
    <input type="submit" name="btnSubmit" id="btnSubmit"
       value="Sign Up!" class="btn" />
  </div>
</form>
</body>
</html>
```

chapter06/tablefree.css

```
h1 {
  font: 1.2em Arial, Helvetica, sans-serif;
}
input.txt {
  color: #00008B;
  background-color: #E3F2F7;
  border: 1px inset #00008B;
  width: 200px;
}
input.btn {
  color: #00008B;
  background-color: #ADD8E6;
  border: 1px outset #00008B;
}
form div {
  clear: left;
  margin: 0;
  padding: 0;
  padding-top: 0.6em;
}
form div label {
  float: left;
```

```
    width: 40%;
    font: bold 0.9em Arial, Helvetica, sans-serif;
}
```

## Discussion

The example above creates a common form layout. As we saw earlier in this chapter, this layout's often achieved using a two-column table in which the label is placed in one cell, the field in another:

chapter06/textonly.html *(excerpt)*

```
<form method="post" action="textonly.html">
  <table>
    <tr>
      <td><label for="fullname">Name:</label></td>
      <td><input type="text" name="fullname" id="fullname"
          class="txt" /></td>
    </tr>
    <tr>
      <td><label for="email">Email Address:</label></td>
      <td><input type="text" name="email" id="email" class="txt"
        /></td>
    </tr>
    <tr>
      <td><label for="password1">Password:</label></td>
      <td><input type="password" name="password1" id="password1"
          class="txt" /></td>
    </tr>
    <tr>
      <td><label for="password2">Confirm Password:</label></td>
      <td><input type="password" name="password2" id="password2"
          class="txt" /></td>
    </tr>
    <tr>
      <td><label for="level">Membership Level:</label></td>
      <td><select name="level">
          <option value="silver">silver</option>
          <option value="gold">gold</option>
        </select></td>
    </tr>
  </table>
  <p>
```

```
        <input type="submit" name="btnSubmit" id="btnSubmit"
            value="Sign Up!" class="btn" />
    </p>
</form>
```

This form has been laid out using a table to ensure that all the fields line up neatly. Without the table, the fields appear immediately after the labels, as Figure 6.9 shows.

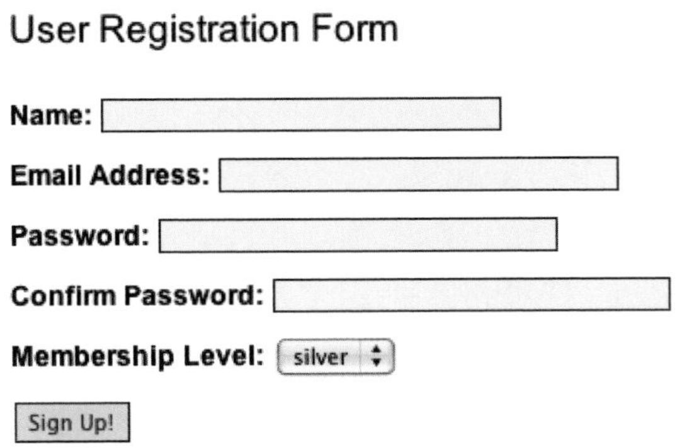

## User Registration Form

Name:

Email Address:

Password:

Confirm Password:

Membership Level: silver

Sign Up!

Figure 6.9. A form laid out sans table

In the markup that's used to create the form shown in Figure 6.9, each form row is located within a `div` element, causing the field to appear immediately after the label:

chapter06/tablefree.html *(excerpt)*

```
<form method="post" action="tablefree.html">
  <div>
    <label for="fullname">Name:</label>
    <input type="text" name="fullname" id="fullname" class="txt"
        />
  </div>
  <div>
    <label for="email">Email Address:</label>
```

```
    <input type="text" name="email" id="email" class="txt" />
  </div>
  ⋮
```

To recreate the effect of the table-based layout using only CSS, there's no need to make any changes to our markup. All we need is some simple CSS:

chapter06/tablefree.css

```css
form div {
  clear: left;
  margin: 0;
  padding: 0;
  padding-top: 0.6em;
}
form div label {
  float: left;
  width: 40%;
  font: bold 0.9em Arial, Helvetica, sans-serif;
}
```

What we're doing here is addressing our `label` element directly in the style sheet. We float it to the left, give it a `width` value, and modify its font settings.

As the `float` property takes an element out of the document flow, we need to give our `div`s a `clear` property with the value `left`, to ensure that each `div` starts below the `label` in the preceding `div`. We also give our `div`s a `padding-top` value, in order to space out the rows, and that's it!

# How do I group related fields?

Large web forms can be made much more usable if the visitor can ascertain which questions are related. We need a way to show the relationships between information—a way that helps users with standard browsers as well as those using text-only devices and screen readers.

## Solution

We can group related fields using the `fieldset` and `legend` elements:

```
<form method="post" action="fieldset.html">
  <fieldset>
    <legend>Personal Information</legend>
    <div>
      <label for="fullname">Name:</label>
      <input type="text" name="fullname" id="fullname"
          class="txt" />
    </div>
    <div>
      <label for="email">Email Address:</label>
      <input type="text" name="email" id="email" class="txt" />
    </div>
    <div>
      <label for="password1">Password:</label>
      <input type="password" name="password1" id="password1"
          class="txt" />
    </div>
    <div>
      <label for="password2">Confirm Password:</label>
      <input type="password" name="password2" id="password2"
          class="txt" />
    </div>
  </fieldset>
  <fieldset>
    <legend>Address Details</legend>
    <div>
      <label for="address1">Address line one:</label>
      <input type="text" name="address1" id="address1"
          class="txt" />
    </div>
    <div>
      <label for="address2">Address line two:</label>
      <input type="text" name="address2" id="address2"
          class="txt" />
    </div>
    <div>
      <label for="city">Town / City:</label>
      <input type="text" name="city" id="city" class="txt" />
    </div>
    <div>
      <label for="zip">Zip / Post code:</label>
      <input type="text" name="zip" id="zip" class="txt" />
```

```
    </div>
  </fieldset>
  <div>
    <input type="submit" name="btnSubmit" id="btnSubmit"
        value="Sign Up!" class="btn" />
  </div>
</form>
```

```css
h1 {
  font: 1.2em Arial, Helvetica, sans-serif;
}
input.txt {
  color: #00008B;
  background-color: #E3F2F7;
  border: 1px inset #00008B;
  width: 200px;
}
input.btn {
  color: #00008B;
  background-color: #ADD8E6;
  border: 1px outset #00008B;
}
form div {
  clear: left;
  margin: 0;
  padding: 0;
  padding-top: 5px;
}
form div label {
  float: left;
  width: 40%;
  font: bold 0.9em Arial, Helvetica, sans-serif;
}
fieldset {
  border: 1px dotted #61B5CF;
  margin-top: 1.4em;
  padding: 0.6em;
}
legend {
  font: bold 0.8em Arial, Helvetica, sans-serif;
```

```
    color: #00008B;
    background-color: #FFFFFF;
}
```

Figure 6.10 shows how the groupings are displayed by the browser.

## User Registration Form

```
┌─ Personal Information ─────────────────────────────────────┐
│                                                            │
│   Name:              [                              ]      │
│                                                            │
│   Email Address:     [                              ]      │
│                                                            │
│   Password:          [                              ]      │
│                                                            │
│   Confirm Password:  [                              ]      │
│                                                            │
└────────────────────────────────────────────────────────────┘

┌─ Address Details ──────────────────────────────────────────┐
│                                                            │
│   Address line one:  [                              ]      │
│                                                            │
│   Address line two:  [                              ]      │
│                                                            │
│   Town / City:       [                              ]      │
│                                                            │
│   Zip / Post code:   [                              ]      │
│                                                            │
└────────────────────────────────────────────────────────────┘

[ Sign Up! ]
```

Figure 6.10. Creating two sections in a form using the `<fieldset>` tag

# Discussion

The `<fieldset>` and `<legend>` tags are a great way to group related information in a form. These tags provide an easy means to group items visually, and are understood by screen readers and text-only devices, which can perceive that the tagged items are logically grouped together. The situation would be quite different if you simply wrapped the related items in a styled `div`; users of a standard browser *would* understand the relationship, in contrast to those unable to see the results of our CSS.

To group form fields, simply wrap the related fields with a `<fieldset>` tag and, immediately after your opening `<fieldset>` tag, add a `<legend>` tag that contains a title for the group:

```
                                          chapter06/fieldset.html (excerpt)

<fieldset>
  <legend>Personal Information</legend>
  <div>
    <label for="fullname">Name:</label>
    <input type="text" name="fullname" id="fullname" class="txt"
        />
  </div>
  <div>
    <label for="email">Email Address:</label>
    <input type="text" name="email" id="email" class="txt" />
  </div>
  <div>
    <label for="password1">Password:</label>
    <input type="password" name="password1" id="password1"
        class="txt" />
  </div>
  <div>
    <label for="password2">Confirm Password:</label>
    <input type="password" name="password2" id="password2"
        class="txt" />
  </div>
</fieldset>
```

Like other HTML tags, <fieldset> and <legend> are displayed with a default style by browsers. The default style surrounds the grouped elements with a box, and the <legend> tag appears in the top-left corner of that box. Figure 6.11 shows the <fieldset> and <legend> tags as they display by default in Firefox on Mac OS X.

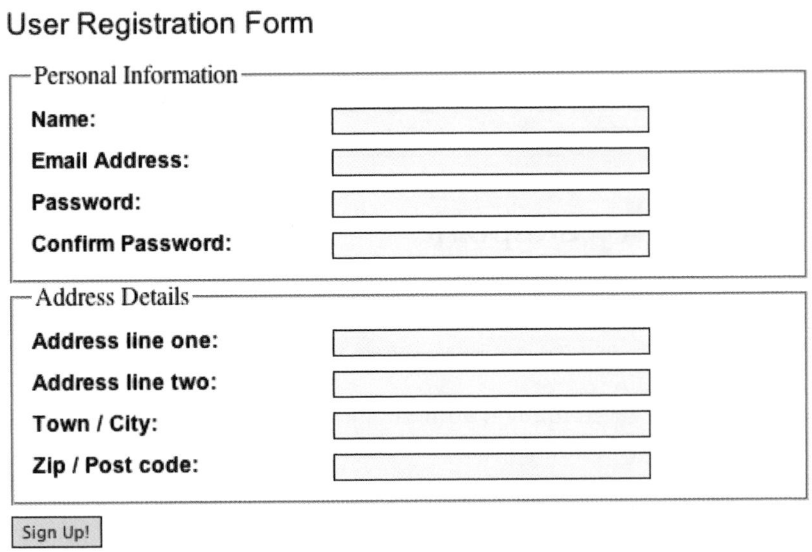

User Registration Form

Figure 6.11. Viewing unstyled `<fieldset>` and `<legend>` tags

# How do I style **accesskey** hints?

Access keys allow users to jump quickly to a certain place in a document or follow a link—all they need to do is press a combination of keys; usually the **Alt** key (or equivalent), and another specific key. You have to let users know what that other key is, of course!

## Solution

The convention that's followed by many computer operating systems is to indicate which letter of a key word is its access key by underlining that letter. For example, on a Windows machine, **Alt+F** opens the **File** drop-down menu. This functionality is indicated by the underlining of the letter "F" in **File**, as shown in Figure 6.12.

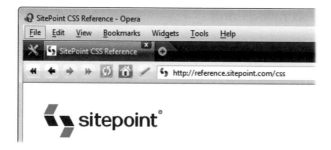

Figure 6.12. The underline beneath the letter "F" in the word **File**

You can use a similar technique on your site, underlining the appropriate letters to identify your access keys:

chapter06/accesskeys.html *(excerpt)*

```
<fieldset>
  <legend><span class="akey">P</span>ersonal
    Information</legend>
  <div>
    <label for="fullname">Name:</label>
    <input type="text" name="fullname" id="fullname" class="txt"
      accesskey="p" />
  </div>
```

chapter06/accesskeys.css *(excerpt)*

```
.akey {
  text-decoration: underline;
}
```

As you can see in Figure 6.13, the access key for each field set is underlined.

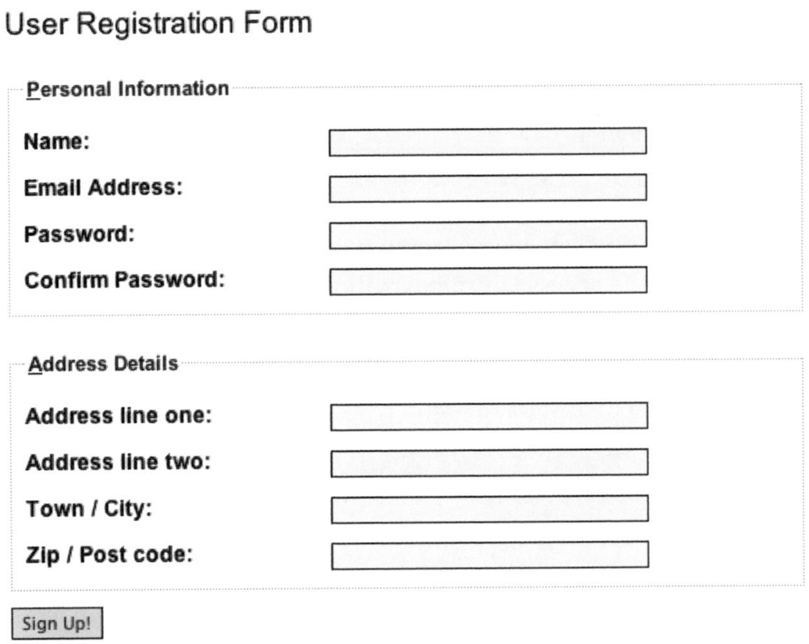

## User Registration Form

**Personal Information**

**Name:** [                    ]

**Email Address:** [                    ]

**Password:** [                    ]

**Confirm Password:** [                    ]

**Address Details**

**Address line one:** [                    ]

**Address line two:** [                    ]

**Town / City:** [                    ]

**Zip / Post code:** [                    ]

[Sign Up!]

Figure 6.13. Indicating access keys with lines under the "P" in **Personal** and "A" in **Address**

# Discussion

Access keys can be very helpful to site users who have mobility problems and are unable to use a mouse, as well as to users who simply prefer using the keyboard over the mouse to navigate. You could provide an access key that allowed these visitors to jump straight to the form by pressing one key, for example, or to go to the search box by pressing another. The convention of underlining the letter that corresponds to the access key will be familiar to visitors who use this functionality, even if other users are unaware what it means.

To add access key functionality to a form field, you simply need to add the attribute `accesskey="x"` to that field, where $x$ is the character you've chosen for the access key:

```
chapter06/accesskeys.html (excerpt)

<div>
  <label for="fullname">Name:</label>
  <input type="text" name="fullname" id="fullname" class="txt"
     accesskey="p" />
</div>
```

In our example, I've added an access key to the first form element of each group. When a user presses the access key, focus will move to that first form field so that users can begin to complete the form. To highlight the access key, I've taken the first letter of the field set `<legend>` (for example, the "P" in "Personal Details") and wrapped it in a span with a class of `akey`:

```
chapter06/accesskeys.html (excerpt)

<legend><span class="akey">P</span>ersonal Information</legend>
```

I've styled the `akey` class, setting the `text-decoration` property to `underline`:

```
chapter06/accesskeys.css (excerpt)

.akey {
  text-decoration: underline;
}
```

Different browsers and operating systems implement access keys in different ways. For example, Internet Explorer, and Firefox 1.5 on Windows use the **Alt** key. However, Firefox version 2 and above on Windows uses **Alt+Shift** (at the time of writing, however, this only works for alphabetical access keys, as opposed to numeric ones). Safari uses **Ctrl**, as does Firefox on Mac OS X (again no numeric shortcuts), and Opera uses **Shift+Esc** but allows users to configure their own key combinations.

 **Access Keys May Be Less Accessible Than They Appear**

When creating access keys, take care to avoid overriding default browser or system keyboard shortcuts!

# How do I use different colored highlights in a `select` menu?

Earlier, we learned how to color the background of a `select` menu in a form. But is it possible to include several colors in the menu to highlight different options?

## Solution

You can assign classes to menu options to apply multiple background colors within the drop-down menu. `color` and `background-color` are the only properties you can set for a menu item.

 **Safari Has No Stripes**

Remember, Safari lacks support for background colors on select options, so this solution will fail to work in that browser.

Here's the code you'll need:

*chapter06/select.html (excerpt)*

```
<form method="post" action="example8.html">
  <div>
    <label for="color">Select your favorite color:</label>
    <select name="color" id="color">
      <option value="">Select One</option>
      <option value="blue" class="blue">blue</option>
      <option value="red" class="red">red</option>
      <option value="green" class="green">green</option>
      <option value="yellow" class="yellow">yellow</option>
    </select>
  </div>
  <div>
    <input type="submit" name="btnSubmit" id="btnSubmit"
        value="Send!" class="btn" />
  </div>
</form>
```

```
                                        chapter06/select.css (excerpt)
option.blue {
  background-color: #ADD8E6;
  color: #000000;
}
option.red {
  background-color: #E20A0A;
  color: #ffffff;
}
option.green {
  background-color: #3CB371;
  color: #ffffff;
}
option.yellow {
  background-color: #FFF280;
  color: #000000;
}
```

Thanks to this code, the drop-down menu in Figure 6.14 looks very colorful indeed.

Figure 6.14. Classes applied to options displaying within a selectmenu, as seen in the Opera browser

## Discussion

We'd normally avoid using such presentational class names in our CSS. For example, giving a heading a class name of blue would be a poor decision, as you might decide later to change the color of all headings to green—you'd then either be left with a bunch of headings that had a class of blue but displayed as green, or you'd have to change all of your markup. However, in the case of a color selection form, like in this example, common sense prevails!

### Style with Substance

Use different background colors on sets of related options, or apply alternating row colors in your `select` menu.

### Alternatively, Use Attribute Selectors

Once again, an alternative to adding class names to your markup would be to use attribute selectors in your CSS. For example, instead of the selector `option.blue`, you could use:

```css
option[value="blue"] {
  background-color: #ADD8E6;
  color: #000000;
}
```

Of course, once again, you'll have to take the lack of support from IE6 into consideration.

# How do I style a form with CSS that allows users to enter data as if into a spreadsheet?

While laying out forms using CSS is possible—and recommended in most cases—there are some circumstances in which data is more easily entered into a form within a table. One obvious example is a spreadsheet-like web application.

Users may already be accustomed to entering data into a spreadsheet using Microsoft Excel or another package. Keep this in mind as you design your application interface—mimicking familiar interfaces often helps users to feel comfortable with your application. Making your form look like a spreadsheet by laying it out in a table and using CSS to format it may be the way to go. Let's take a look at the code:

chapter06/spreadsheet.html *(excerpt)*

```html
<form method="post" action="spreadsheet.html">
<table class="formdata" summary="This table contains a form to
    input the yearly income for years 1999 through 2002">
  <caption>Complete the Yearly Income 1999 - 2002</caption>
```

```
<tr>
  <th></th>
  <th scope="col">1999</th>
  <th scope="col">2000</th>
  <th scope="col">2001</th>
  <th scope="col">2002</th>
</tr>
<tr>
  <th scope="row">Grants</th>
  <td><input type="text" name="grants1999" id="grants1999" />
    </td>
  <td><input type="text" name="grants2000" id="grants2000" />
    </td>
  <td><input type="text" name="grants2001" id="grants2001" />
    </td>
  <td><input type="text" name="grants2002" id="grants2002" />
    </td>
</tr>
<tr>
  <th scope="row">Donations</th>
  <td><input type="text" name="donations1999" id="donations1999"
      /></td>
  <td><input type="text" name="donations2000" id="donations2000"
      /></td>
  <td><input type="text" name="donations2001" id="donations2001"
      /></td>
  <td><input type="text" name="donations2002" id="donations2002"
      /></td>
</tr>
<tr>
  <th scope="row">Investments</th>
  <td><input type="text" name="investments1999"
      id="investments1999" /></td>
  <td><input type="text" name="investments2000"
      id="investments2000" /></td>
  <td><input type="text" name="investments2001"
      id="investments2001" /></td>
  <td><input type="text" name="investments2002"
      id="investments2002" /></td>
</tr>
<tr>
  <th scope="row">Fundraising</th>
  <td><input type="text" name="fundraising1999"
      id="fundraising1999" /></td>
```

```
    <td><input type="text" name="fundraising2000"
        id="fundraising2000" /></td>
    <td><input type="text" name="fundraising2001"
        id="fundraising2001" /></td>
    <td><input type="text" name="fundraising2002"
        id="fundraising2002" /></td>
  </tr>
  <tr>
    <th scope="row">Sales</th>
    <td><input type="text" name="sales1999" id="sales1999" /></td>
    <td><input type="text" name="sales2000" id="sales2000" /></td>
    <td><input type="text" name="sales2001" id="sales2001" /></td>
    <td><input type="text" name="sales2002" id="sales2002" /></td>
  </tr>
  <tr>
    <th scope="row">Miscellaneous</th>
    <td><input type="text" name="misc1999" id="misc1999" /></td>
    <td><input type="text" name="misc2000" id="misc2000" /></td>
    <td><input type="text" name="misc2001" id="misc2001" /></td>
    <td><input type="text" name="misc2002" id="misc2002" /></td>
  </tr>
  <tr>
    <th scope="row">Total</th>
    <td><input type="text" name="total1999" id="total1999" /></td>
    <td><input type="text" name="total2000" id="total2000" /></td>
    <td><input type="text" name="total2001" id="total2001" /></td>
    <td><input type="text" name="total2002" id="total2002" /></td>
  </tr>
</table>
<div><input type="submit" name="btnSubmit" id="btnSubmit"
        value="Add Data" /></div>
</form>
```

chapter06/spreadsheet.css

```css
table.formdata {
  border: 1px solid #5F6F7E;
  border-collapse: collapse;
  margin: 1em 0 2em 0;
}
table.formdata th {
  border: 1px solid #5F6F7E;
  background-color: #E2E2E2;
  color: #000000;
```

```
    text-align: left;
    font-weight: normal;
    padding: 0.2em 0.4em 0.2em 0.4em;
    margin: 0;
}
table.formdata td {
    margin: 0;
    padding: 0;
    border: 1px solid #E2E2E2;
}
table.formdata input {
    width: 80px;
    padding: 0.2em 0.4em 0.2em 0.4em;
    margin: 0;
    border: none;
}
```

The styled form, which looks very spreadsheet-like, is shown in Figure 6.15.

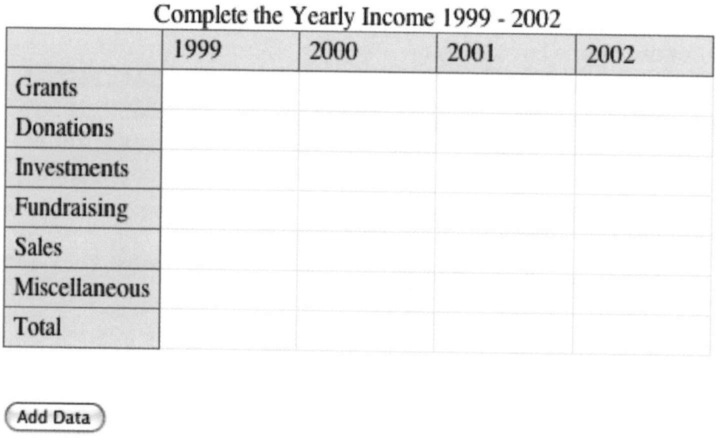

| Complete the Yearly Income 1999 - 2002 | | | | |
|---|---|---|---|---|
| | 1999 | 2000 | 2001 | 2002 |
| Grants | | | | |
| Donations | | | | |
| Investments | | | | |
| Fundraising | | | | |
| Sales | | | | |
| Miscellaneous | | | | |
| Total | | | | |

Add Data

Figure 6.15. A form styled to resemble a spreadsheet

# Discussion

The aim here is to create a form that looks similar to a spreadsheet, such as the Excel spreadsheet shown in Figure 6.16. Recently, I created forms similar to this for a web application that had many tables of data. The client wanted the table to turn into an editable table when it was selected for editing; so while it retained the appearance of the original data table, the contents could be edited by the user.

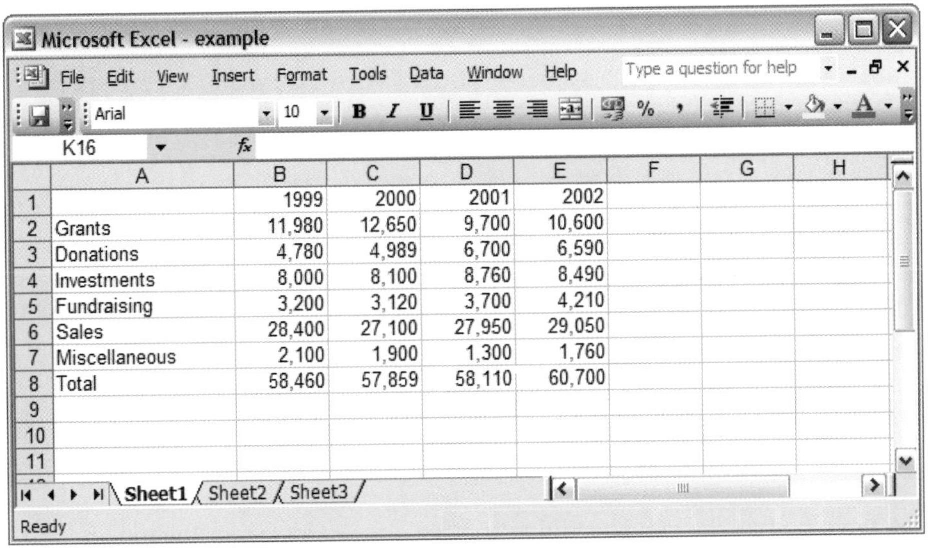

Figure 6.16. A spreadsheet displaying in Excel

The first step to achieve this effect is to lay out the form within a structured table, using table headings (th elements) where appropriate, and adding a caption and summary for accessibility purposes. The complete code for this form is provided in the solution above. Before we add any CSS, the form should display as shown in Figure 6.17.

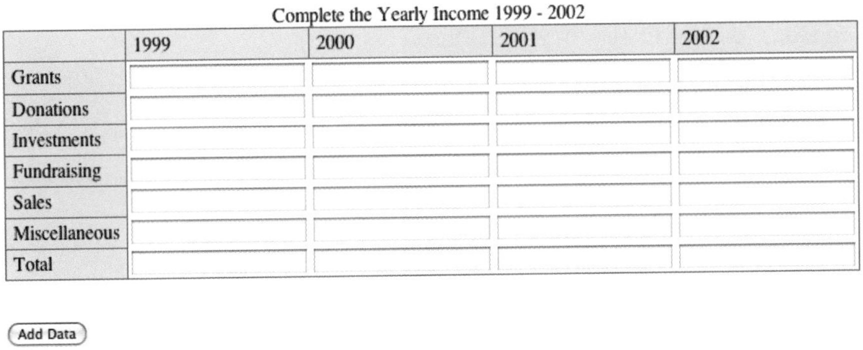

Figure 6.17. The unstyled form, ready for CSS formatting

To create the style rules for this form, we must establish for the table a `class` that contains all the spreadsheet fields. I've given the table a class name of `formdata`:

chapter06/spreadsheet.html *(excerpt)*

```
<table class="formdata" summary="This table contains a form to
    input the yearly income for years 1999 through 2002">
```

In the style sheet, class `formdata` has a single-pixel border in a dark, slate gray, and the `border-collapse` property is set to `collapse`:

chapter06/spreadsheet.css *(excerpt)*

```
table.formdata {
  border: 1px solid #5F6F7E;
  border-collapse: collapse;
}
```

Next, we can style the table headings. I've used the `<th>` tag for the top and left-hand column headings, so to style these, all I need to do is address the `<th>` tags within a table of class `formdata`:

chapter06/spreadsheet.css *(excerpt)*

```
table.formdata th {
  border: 1px solid #5F6F7E;
  background-color: #E2E2E2;
  color: #000000;
  text-align: left;
  font-weight: normal;
  padding: 0.2em 0.4em 0.2em 0.4em;
  margin: 0;
}
```

| Complete the Yearly Income 1999 - 2002 | | | |
|---|---|---|---|
| | **1999** | **2000** | **2001** | **2002** |
| **Grants** | | | | |
| **Donations** | | | | |
| **Investments** | | | | |
| **Fundraising** | | | | |
| **Sales** | | | | |
| **Miscellaneous** | | | | |
| **Total** | | | | |

[ Add Data ]

Figure 6.18. The form display after the `table` and `th` elements are styled

To produce an editable table, we need to hide the borders of the form fields and add borders to the table cells. As the only `input` elements within the table are the text fields that we want to style, we can simply address all `input` elements in the table with a class of `formdata`; this saves us having to add classes to all our fields.

We add a border to the `td` element, and set the borders on the `input` element to 0. We specify a width for the `input` element, as we know that the type of data that will be added will only need a small field. We then add some padding so that text that's typed into the form field will stop well short of the border:

*chapter06/spreadsheet.css (excerpt)*

```css
table.formdata td {
  margin: 0;
  padding: 0;
  border: 1px solid #E2E2E2;
}
table.formdata input {
  width: 80px;
  padding: 0.2em 0.4em 0.2em 0.4em;
  margin: 0;
  border-width: 0;
  border-style: none;
}
```

That's all there is to it! If you use this technique, make sure that your users understand that the table is editable. Removing borders from form fields will only help users if they can work out how to complete the form—let alone realize that it exists!

**Some Browsers Still Display Input Element Borders**

Certain browsers—most notably older versions of Safari on Mac OS X—will display the input element borders, so while the effect will be less neat, it will still be completely usable.

# How do I highlight the form field that the user clicks into?

Applications such as Excel highlight the focused form field when the user clicks on it or tabs to it. Is it possible to create this effect in our web form?

## Solution

We can create this effect using pure CSS, thanks to the :focus pseudo-class. While this solution works in modern browsers, including Internet Explorer 8, it fails to work in either Internet Explorer 6 or 7:

*chapter06/spreadsheet2.css (excerpt)*

```
table.formdata input {
  width: 80px;
  padding: 0.2em 0.4em 0.2em 0.4em;
  margin: 0;
  border: 2px solid #FFFFFF;
}
.formdata input:focus {
  border: 2px solid #000000;
}
```

Figure 6.19 shows how this code displays.

| Complete the Yearly Income 1999 - 2002 | | | | |
|---|---|---|---|---|
| | 1999 | 2000 | 2001 | 2002 |
| Grants | | | | |
| Donations | | | | |
| Investments | | | | |
| Fundraising | | | | |
| Sales | | | | |
| Miscellaneous | | | | |
| Total | | | | |

( Add Data )

Figure 6.19. Highlighting the form field in focus in Firefox

## Discussion

This solution for adding a border (or changing the background color) of the form field when it receives focus is a simple one. In fact, it's as simple as adding the pseudo-class selector :focus to your style sheet to display a different style for the input element when the user clicks into it.

Unfortunately, as I've already mentioned, Internet Explorer 6 lacks support for the :focus pseudo-class, so this effect may fail to display for some of your application's users.

There is a way around this problem that, unfortunately, requires a little JavaScript. Add the following JavaScript after the table in your document:

chapter06/spreadsheet2.html *(excerpt)*

```
<script type="text/javascript">
var editcells =
  document.getElementById('form1').getElementsByTagName('input');
for (var i = 0; i < editcells.length; i++) {
  editcells[i].onfocus = function() {
    this.className += ' hilite';
  }
  editcells[i].onblur = function() {
```

```
      this.className = this.className.replace('hilite', '');
  }
}
</script>
```

Once you've added this code, you'll need to add the class `hilite` to your CSS file, using the same rules we used for the `:focus` pseudo-class:

*chapter06/spreadsheet2.css (excerpt)*

```
.formdata input:focus, .formdata input.hilite {
  border: 2px solid #000000;
}
```

Your field highlighting will now work in Internet Explorer 6, as well as those browsers that support the `:focus` pseudo-class.

## Summary

In this chapter, we've looked at a variety of ways to style forms using CSS, from simply changing the look of form elements, to using CSS to lay forms out. We've seen how CSS can greatly enhance the appearance and usability of forms. We've also touched on the accessibility of forms for users of alternative devices, and we've seen how, by being careful when marking forms up, you can make it easier for all visitors to use your site or web application.

# Cross-browser Techniques

This chapter contains solutions for making your sites work well in many browsers. It's unlikely that every visitor to your site is using the same browser or even the most up-to-date version, so you'll want to ensure that all users enjoy their experience of your site regardless of which browser they use.

As we've seen, you can use CSS to separate the structure and content of your documents from the presentation of your site. If you take this approach, visitors who use devices that can't render your design—either because they're limited from a technical standpoint, such as some PDA or phone browsers, or as a result of their own functional advantages, such as screen readers that speak your pages' text for the benefit of visually impaired users—will still be able to access the content. CSS gives you the freedom to meet the needs of these users *and* to create beautiful designs for the majority of users, whose browsers do support CSS.

In addition to discussing the nuances of different browsers and devices, this chapter will provide you with techniques to troubleshoot CSS bugs in browsers that support CSS. Keep in mind that it's impossible for this chapter to cover every known CSS bug—even if it tried, as new bugs and new bug fixes appear all the time. What I've tried to do here is explain some of the main culprits that cause browser-related problems with CSS. I've explained how those problems might be solved, where you can go to receive up-to-date bug-squashing advice, and how to step through a problem, isolate its cause, and ask for help in a way that's likely to be rewarded with a useful answer.

The good news is that with each edition of this book, I can see how our jobs as front-end developers are becoming easier. The problems we see today are mainly with really old browsers such as Internet Explorer 6, but an ever-decreasing number of people are using these browsers. New releases of browsers tend to comply with standards very well indeed and these days—when I check my work in the latest version of Internet Explorer, Safari, Firefox, Opera, and Chrome—the most common result is that it displays in exactly the same way in all the browsers. This is what we've wanted for a very long time and we really are finally achieving that now.

# In which browsers should I test my site?

Once upon a time, web designers only worried about whether or not their sites looked good in Internet Explorer and Netscape Navigator; those days are now long gone. While Internet Explorer currently has the largest share of the browser market, several other important browsers are in use, including screen readers and browsers for mobile devices.

## Solution

The answer is to test your sites in as many browsers as you can. The types of browsers that you're able to install will depend on the operating systems to which you have access. Table 7.1 lists the major browsers that can be installed on Windows, Mac OS X, and Linux. At the very least, you should test in Internet Explorer 6, 7, and 8; Firefox, Opera, Safari, and Chrome.

## The Engines That Drive Browsers

You may have come across the term **browser rendering engine**. If a browser is the complete software package, including the application interface and features—the browser rendering engine is the part that interprets the HTML and CSS, and renders the web pages for you to view. Some engines are separate software products that are used by more than one browser. For example, the Gecko[1] engine developed by the Mozilla Foundation is used by Firefox, as well as Camino and the last versions of Netscape Navigator, among others. The WebKit[2] engine powers Safari and Chrome, and is derived from the KHTML[3] engine that powers the Konqueror web browser.

You may be thinking that if two browsers use the same rendering engine, you only need to test in one. While true to a certain extent there can still be differences, especially across versions and operating systems. Some browsers, like Internet Explorer and Opera, use their own internal engines.

## Tracking Down Obscure and Obsolete Browsers

If you're looking for versions of Internet Explorer older than 6, you'll be able to find and download them—including many other older and uncommon browsers—from http://browsers.evolt.org/.

The browsers you're able to install and test on may be limited by your operating system. Table 7.1 shows a list of common browsers, the rendering engine they use, the operating systems they're available for, and where you can download them.

---

[1] https://developer.mozilla.org/en/Gecko

[2] http://webkit.org/

[3] http://konqueror.kde.org/features/browser.php

## Table 7.1. Browsers, Engines, and Operating Systems

| Browser (Engine) | Win | Mac | Linux | Download From |
|---|:---:|:---:|:---:|---|
| Internet Explorer 6, 7, and 8 | ✓ | | | http://www.microsoft.com/windows/internet-explorer/ |
| Firefox (Gecko) | ✓ | ✓ | ✓ | http://www.mozilla.com/ |
| Camino (Gecko) | | ✓ | | http://www.caminobrowser.org/ |
| Opera | ✓ | ✓ | ✓ | http://www.opera.com/ |
| Safari (WebKit) | ✓ | ✓ | | http://www.apple.com/safari/ |
| Chrome (WebKit)[a] | ✓ | ✓ | ✓ | http://www.google.com/chrome/ |
| Konqueror (KHTML) | | | ✓ | http://konqueror.kde.org/ |

[a] At the time of writing the Mac OS X and Linux versions were in development and yet to be officially released.

# How can I test in many browsers when I only have access to one operating system?

Unless you have an entire test suite in your office, you'll probably find that you're unable to install certain browsers because they're operating-system specific.

## Solution

There are a variety of ways to run an additional operating system on your computer, thereby giving you the ability to install and use the browsers developed for that operating system.

### Windows Users

Windows users are in a good position to test on a wide variety of browsers. Internet Explorer, in its various incarnations, accounts for roughly 60–70% of the general browsing public, and most of the other major browsers offer Windows versions. Unfortunately, when it comes to testing on Mac OS X browsers such as Safari, the options available in Windows are limited.

## Testing Mac Browsers

Mac OS X is the most difficult platform to emulate at present. Having a Mac around is therefore almost essential for any serious web designer—though it's unnecessary for your Mac to be particularly fast or have an enormous amount of memory if all you use it for is testing sites in Safari.

In mid-2007, Apple surprised the web community by releasing a version of its Safari browser for Windows. Unfortunately, Safari for Windows is unreliable when it comes to pages being rendered identically to its older (and more popular) Mac-based cousin. It can, however, be useful as an indication of where possible rendering problems may lie.

The same can be said for the Windows version of Google Chrome. Even though it uses the same rendering engine as Safari (WebKit), you still need to test with the Mac version of Safari.

## Testing Linux Browsers

While there's currently no way to emulate a Mac on a Windows computer, various options are available for viewing sites in Linux-specific browsers.

### Linux Live CDs

Live CDs are versions of Linux that run completely from a CD, and can be run as a testing environment on your computer without you needing to actually install Linux onto your hard disk. One of the most well-known of the Live CDs is Knoppix, which can be downloaded from the Knoppix web site.[4] Knoppix comes with the KDE desktop environment, which includes Konqueror. Another popular distribution that comes as a live CD is Ubuntu,[5] which has the Gnome desktop as standard. A comprehensive list of other Live CDs is available at FrozenTech.[6]

### Dual Booting with Linux

Another option, if you want to run another operating system, is to dual boot your computer. You can install Windows and Linux, then select the platform you want to boot into when you start up your machine. A good walk-through of the process

---

[4] http://www.knoppix.net/
[5] http://www.ubuntu.com/
[6] http://www.frozentech.com/content/livecd.php

you'll need to use to set up your dual-boot system up can be found at https://help.ubuntu.com/community/WindowsDualBoot.

### Virtualization

The alternative to dual booting is virtualization: running other operating systems as virtual machines simultaneously inside the currently running operating system. Parallels Workstation[7] and VMWare Workstation[8] are commercial applications that can both run Linux virtual machines from Windows, but may be an expensive option just for testing Linux browsers. A better solution may be the Windows version of VirtualBox,[9] which is a free, open-source application that can also run Linux virtual machines.

## Mac Users

Mac users who have Intel Macs can feel smug—your environment can easily be used to test sites in all three operating systems. If you're a designer who wants to be able to work on only one machine, Macs are well worth investigating, and I say that as a Linux desktop user!

### Dual Boot with Boot Camp

Mac users wishing to install Windows can use the Boot Camp software, to dual boot your Mac with Windows.[10] Unlike virtual machine software, Boot Camp will require you to reboot into Windows—it's unable to run Windows inside a window on your desktop—but it does offer a handy way to test your work. Boot Camp is included in Mac OS X from version 10.5 (Leopard).

### Virtualization

Since Apple launched its Intel-based machines, customers have been able to run Windows and Linux virtual machines via third-party applications inside Mac OS X. You can even run multiple versions of Windows, so you can test Internet Explorer 6, 7, and 8 on the same computer!

---

[7] http://www.parallels.com/products/workstation/

[8] http://www.vmware.com/products/ws/

[9] http://www.virtualbox.org/

[10] http://www.apple.com/macosx/bootcamp/

Parallels Desktop for Mac, pictured in Figure 7.1,[11] has traditionally been a popular solution for Mac OS X. VMWare Workstation has been a favorite virtualization solution for Windows and in 2007 the company released VMWare Fusion for Mac OS X.[12] If you're after a free option try the Mac OS X version of the open-source VirtualBox.[13]

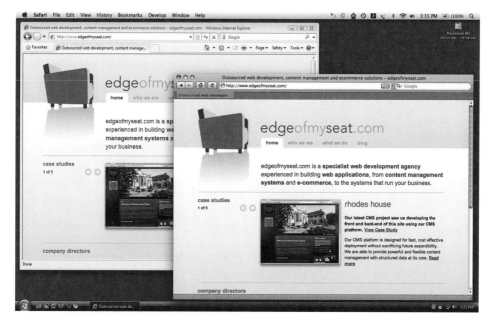

Figure 7.1. Internet Explorer 8 and Safari on Mac OS X using Parallels

## Linux Users

Linux users are in much the same boat as Windows users when it comes to testing on Mac-only browsers. On the bright side, Virtualization and dual booting offer convenient ways for Linux users to run various versions of Internet Explorer.

### Testing Mac Browsers

Linux is in the same situation as Windows with regards to testing Mac Browsers; you really need to have a Mac available for testing.

---

[11] http://www.parallels.com/
[12] http://www.vmware.com/products/fusion/
[13] http://www.virtualbox.org/

Safari and Chrome both use the WebKit rendering engine that was based on the KHTML rendering engine, used by (and originally developed by) the KDE browser, Konqueror. Konqueror tends to render things in a similar way to Safari, and the Linux version of Chrome (still under development at the time of writing) should too. This is certainly no substitute for having a Mac on hand to use for testing, but it can provide a rough indication of how your pages will render in Safari.

### Testing Windows Browsers

As with Windows, the easiest option for Linux users who want to test sites on Windows browsers is usually to dual boot their machines, but a number of tools that facilitate side-by-side testing with Windows browsers on Linux are available.

### Virtualization

VMWare Workstation and Parallels Workstation are commercial products that will allow you to run Windows virtual machines on Linux. However, the free, open-source VirtualBox[14] is also an option.

### Dual Booting

Linux users also have the option of dual booting their system as a way to install a version of Windows—as much as it may pain them to do so!

# Is there a service that can show me how my site looks in various browsers?

Being able to test your site in a variety of browsers is the best way to check that it works well in all of them; however, unless you can set up a test suite in your office, it's likely that there'll be some browsers to which you'll lack access to.

## Solution

There are now many services available for checking how your site displays and functions in multiple browsers on multiple operating systems that you may have no access to normally. Generally these take the form of screenshot services: submit a URL and the service will return a collection of screenshots of the web page open

---

[14] http://www.virtualbox.org/wiki/Linux_Downloads

in various browser-operating system combinations, and at different screen resolutions.

Some services also offer remote access to a machine where you're able to test your site's functionality on alternative platforms. This kind of service is particularly helpful if you've used JavaScript and need to interact with your page to see how it looks and functions.

Here's a list of a few available services:

**BrowserCam**

BrowserCam (http://www.browsercam.com/) is a screenshot-generating testing service that also has a remote access option. A free trial is available.

**Litmus**

Litmus (http://litmusapp.com/) is a professional web page and HTML email testing service that generates screenshots and has a few other features for HTML email testing. There is a free account type available as well as paid accounts.

**CrossBrowserTesting.com**

CrossBrowserTesting.com (http://crossbrowsertesting.com/) is a commercial testing service that allows you to remotely access machines running various browser and operating system combinations.

**Browser Shots**

Browser Shots (http://browsershots.org/) is a free screenshot service with a large variety of browsers, but is quite slow.

It's definitely a sign of the times that Adobe and Microsoft have recently released their own browser testing software.

**Adobe BrowserLab**

Adobe BrowserLab (https://browserlab.adobe.com/index.html) is a screenshot-generating service that allows you to compare screenshots side by side, as well as overlay screenshots on top of one another with slight transparency to make differences easy to spot. It currently only supports Internet Explorer, Firefox, and Safari. BrowserLab also has an extension for Dreamweaver.

**Microsoft SuperPreview**

Microsoft SuperPreview (http://expression.microsoft.com/en-us/dd565874.aspx) is a Windows application that can provide side-by-side and overlapping previews of web pages. At the time of writing it only supports IE6,7, and 8, but wider browser support is planned.

## Discussion

Another way to check that your site works in browsers that you lack access to is to request a site check on a mailing list. Most web design and development mailing lists and forums, including the SitePoint Forums,[15] are quite familiar with having users ask for people to check their sites, and you can return the favor by viewing other people's sites in the browsers that you use.

# Can I install multiple versions of Internet Explorer on Windows?

There are major differences between Internet Explorer versions 6, 7, and 8 in terms of the ways they render CSS, but Windows normally allows only one version of Internet Explorer to be installed at a time. How can we test sites in older, but still used, versions of Internet Explorer?

## Solution

Microsoft's Virtual PC software enables us to test Internet Explorer 6, 7, and 8 on one Windows computer, and is available as a free download. You'll need to take a few steps so that your Windows machine will run Internet Explorer 8 as the main browser, with virtual machines running Internet Explorer 6 and 7, but this is a great way to test your work.

1.  Upgrade to Internet Explorer 8 if you've yet to do so already.

2.  Download and install Virtual PC 2007 from Microsoft's Virtual PC site.[16]

---

[15] http://www.sitepoint.com/forums/
[16] http://www.microsoft.com/windows/virtualpc/default.mspx

3. Download a time-limited Virtual PC virtual machine image for IE6 and IE7 from Microsoft's Download Center.[17] This image comes with Microsoft Windows and Internet Explorer pre-installed. The beauty of using this image is that there's no need for you to pay for an additional Windows license to run it.

4. To use the virtual machine image, extract the archive and start up Virtual PC. Browse for the image files, and your separate version of Windows will start up in a window on your desktop.

### IE7 mode in IE8

Internet Explorer 8 Developer Tools panel has a feature that allows you to switch to the IE7 rendering mode. This feature was added to support backwards compatibility—a safeguard against web sites that fail to work in IE8. In those cases the browser can revert to behaving as IE7, possibly fixing the problem. It's also a quick way to test your site in IE7, if you'd rather avoid running a Virtual PC machine image (or perhaps are running a single Windows virtual machine on a Mac).

At the time of writing, Microsoft has no virtual machine images available for earlier versions of Internet Explorer; however, if you actually need to test in versions earlier than 6, some stand-alone versions are available to help you spot CSS rendering issues. You can download an installer of multiple stand-alone versions of Internet Explorer at Tredosoft,[18] but be warned, these browsers can be temperamental and prone to crashing. They're also unreliable for testing JavaScript, since they use the currently installed JScript engine, rather than the older versions of JScript that would normally be installed with these versions of Internet Explorer. However, these browsers are reliable enough for CSS developers who want to test their work in really old versions of Internet Explorer.

---

[17] http://go.microsoft.com/fwlink/?LinkId=70868
[18] http://tredosoft.com/Multiple_IE

**Stand-alone Versions of IE**

There are installers that promise to allow you to run multiple versions of Internet Explorer on one computer, but I'd advise you to avoid these. Due to the fact that IE is part of Windows, you can never have completely separate versions of IE running on the same machine and you'll find issues such as conditional comments failing to work correctly. To test in multiple versions of IE you either need more than one computer, or to use the virtual machines as described above.

# How do I decide which browsers should get the full design experience?

As we'll discover in this chapter, it's possible to provide older browsers with different style sheets and to target different Internet Explorer versions using conditional comments. The great aspect about creating your layout using CSS is that there's no need to lock anyone out of your content, regardless of how old and crumbly the browser is that they're using. That said, you should understand that you're under no obligation to present the same experience to an IE5 user as you would to users of IE8 or the latest version of Firefox.

## Solution

Your agreement with your client, or your company policy, will of course dictate to some extent what you can decide to support; however, if you're in the position to advise you might like to use the YUI Graded Browser Support chart[19] as backing for a sensible approach to browser support. This chart is essentially what Yahoo use to decide how they'll support the different browsers visiting their site, and with the Yahoo home page being the most trafficked site in the world they have excellent data to back up their decisions.

I believe that a modern approach to dealing with old browsers is to avoid completely locking anyone out of your site; as you'll see below it's possible to serve really old browsers plain, HTML text if required and avoid serving a CSS layout at all. For slightly newer browsers that perhaps stop short of supporting the full CSS 2.1 specification or CSS3 as that becomes commonplace, you can serve a reduced design

---

[19] http://developer.yahoo.com/yui/articles/gbs/

experience—an approach I think that's beginning to become possible for IE6. In the section called "How do I achieve PNG image transparency in Internet Explorer 6?" we look at two ways to deal with IE6's lack of transparency support for PNG images. When coming up against this issue you have two options: try and give IE6 the full design experience, including transparency, or provide it with a simpler version using GIF file images. Looking at the recommendations of the YUI Graded Browser Support chart may well help you decide which to do and give you a way to explain this to the end client.

# How do I display a basic style sheet for really old browsers?

CSS is now used so extensively on the Web that users of really old browsers, such as Netscape 4, are destined to have fairly poor online experiences, regardless of which sites they visit. However, we can still be kind to users of these old browsers by at least ensuring there are no crashes as a result of our advanced use of CSS, and that the content remains readable. To do this, we serve a very simple style sheet to these browsers, and attach our real style sheet using a technique unsupported by older browsers.

## Solution

Netscape 4, Internet Explorer 4, and other old browsers lack support for the @import method of linking to a style sheet and one of the features of CSS is that it will ignore a directive it's unable to understand. We can use this fact to our advantage: serving one set of styles to these browsers, and leaving newer browsers that understand @import to read the full style sheet.

In the head of your document, attach a basic style sheet using the link element—this can be read by all browsers that support CSS. Then, attach your full style sheet (or style sheets) using the @import method, which will be ignored by the old browsers:

**chapter07/basicstyles.html**

```
<!DOCTYPE html PUBLIC "-//W3C//DTD XHTML 1.0 Strict//EN"
    "http://www.w3.org/TR/xhtml1/DTD/xhtml1-strict.dtd">
<html xmlns="http://www.w3.org/1999/xhtml" xml:lang="en" lang="en">
  <head>
    <meta http-equiv="content-type" content="text/html;
        charset=utf-8" />
    <title>Serving a basic stylesheet</title>
    <link rel="stylesheet" href="basic_basic.css" type="text/css"
        media="screen"  />
    <style type="text/css" media="screen">
      @import "basic_default.css";
    </style>
  </head>

  <body>
    <div class="content">
      <h1>Serving a basic style sheet to old browsers</h1>
      <p>CSS is now used so extensively on the Web that …</p>
    </div>
  </body>
</html>
```

The basic style sheet shown below—**basic_basic.css**—defines some simple styles to boost the page's readability. You could make this style sheet slightly more advanced if you wish, assuming you have a copy of Netscape 4 to test on,[20] and can check that anything you add is safe for that browser. However, at the current time very few people use these old browsers. Presenting them with a basic document should be fine—it will at least ensure that the site is readable for them, in contrast to much of the rest of the Web.

**chapter07/basic_basic.css**

```
body {
  background-color: #fff;
  color: #000;
  margin: 0;
  padding: 5%;
```

[20] You can download version 4.8 for Windows from the evolt.org browser archive, [http://browsers.evolt.org/?navigator/32bit/4.8/] which can still be run in Windows XP or Vista.

```
}

body, h1, h2, h3, h4, h5, h6, ol, ul, li, p {
  font-family: verdana, arial, helvetica, sans-serif;
  color: #000;
}
```

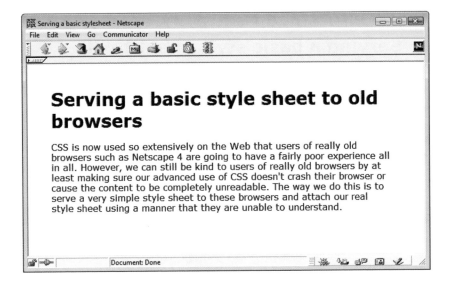

Figure 7.2. The page displaying in Netscape 4.8

Keep in mind that the newer browsers will read both the linked and imported style sheets, so within your site's main style sheet, you'll need to override any of the basic styles that you want to appear differently in newer browsers, as well as applying the styles you want users of newer browsers to see.

In the code below, I've added a few rules to demonstrate the effects of this approach, which can be seen in Figure 7.2 and Figure 7.3:

chapter07/basic_default.css

```
h1 {
  color: #cc0022;
  margin: 0;
}

.content {
```

```
    background-color: #ececec;
    padding: 0.6em;
}
```

Figure 7.3. The same page displaying in Google Chrome

## Discussion

Browsers that offer very minimal CSS support are problematic because they understand just enough CSS to attempt to render your styles, but not enough to be able to do so properly! The advanced CSS in use on an average site today is likely to display poorly or even crash a very old browser, so hiding these styles with the help of @import prevents this. There's no need to even add a basic style sheet—if you simply use @import on its own, those old browsers will display the document using the browser's internal styles.

However, the use of the basic linked style sheet offers an additional benefit: it lets us avoid the "Flash of Unstyled Content" phenomenon.[21] This annoying bug causes Internet Explorer users to see the site with the default Internet Explorer styles for a split-second before the styles from your style sheet load in. Adding a link before

---

[21] http://www.bluerobot.com/web/css/fouc.asp/

the import—as we do in this solution—also solves that problem. So we're able to be kind to a couple of generations of crumbly browsers with one trick!

# What is quirks mode and how do I avoid it?

You're developing a site using XHTML and CSS, testing in Internet Explorer, and it all seems to be going well … then you look at the layout with Firefox and Safari and realize it is displaying very differently to the way it's rendering in Internet Explorer. What's going on?

## Solution

Internet Explorer bugs aside, the most likely issue is that Internet Explorer is rendering your document in **quirks mode**. Many modern browsers have two rendering modes. Quirks mode renders documents according to the buggy implementations of older browsers such as Netscape 4 and Internet Explorer 4 and 5. Standards or **compliance mode** renders documents as per the W3C specifications (or as close to it as they can).

- Documents that use older doctypes, are poorly formed, or lack a doctype declaration at all, display using quirks mode.
- Internet Explorer 6 will render in quirks mode if you include anything at all above the DOCTYPE statement—including the XML prolog required for an XHTML doctype.
- Documents that are using strict HTML 4 or XHTML doctypes render using compliance mode.

The way browsers switch between quirks mode and compliance mode rendering based on the document's doctype is called **doctype switching**. The solution is simple; use a doctype that will trigger compliance mode and make sure there's nothing before your doctype declaration to keep IE6 happy. Here is the list of doctypes that will force the browsers that support doctype switching—browsers from Internet Explorer 6, Internet Explorer 5 Mac, Opera 7, Safari, Firefox, and Chrome—into compliance mode.[22]

---

[22] A full list of doctypes and their effects on various browsers is available at http://gutfeldt.ch/matthias/articles/doctypeswitch/table.html.

### HTML 4.01 Transitional

```
<!DOCTYPE HTML PUBLIC "-//W3C//DTD HTML 4.01 Transitional//EN"
    "http://www.w3.org/TR/html4/loose.dtd">
```

### HTML 4.01 Frameset

```
<!DOCTYPE HTML PUBLIC "-//W3C//DTD HTML 4.01 Frameset//EN"
    "http://www.w3.org/TR/html4/frameset.dtd">
```

### HTML 4.01 Strict

```
<!DOCTYPE HTML PUBLIC "-//W3C//DTD HTML 4.01//EN"
    "http://www.w3.org/TR/html4/strict.dtd">
```

### XHTML 1.0 Transitional

```
<!DOCTYPE html PUBLIC "-//W3C//DTD XHTML 1.0 Transitional//EN"
    "http://www.w3.org/TR/xhtml1/DTD/xhtml1-transitional.dtd">
```

### XHTML 1.0 Frameset

```
<!DOCTYPE html PUBLIC "-//W3C//DTD XHTML 1.0 Frameset//EN"
    "http://www.w3.org/TR/xhtml1/DTD/xhtml1-frameset.dtd">
```

### XHTML 1.0 Strict

```
<!DOCTYPE html PUBLIC "-//W3C//DTD XHTML 1.0 Strict//EN"
    "http://www.w3.org/TR/xhtml1/DTD/xhtml1-strict.dtd">
```

### XHTML 1.1

```
<!DOCTYPE html PUBLIC "-//W3C//DTD XHTML 1.1//EN"
    "http://www.w3.org/TR/xhtml11/DTD/xhtml11.dtd">
```

An XHTML document is supposed to have an XML prolog at the top like so:

```
<?xml version="1.0" encoding="utf-8"?>
<!DOCTYPE html PUBLIC "-//W3C//DTD XHTML 1.0 Strict//EN"
    "http://www.w3.org/TR/xhtml1/DTD/xhtml1-strict.dtd">
<html xmlns="http://www.w3.org/1999/xhtml" lang="en-US">
⋮
</html>
```

Unfortunately, this will cause IE6 to choose quirks mode, so you need to remove it:

```
<!DOCTYPE html PUBLIC "-//W3C//DTD XHTML 1.0 Strict//EN"
    "http://www.w3.org/TR/xhtml1/DTD/xhtml1-strict.dtd">
<html xmlns="http://www.w3.org/1999/xhtml" lang="en-US">
⋮
</html>
```

## Discussion

The best known quirks mode behavior is that of Internet Explorer. When in quirks mode, IE renders the page with the broken CSS Box Model implementation used by Internet Explorer 5 and 5.5. So, instead of the padding and border being added to the width of the box (making a 200 pixel width plus 20 pixels either side a real width of 240 pixels), it renders the box at the set width of 200 pixels and takes the padding away from that. Figure 7.4 illustrates the difference.

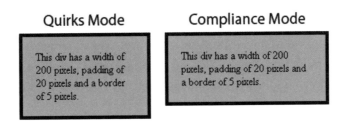

Figure 7.4. The difference between quirks mode and compliance mode in Internet Explorer

If you're building a new site, I recommend that you aim to meet the requirements of compliance mode, whichever doctype you're using. New browsers will be likely to support the W3C standards and will render pages using those standards whether or not they support any doctype switching. There are too many quirky behaviors to deal with when browsers use quirks mode, so avoid the problem from the start.

# How can I specify different styles for Internet Explorer 6 and 7?

At the time of writing, a big problem for CSS developers is the large number of people still using Internet Explorer 6—a browser that provides poor, buggy support for much of the CSS specification. While Microsoft fixed most of the well-known bugs and added support for more of the CSS 2.1 spec in Internet Explorer 7, it's still less able than modern browsers like IE8. So, we've been left with a group of users who are unable to or resist upgrading beyond Internet Explorer 6, and although trends show IE7 users are slowly upgrading to IE8, IE7 will still be around for some time yet.

## Solution

The best method we can use to target our style rules to specific Internet Explorer versions is conditional comments. Conditional comments are an Internet Explorer proprietary feature that enable you to wrap markup in HTML comments and specify a condition that governs when the browser should read the HTML and when it should ignore it. You can use conditional comments to reveal a style sheet link `<tag>` only to specific IE versions.

First, create the style sheet containing the Internet Explorer-specific CSS fixes—there's no need to duplicate your entire style sheet, just override or add the rules necessary to fix problems in Internet Explorer. Then, include the link to the style sheet within a conditional comment in the head of your document, like this:

```
<!--[if IE 6]>
<link rel="stylesheet" type="text/css" href="ie6fixes.css" />
<![endif]-->
```

The above code will reveal the **ie6fixes.css** style sheet only to IE6. The following code will only reveal the style sheet to IE7:

```
<!--[if IE 7]>
<link rel="stylesheet" type="text/css" href="ie7fixes.css" />
<![endif]-->
```

This code will reveal a style sheet to all versions of Internet Explorer less than or equal to version 7:

```
<!--[if lte IE 7]>
<link rel="stylesheet" type="text/css" href="iefixes.css" />
<![endif]-->
```

The conditional comments need to go into the `head` of your document—you must include them after your main style sheet, otherwise rules in your IE-only style sheet will be overwritten by rules in your main style sheet.

There are many more options available in the syntax of the condition. If you want to know more about conditional comments the SitePoint CSS Reference has a useful page.[23] In the solutions that follow, we'll look at the use of conditional comments to serve Internet Explorer 6 an additional style sheet, as well as a JavaScript file.

# How do I deal with the most common issues in IE6 and 7

Internet Explorer 6 (and to a lesser extent, 7) are the browsers that you're most likely to have problems with today. By using methodical working practices you should be able to make your sites work well in these browsers, but still be able to push ahead with complex layouts taking advantage of the excellent CSS support in modern browsers.

## Solution

The following are my suggestions for a CSS working method, along with tips to help you make IE6 and 7 behave.

---

[23] http://reference.sitepoint.com/css/conditionalcomments/

# The Development Process

Here's how I work to avoid as many IE6 and 7 issues as possible.

## Develop Using an Up-to-date Browser

You should initially develop your layout in a browser that complies with the CSS specification well; for example, the latest versions of Firefox, Opera, and Safari. Browsers are becoming *more* standards-compliant, not less, so you want to ensure that the CSS you write today complies with the specification because it's more likely to behave in future browsers. I never look at the layout in Internet Explorer while building a web site. If I do I might be tempted to start hacking at my markup or adding in unnecessary elements in my CSS. I want to ensure the site works right in browsers that are standards-compliant first, before worrying about those that fall short.

## Validate Your Markup and CSS

If you begin with valid markup and CSS you'll find problems far easier to fix. Browsers handle markup and CSS errors differently. One browser's interpretation of an unclosed `<div>` tag or missing semi-colon in a style rule may cause frustrating problems later on in development. So before going any further, visit the W3C CSS and Markup Validation Service and check your document for errors.[24]

## Check in Other Modern Browsers

Now have a look in other modern browsers: Firefox, Opera, Safari, Chrome, and Internet Explorer 8. I very rarely need to make changes for these browsers in my own work. When I do, it tends to be just a small change to how I've implemented a particular layout element, enabling it to work in all modern browsers. Never do I expect to need to use hacks or alternate style sheets for modern browsers; there's always a simpler way to fix the problem.

## Check in Internet Explorer 6 and 7

At this point you know your CSS is valid and works in up-to-date browsers, so from this point on anything that's a problem in an old browser you can fix using appro-

---

[24] http://validator.w3.org/

priate methods for that old browser. I believe strongly that you should avoid cluttering your markup or CSS with bug fixes for ancient browsers.

There will probably be some problems in IE6 when you first look at your layout. These might be small predicaments such as incorrect padding between page elements or larger issues such as huge sections of your page disappearing or displaying in an odd place. There's no need to panic! Most IE6 issues can be easily resolved by specifying some different style rules for this particular browser.

The same goes for IE7, although I find there are less layout problems to fix in this browser.

### Add Browser-specific Style Sheets Using Conditional Comments

At this point I would suggest that you add an additional style sheet as described in the previous section using conditional comments, to target IE6, 7, or both. You add this style sheet to your document head—after the existing style sheets in your HTML—so that any rules you place in your IE6- and IE7-specific style sheet will overwrite the same rules in the main style sheet.

## Fixing Internet Explorer Problems

You can now work through any problems that you can see in IE6 and 7 in a methodical way, applying fixes in your alternate style sheet, safe in the knowledge they'll only ever be applied by the browsers that need them. The following tips solve most of the issues that we see in IE6. For IE7 I usually find that there's no need for all of the rules used for IE6, but sometimes some of them are still required. It's rare that I find a brand new issue in IE7 that I'd yet to see in IE6 and the fixes are generally the same.

### Check Your DOCTYPE

Make sure that you're using a correct doctype as the first line in your markup, as explained above in "What is quirks mode and how do I avoid it?". An incorrect doctype can cause your pages to display very strangely indeed. So before doing anything else make sure the page is rendering in standards mode in all browsers, including IE6 and 7.

### Fixing the Lack of `min-height` Support in IE6

Internet Explorer 6 has no support for `min-height` (the minimum height an element should take), but it incorrectly interprets `height` as `min-height`. So, though `height` is used to specify a fixed height in other browsers, Internet Explorer 6 takes it to mean the minimum height, so a block element will expand taller than its specified height if need be.

To work around this issue, we simply use the `height` property in our IE6-specific style sheet wherever we've used `min-height` in our main style sheet.

### Trigger the `hasLayout` Property

IE6 and 7 have a mysterious scripting property called `hasLayout` that's an internal component of the rendering engine, and the source of many seemingly bizarre rendering bugs. When an element is responsible for sizing and arranging its contents it's said to have a layout. If an element lacks having layout then it relies on its parent, or an ancestor element, to take care of its size and position. When an element lacks a layout it potentially causes weird things to occur—like content disappearing and the layout behaving erratically. Some elements, like table cells, automatically have a layout; however, `div` elements do not. Specifying some CSS properties, like setting `float` to `left` or `right`, also cause an element to gain a layout. Causing an element to gain a layout makes most of these problems disappear. The trick is to find a CSS property that will cause an element to gain a layout without having a detrimental effect on your layout.

In IE6 I find the simplest way to trigger a layout on an element is to give it a `height` value of `1%`. As I just mentioned, IE6 treats `height` as `min-height`, so a `height` of `1%` actually renders as a minimum height of 1%—so this is perfectly safe to apply and the box will still be sized to suit its contents. Obviously you need to do this in your IE6-specific style sheet.

IE7, in contrast, supports the `height` property correctly, so we're unable to use it as we might with IE6. However, setting the `min-height` property to any value, even to `0`, in IE7 causes the element to gain a layout. This is a safe approach because the default value for `min-height` is `0` anyway.

It isn't always apparent which element is going to need the layout trigger applied, but if you work methodically you may well find the one that causes everything to jump into shape. I usually work from the innermost container out, so if I have a `div` nested inside two more `div`s I'd add the height to the inner `div` and refresh to see if it made a difference. Otherwise, I'd remove it and try the next `div`, and so on.

### Adding Position: Relative to Elements

If gaining a layout fails to work sometimes setting `position` to `relative` on an element will fix a problem. Keep in mind that setting `position` to `relative` on an element will mean all its child elements will now use that element for a positioning context. Otherwise this should be safe to do.

### If All Else Fails

The above tips should fix the worst problems, but you may still be left with slight alignment, margin, or padding issues. At this point remind yourself that what you're dealing with are old, buggy browsers and you should feel quite at liberty, in your IE6- and IE7-specific style sheets, to manipulate elements by adjusting the margin, padding, or positioning until it does work. This will have no effect on any other browser if you've used conditional comments so no harm is done. Hopefully it will be unnecessary to do too much of this because obviously this will need to be redone if the layout ever changes; sometimes, with a very complex layout, you do need to just hammer bits into place!

# How do I achieve PNG image transparency in Internet Explorer 6?

One of the exciting additions to Internet Explorer 7 was support of PNG transparency. As I showed in Chapter 3, when we discussed background images, PNG image transparency can give you true transparency: it allows overlaid images to display across different background colors without showing a pixilated halo, and enables designers to create effects using opaque background layers. However, if you simply go ahead and use transparent PNGs, users of Internet Explorer 6 will see solid images like those shown in Figure 7.5. Is there anything that can be done to make transparent PNGs to play nicely with Internet Explorer 6?

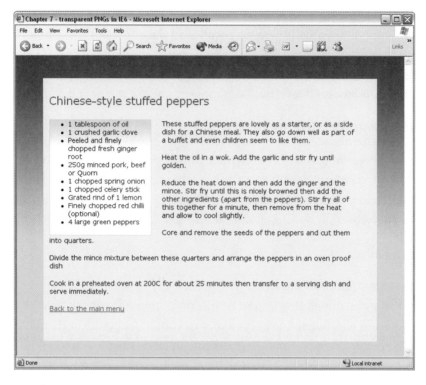

Figure 7.5. Internet Explorer 6 displaying the transparent PNG images as solid images

## Solution

There is a way to make transparent PNGs appear to work in Internet Explorer 6, but it involves the use of JavaScript. The solution was originally devised by Aaron Boodman[25] and edited by Drew McLellan in order to support background images.[26]

First, create a 1x1px transparent GIF, and save it as **x.gif**.

Now, create a new JavaScript file (which we'll include only for Internet Explorer 6), and add the following JavaScript:

[25] http://webapp.youngpup.net/?request=/snippets/sleight.xml
[26] http://allinthehead.com/retro/289/sleight-update-alpha-png-backgrounds-in-ie

```javascript
function addLoadEvent(func) {
  var oldonload = window.onload;
  if (typeof window.onload != 'function') {
    window.onload = func;
  } else {
    window.onload = function() {
      if (oldonload) {
        oldonload();
      }
      func();
    }
  }
}


var bgsleight = function() {

function fnLoadPngs() {
var rslt = navigator.appVersion.match(/MSIE (\d+\.\d+)/, '');
var itsAllGood = (rslt != null && Number(rslt[1]) >= 5.5);
for (var i = document.all.length - 1, obj = null; (obj =
    document.all[i]); i--) {
  if (itsAllGood &&
      obj.currentStyle.backgroundImage.match(/\.png/i) != null) {
    fnFixPng(obj);
    obj.attachEvent("onpropertychange", fnPropertyChanged);
  }
  if ((obj.tagName=='A' || obj.tagName=='INPUT') &&
      obj.style.position == ''){
  obj.style.position = 'relative';
  }
 }
}

function fnPropertyChanged() {
 if (window.event.propertyName == "style.backgroundImage") {
  var el = window.event.srcElement;
   if (!el.currentStyle.backgroundImage.match(/x\.gif/i)) {
    var bg = el.currentStyle.backgroundImage;
    var src = bg.substring(5,bg.length-2);
    el.filters.item(0).src = src;
    el.style.backgroundImage = "url(/img/shim.gif)";
```

```
    }
   }
  }

function fnFixPng(obj) {
 var mode = 'scale';
 var bg = obj.currentStyle.backgroundImage;
 var src = bg.substring(5,bg.length-2);
 if (obj.currentStyle.backgroundRepeat == 'no-repeat') mode =
     'crop';
  obj.style.filter =
      "progid:DXImageTransform.Microsoft.AlphaImageLoader(src='"
      + src + "', sizingMethod='" + mode + "')";
  obj.style.backgroundImage = "url(/img/shim.gif)";
  }

  return {
  init: function() {
   if (navigator.platform == "Win32" && navigator.appName ==
       "Microsoft Internet Explorer" && window.attachEvent) {
   addLoadEvent(fnLoadPngs);
   }
  }
 }
}();

bgsleight.init();
```

Use a conditional comment to include the new JavaScript file so that it's used only by Internet Explorer:

**chapter07/bgsleight.html** *(excerpt)*

```
<!--[if IE 6]>
<script type="text/javascript" src="bgsleight.js"></script>
<![endif]-->
```

If you save your page and view it in Internet Explorer at this point, you'll see that the background attached to the div element with ID content has disappeared. To make it display again, we'll need to give it a height. A height of just 1% will do—Internet Explorer will treat that as min-height, and will expand the div to contain all of its contents. As we want only Internet Explorer to see this height value, we can either put it in a `style` element in the document's `head`, or add it to a separate Internet Explorer 6-only style sheet that's linked to from within the conditional comments:

*chapter07/bgsleight.html (excerpt)*

```
<!--[if IE 6]>
<style type="text/css">
#content {
  height: 1%;
}
</style>
<script type="text/javascript" src="bgsleight.js"></script>
<![endif]-->
```

Refresh your page in Internet Explorer, and the opaque background will display over the background color, as shown in Figure 7.6.

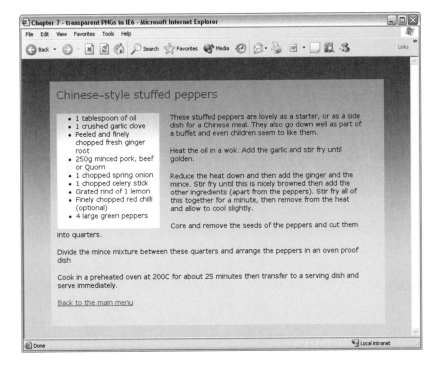

Figure 7.6. Internet Explorer 6 displaying the transparent PNG images

## Discussion

This hack can be problematic. You may find that areas of the page appear as if covered by the background image, making links unclickable and text input fields unable to accept focus. If that happens, you'll usually find that adding `position: relative;` to the element fixes the problem, but it will also add a layer of complication to your work. That said, this option does enable the design flexibility that results from the use of proper transparency, and with a bit of care you can make it work well.

### Avoiding the Hack

Another way to deal with the issue would be to create different images for Internet Explorer 6, and add an Internet Explorer 6 style sheet that used non-transparent images to override the PNGs used for other browsers. The site would look different in Internet Explorer 6, but now that IE6 is two versions old and is losing market share, it's an acceptable solution. In sites we're building today we often use a combination of the two methods: using the hack for places where it would be hard to do a GIF version, but using GIFs where we're able to.

# How do I ensure my standards–compliant web site displays correctly in Internet Explorer 8?

As mentioned previously, Internet Explorer 8 is capable of rendering web sites as if it were IE7, including all the strange `hasLayout` discrepancies that have caused us trouble over the years. How do you make sure that IE8 uses it's best rendering mode—rather than reverting to IE7—when displaying your web site?

## Solution

IE8 is a very capable browser, so if you're developing a brand new site you'll want IE8 to display your site to the best of its ability. Where CSS is concerned I've found very few day-to-day problems when comparing IE8 to Firefox 3 and Safari 3 or 4. As usual, by default, IE8 will use doctype switching to determine whether to render your web page in compliance mode or quirks mode. However, in an attempt to safeguard backwards compatibility and to "not break the Web", Microsoft introduced **Compatibility View** and the x-ua-compatible header that can instruct the browser to render sites in its most standards-compliant way or in a way that emulates how IE7 renders web pages.

Compatibility view is enabled in the browser, while the x-ua-compatible header is set in the markup, using a <meta/> tag, or via a HTTP header sent by the server. Compatibility view is enabled if the user clicks the **Compatibility View** button, or if the web site appears on the Windows Internet Explorer 8 Compatibility View List, which is a list of sites that should be rendered in compatibility view mode. This list is maintained by Microsoft, and the IE8 user can choose to subscribe to the list.[27]

The x-ua-compatible header is a directive that will override all compatibility view settings in the browser. Here's an example of the meta tag:

```
<meta http-equiv="X-UA-Compatible" content="IE=8" />
```

The above tag ensures that IE8 displays the page in its most standards-compliant mode. If you set the content value to IE=EmulateIE7 the browser will render the document using the IE7 rendering engine. If you set it to IE=Edge Internet Explorer 8 and beyond will always use the most standards-compliant rendering mode no matter what the version.

My suggestion is that if you're building a new site you either ignore the x-ua-compatible header or set it to IE=Edge. If you use a proper doctype and ignore the the x-ua-compatible header altogether Internet Explorer will render the site as best it can—hopefully you're building a standards-compliant site and will have no need to worry about ending up on that list! Alternatively, setting the value of x-ua-compatible to IE=Edge is recommended against setting it to IE=IE8 or another value. This means that when IE9 comes out your site will avoid becoming frozen in IE8-style rendering, for example.

For detailed information see Faruk Ates excellent blog post on the subject: *IE8 and the X-UA-Compatible situation.* [28]

---

[27] You can download it from the Microsoft web site to see what sites are on the list:
http://www.microsoft.com/downloads/details.aspx?FamilyID=b885e621-91b7-432d-8175-a745b87d2588&displaylang=en
[28] http://farukat.es/journal/2009/05/245-ie8-and-the-x-ua-compatible-situation

# What do I do if I think I've found a CSS bug?

We all find ourselves in situations where our CSS just will *not* work! Though you've tried every solution you can think of, some random bit of text continues to appear and disappear in Internet Explorer 6, or part of your layout spreads across half the content in Safari. Before the bug drives you mad, take a deep breath and relax. There is a solution!

## Solution

This is a solution that helps you find the solution!

1. **Take a Break**

   Once we've become frustrated over battling a problem, to apply any kind of rational process for finding a solution is difficult at best. So take a break. Go for a walk, tidy your desk, or do some housework. If you're at work with your boss looking over your shoulder so that you're unable to make it to the coffee machine in peace, work on another task—answer some mail, tidy up some content. Do anything to take your mind off the problem for a while.

2. **Validate Your Style Sheet and Document**

   If you've yet to do so, your next step should be to validate the CSS and the markup. Errors in your CSS or markup may well cause problems and, even if your bug is actually caused by another issue, they often make it more difficult to find a solution.

3. **Isolate the Problem**

   Can you make your bug occur in isolation from the rest of your document? CSS bugs often display only when a certain group of conditions is met, so trying to find out exactly where the problem occurs may help you work out how it can be fixed. Try and reproduce the problem in a document different from the rest of your layout.

4.  **Search the Web**

If what you have is a browser bug, it's likely that another user has seen it before. There are plenty of great sites that detail browser bugs and explain how to overcome them. I always check the following sites when I'm up against a problem:

- CSS Pointers Group, at http://css.nu/pointers/bugs.html
- Position is Everything, at http://www.positioniseverything.net/
- The Browser Bug Category on the css-d wiki, at http://css-discuss.incutio.com/?page=CategoryBrowserBug

The SitePoint CSS Reference[29] has much useful browser support information for each CSS property and selector. Also, try searching the css-discuss archives,[30] and, of course, Google!

5.  **Ask for Help**

If you've yet to find a solution as you've moved through the above steps, ask for help. Even the most experienced developers hit problems that they're unable to see past. Sometimes, just talking through the issue with a bunch of people with fresh eyes can help you resolve the problem, or come up with new ideas to test—even if no one has an immediate solution.

When you post to a forum or mailing list, remember these rules of thumb:

- If the list or forum has archives, search them first, just in case you're about to ask one of those questions that's asked at least once a day.

- Make sure that your CSS and HTML validates; otherwise, the answer you'll receive is most likely to be, "go and validate your document and see if that helps."

- Upload an example to a location to which you can link from your forum post. If you manage to reproduce the problem outside a complex layout, so

---

[29] http://reference.sitepoint.com/css/
[30] http://www.css-discuss.org/

much the better—this will make it easier for others to work out what's going on.

- Explain the solutions you've tried so far. This saves the recipients of your message from pursuing those same dead-ends, and shows that you've attempted to fix the problem yourself before asking for help.

- Give your message a descriptive subject line. People are more likely to read a post entitled, "Duplicate boxes appearing in IE5" than one that screams, "HELP!" Good titles also make the list archives more useful, as people can see at a glance the titles of posts in a thread.

- Be polite and to the point.

- Be patient while you wait for answers. If you fail to receive a reply after a day or so and it's a busy list, it's usually acceptable to post again with the word "REPOST" in the subject line. Posts can be overlooked in particularly large boards, and this is a polite way to remind users that you've yet to receive any assistance with your problem.

- When you receive answers, try implementing the poster's suggestions. Avoid becoming upset or angry if the recommendations fail to work, or you feel that the poster is asking you to try very basic things. I've seen threads go on for many posts as different posters weigh in to help a user solve a problem, and continue the discussion until a solution is found. Give people a chance to help!

- If you find a solution—or you have no success and decide instead to change your design to avoid the problem—post to the thread to explain what worked and what failed. This shows good manners towards those who helped you, but will also aid anyone who searches the archive for information on the same problem. It's very frustrating to search an archive and find several possible solutions to a problem, but to be unsure which (if any) was successful!

Many web design and development mailing lists are used by people who are very knowledgeable about CSS. In my opinion, the best CSS-specific list is css-discuss.[31] It's a high-traffic list, but the people on it are very accommodating, and you can pick up a lot just by reading the posts and browsing the archives. SitePoint also has a great, active CSS forum full of obliging and experienced people.[32]

# What do the error and warning messages in the W3C Validator mean?

Validating your documents and CSS is an important step in ensuring that your site renders correctly in standards-complaint browsers. Sometimes, however, the error and warning messages can be very confusing.

## Solution

You can validate your (X)HTML documents online at the W3C Validator;[33] CSS documents can be validated at the W3C CSS Validator.[34] Many authoring tools, such as Dreamweaver, have inbuilt validators, and plugins are available for browsers such as Firefox to help you validate your pages.[35]

With both CSS and HTML documents, start validating at the top. Sometimes, you'll run a document through the validator and receive a huge list of errors. However, when you fix the first error that the validator has encountered, many of the subsequent errors often disappear. This is especially likely to occur in an (X)HTML document. If you have forgotten to close a tag correctly, the validator believes that the tag is still open, and it will give you a whole list of errors to tell you that element X is not allowed within element Y. Close the offending tag and those errors will instantly be resolved.

A related problem is found in documents with an HTML (non-XHTML) doctype, where the developer has closed a tag using XML syntax, like this:

---

[31] http://www.css-discuss.org/
[32] http://www.sitepoint.com/launch/cssforum/
[33] http://validator.w3.org/
[34] http://jigsaw.w3.org/css-validator/
[35] http://users.skynet.be/mgueury/mozilla/

```
<link rel="stylesheet" href="stylesheet.css" type="text/css" />
```

If you've done this in a document that lacks an XHTML doctype, you'll receive errors indicating that there's a closing `</head>` element in the wrong place. To make the document obey the HTML standard, simply remove the slash from the tag:

```
<link rel="stylesheet" href="stylesheet.css" type="text/css">
```

## Errors and Warnings

A CSS document is not valid CSS if it contains errors such as invalid syntax, missing semicolons, and so on. You'll need to fix these errors to have the document validate, and to ensure that your style sheet behaves as expected.

If your style sheet is error-free, it will validate. A valid document, however, may still contain warnings when you run it through the validator. Whether you take notice of these warnings or not is entirely up to you. The most common warning states that you've failed to specify an acceptable background color for a specific element. This could indicate a problem with your design—for example, part of the text on your page may be rendered unreadable—or it could simply indicate an aspect of your design that has the potential to cause problems, even if you've intentionally designed it that way (for instance, you're expecting the background of an element beneath the element in question to show through). Warnings should act as a reminder to check you've covered everything, but remember that a style sheet that validates *with* warnings is still perfectly valid!

# Summary

This chapter has covered a wide range of solutions to problems that you may have yet to experience. This will almost certainly be the case if you've only designed sites using tables, rather than CSS, for positioning. It's at that point that the more interesting browser bugs start to rear their ugly heads, and testing in a wide range of browsers, and browser versions, becomes very important indeed.

What I hope to have shown you in this chapter is how I go about testing sites, finding bugs, and gaining help. I've also aimed to broaden your options in terms of displaying your pages appropriately for different users. If you're reading through this book chapter by chapter, you might find that much of this information makes more sense in light of Chapter 9, which deals with the use of CSS for layout.

Chapter

# 8

# Accessibility and Alternative Devices

CSS allows us to separate the structure and content of our documents from the presentation of the site. This means that visitors using devices that are unable to render the site's design—either because they're limited from a technical standpoint, such as some mobile device browsers, or as a result of their own functional advantages, such as screen readers that speak a page's text for the benefit of visually impaired users—will still be able to access the content. However, we're still free to create beautiful designs for the majority of users who do have browsers that support CSS.

While these considerations will improve the experience for users of assistive technology, you still need to take care of visitors who can see the site's design, but have particular accessibility-related needs. Making your site accessible to everyone requires more than simply using CSS for layout. For example, many people who suffer some kind of vision loss can only read text that's clearly laid out and can be enlarged. This chapter also covers the use of alternative style sheets (also called alternate style sheets), style sheets for different media (such as print style sheets), and targeted CSS for mobile devices.

# What should I be aware of in terms of accessibility when using CSS?

The accessibility of your site involves more than just considering the users of screen readers. The design choices you make will impact users with a range of issues; for example, older people with poor eyesight, people with dyslexia, and those who are unable to use a mouse because of a physical disability. These users will most likely be viewing your site as designed in a regular web browser, and so your choices when designing and building the site will impact on their experience.

## Solution

This is more a short checklist—rather than a hard and fast solution—with many points having already been mentioned in previous chapters of this book.

### Set Background Colors When Using Background Images

If you've used a background image in your design underneath some text—perhaps giving a background color to a column or box—make sure that you also add a background color. That way, if the image fails to load, the color will ensure that the text on top remains at a high enough contrast to be read.

### If You Set a Foreground Color, You Need to Set a Background Color, and Vice Versa

In the interests of readability, color settings should always be considered in tandem: that is, the foreground and background colors should be chosen together so that they contrast sufficiently. If you were to only set one color, say the background, and a user's default foreground color lacks contrast with your choice of color, it may leave your text unreadable. For example, if the user has set their background color to black and foreground to white, and you then set the main text color to black, the text will seem to disappear! If you want users to be able to make their own choices as to colors then you should leave all colors unset and very few web designers would feel able to do that!

## Check Color Contrasts

Take care to check the contrast of text against background colors. For users with any kind of visual impairment a low contrast between the text and the background can make the text very hard to read. You should also consider those users with color blindness who may find certain combinations of foreground and background colors difficult to distinguish. WCAG 2.0 Success Criterion 1.4.3[1] requires that, in general, text and images of text should have a contrast ratio of at least 4.5:1. To help you assess whether your chosen colors will pass this ratio you can use the handy Luminosity Contrast Ratio Analyser written by Jez Lemon.[2]

## Backgrounds Should Only Be Decorative

It's so easy to use background images in CSS that we can fall into the trap of using them everywhere. It's worth remembering, however, that anyone who is unable to load images and/or CSS will be unaware the image exists at all if it is set as a background image. This is acceptable if the image is purely for visual display, but if it's important to the content it's more appropriate to put the image inline with descriptive `alt` text; that way, users who are unable to see the image understand it's there and what it represents.

## Check `line-height` for Readability

Increasing the `line-height` used on your site can help readability—but take care here as very wide gaps between lines can also make it hard to read. A value between `1.2` and `1.6` should work well, and if you leave off the unit (for example, `em` or `%`) the `line-height` can scale correctly according to the text size.

# How do I test my site in a text-only browser?

Checking your site using a text-only browser is an excellent way to find out how accessible it really is. If you find it easy to navigate your site using a text-only browser, it's likely that visitors using screen readers will too.

---

[1] http://www.w3.org/TR/2008/REC-WCAG20-20081211/#visual-audio-contrast-contrast
[2] http://juicystudio.com/services/luminositycontrastratio.php

# Solution

You can view pages from your site using Lynx, a text-only browser, through the online Lynx Viewer.[3] While this is a useful test, Lynx is free to download and install, so you may as well install a copy on your system. This option provides the added advantage of testing pages before you upload them to the Web.

## Linux/Unix Users

You may find that Lynx is already installed on your system; otherwise, you should be able to obtain a copy easily via your package management system. Alternatively, you can download the source from the Lynx software distribution site.[4]

## Windows Users

Installing Lynx on Windows used to be a tricky process, but now an installer is available from csant.info.[5] Download and run the installer, which will also make Lynx available from your **Start** menu.

## Mac OS X Users

Lynx for Mac OS X is available from the Apple web site.[6]

# Discussion

Lynx behaves consistently across all platforms, but you'll need to learn a few simple commands in order to use it for web browsing. Figure 8.1 shows a typical site displayed in Lynx.

To open a web page, hit **G** and enter the URL. Press **Enter**, and Lynx will load that URL. If the site that you're trying to visit uses any form of cookies, Lynx will ask you if you wish to accept them. Type **Y** for yes, **N** for no, **A** to accept cookies from that site always, or **V** to ensure that you never accept cookies from that site.

---

[3] http://www.delorie.com/web/lynxview.html

[4] http://lynx.isc.org/release/

[5] http://www.csant.info/lynx.htm

[6] http://www.apple.com/downloads/macosx/unix_open_source/lynxtextwebbrowser.html

Use the arrow keys to navigate. The up and down arrow keys will let you jump from link to link. The right arrow key will follow the link that you're currently on, while the left arrow key will take you back to the previous page.

Figure 8.1. Viewing a site in Lynx

To complete a form, navigate to each form field using the down arrow key and, once you're there, type into the field as normal.

You can use Lynx to view local files, which is useful during development. If you're running a local web server, such as Apache or IIS, you can just point Lynx to localhost URLs. Note, though, that the browser will also read an HTML file directly if you provide it with the path and filename.

For more information on how to use Lynx, hit **H** to display the help system, which you can navigate as you would any site.

**See Accessibility in Action**

Spend some time visiting your favorite sites in a text-only browser—you'll soon start to appreciate the importance of ensuring you have `alt` text on images, and a well-structured document.

# How do I test my site in a screen reader?

The best way to understand the experience of visiting your site with a screen reader is to try it out for yourself; however, the most popular and well-known screen reader in use today, JAWS, is expensive (though a demonstration version exists that will run for 40 minutes) and entails a steep learning curve. What other options do web developers have to test their sites in a screen reader?

## Solution

The free Firefox extension, Fire Vox, can give you an excellent impression of the way a site sounds when it's read through a screen reader, and is available as a download for those running Firefox on Windows, Mac OS X, or Linux. Download Fire Vox from the author, Charles L. Chen's web site,[7] and follow the installation instructions for your operating system. The brief tutorial offered on the site will help you start using Fire Vox.

## Discussion

While trying out a screen reader is a great way to gain a feel for the experience a visually impaired user has online, it's impossible for those of us with good vision to really understand the experience, or even, with the limited use of screen readers in site testing, to become as adept with the software as those who rely on it to use the Web. So unless you have time to learn to use the software properly, testing sites with a screen reader should be seen as an activity to help you gain insight into these users' experiences, rather than as a true test of your site's screen reader compatibility.

---

[7] http://www.firevox.clcworld.net/downloads.html

# How do I create style sheets for specific devices?

It's possible to show different CSS to various browsers, but what about other devices?

## Solution

CSS 2.1 includes a specification for **media types**, which allow web page authors to restrict a style sheet, or section of a style sheet, to a given medium.

You can tag a style sheet with any of these media types. For example, the following markup tags the linked style sheet for use by browsers rendering to a computer screen only:

```
<link rel="stylesheet" type=text/css" href="screen.css"
    media="screen" />
```

Embedded style sheets can also be tagged this way:

```
<style type="text/css" media="all">
⋮
</style>
```

In both these examples, the media attribute has a value of the media type for which the style sheet has been created. This style sheet will only be used by devices that support the specified media type.

## Discussion

The following list of media types is taken from the CSS 2.1 specification.[8]

| | |
|---|---|
| **all** | suitable for all devices |
| **braille** | intended for tactile feedback devices, such as braille browsers |
| **embossed** | intended for paged braille printers |

---

[8] http://www.w3.org/TR/CSS21/media.html#media-types

**handheld**     intended for handheld devices (typically small-screen, limited-bandwidth devices)

**print**          intended for paged material and for documents viewed on screen in Print Preview mode

**projection**   intended for projected presentations (this is used by Opera in full-screen mode)

**screen**       intended primarily for color computer screens

**speech**      intended for speech synthesizers (note that CSS2 had a similar media type called `aural` for this purpose)

**tty**            intended for media using a fixed-pitch character grid (such as tele-types, terminals, or portable devices with limited display capabilit-ies); authors should not use pixel units with the `tty` media type

**tv**             intended for television-type devices (low resolution, color, limited-scrollability screens with sound available)

In addition to the `media` attribute described above, we can address multiple media types in one style sheet using the `@media` at-rule.

Here's an example of this approach in action. The style sheet below dictates that printed documents will print with a font size of ten points, while on the screen, the font will display at a size of 12 pixels. Both print and screen devices will display the text in black:

```
@media print {
  body {
    font-size: 10pt;
  }
}
@media screen {
  body {
    font-size: 12px;
  }
}
@media screen, print {
  body {
```

```
      color: #000000;
   }
}
```

Currently, there are very few devices that fully support the media types you would expect them to and it's likely that this method of targeting specific devices will be superseded by the Media Queries module of CSS3.[9] Opera Mobile and Safari for the iPhone, for example, have dropped support for the handheld media type because their parent companies believe they're fully featured browsers, unlike the typically low-powered browsers you find on handheld devices. Instead, they've opted to support media queries, which offer a far more powerful way of targeting modern mobile devices that can fully render CSS well, but have limitations due to device screen size.[10]

However media types are still very relevant; the one that's most usefully supported by modern browsers is the print media type. The next solution discusses how you can use this media type to create print versions of your pages.

 **No Need to Start from Scratch**

If you're creating a style sheet for a new media type, the easiest way is to save a copy of your existing style sheet under a new name. That way, you already have all your selectors at hand, and can simply change the styles that you've created for each.

# How do I create a print style sheet?

Web pages rarely print well, as techniques that are designed to make a page look good on a screen are usually different from those used to create a document that prints well. However, it's possible to use the CSS media types to provide a style sheet that's applied when the document is printed.

---

[9] http://reference.sitepoint.com/css/mediaqueries/

[10] For example, using CSS media queries you can specify styles for screens that have a maximum width of 480px. You can read more at the Opera Developer Community site [http://dev.opera.com/articles/view/opera-mobile-9-5-the-developer-angle/] and the Apple Safari Dev Center site [http://developer.apple.com/safari/].

# Solution

We can create a special print style sheet for our visitors like so:

chapter08/print-stylesheet.html

```html
<!DOCTYPE html PUBLIC "-//W3C//DTD XHTML 1.0 Strict//EN"
    "http://www.w3.org/TR/xhtml1/DTD/xhtml1-strict.dtd">
<html xmlns="http://www.w3.org/1999/xhtml" lang="en-US">
<head>
<title>Print Style Sheet</title>
<meta http-equiv="content-type"
    content="text/html; charset=utf-8" />
<link rel="stylesheet" type="text/css" href="main.css"
    title="default" />
<link rel="stylesheet" type="text/css" href="print.css"
    media="print" />
</head>
<body>
<div id="banner"></div>
<div id="content">
  <h1>Chinese-style stuffed peppers</h1>
  <p>These stuffed peppers are lovely as a starter, or as a side
    dish for a Chinese meal. They also go down well as part of a
    buffet and even children seem to like them.</p>
  <h2>Ingredients</h2>
  ⋮
</div>
<div id="navigation">
  <ul id="mainnav">
    <li><a href="#">Recipes</a></li>
    <li><a href="#">Contact Us</a></li>
    <li><a href="#">Articles</a></li>
    <li><a href="#">Buy Online</a></li>
  </ul>
</div>
</body>
</html>
```

chapter08/main.css

```css
body, html {
  margin: 0;
  padding: 0;
```

```
}
#navigation {
  width: 200px;
  font: 90% Arial, Helvetica, sans-serif;
  position: absolute;
  top: 41px;
  left: 0;
}
#navigation ul {
  list-style: none;
  margin: 0;
  padding: 0;
  border: none;
}
#navigation li {
  border-bottom: 1px solid #ED9F9F;
  margin: 0;
}
#navigation li a:link, #navigation li a:visited {
  display: block;
  padding: 5px 5px 5px 0.5em;
  border-left: 12px solid #711515;
  border-right: 1px solid #711515;
  color: #FFFFFF;
  background-color: #b51032;
  text-decoration: none;
}
#navigation li a:hover {
  color: #FFFFFF;
  background-color: #711515;
}
#content {
  margin-left: 260px;
  margin-right: 60px;
}
#banner {
  height: 40px;
  background-color: #711515;
  border-bottom: 1px solid #ED9F9F;
  text-align: right;
  padding-right: 20px;
  margin-top: 0;
}
#banner ul {
```

```
    margin: 0;
    padding: 0;
}
#banner li {
    display: inline;
}
#banner a:link, #banner a:visited {
    font: 80% Arial, Helvetica, sans-serif;
    color: #FFFFFF;
    background-color: transparent;
}
#content p, #content li {
    font: 80%/1.6em Arial, Helvetica, sans-serif;
}
#content p {
    margin-left: 1.5em;
}
#content h1, #content h2 {
    font: 140% Georgia, "Times New Roman", Times, serif;
}
#content h2 {
    font: 120% Georgia, "Times New Roman", Times, serif;
    padding-bottom: 3px;
}
```

chapter08/print.css

```
body, html {
    margin: 0;
    padding: 0;
}
#navigation {
    display: none;
}
#content {
    margin-left: 20pt;
    margin-right: 30pt;
}
#banner {
    display: none;
}
#content p, #content li {
    font: 12pt/20pt "Times New Roman", Times, serif;
}
```

```
#content p {
  margin-left: 20pt;
}
#content h1, #content h2 {
  font: 16pt Georgia, "Times New Roman", Times, serif;
  color: #4b4b4b;
  background-color: transparent;
}
#content h2 {
  font: 14pt Georgia, "Times New Roman", Times, serif;
  padding-bottom: 2pt;
  border-bottom: 1pt dotted #CCCCCC;
}
```

## Discussion

Creating a print style sheet can be very helpful to your visitors, particularly if your page has many graphics. Printing from a site featuring multiple graphics can be costly in terms of printer ink and slow on older printers. And some sites fail to print well at all because of the color combinations or layouts used. For example, Figure 8.2 shows a page that has a simple two-column CSS layout, with navigation in the sidebar, and a main content area that contains a recipe.

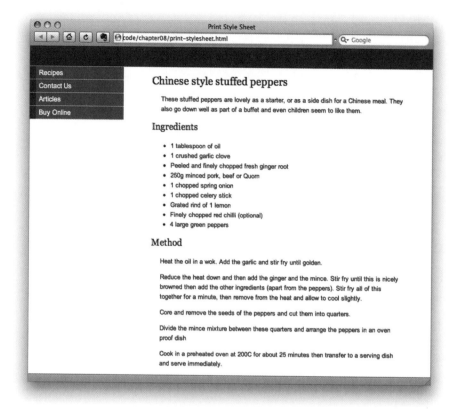

Figure 8.2. Displaying a two-column layout in the browser

Figure 8.3 shows this layout in Print Preview.

These figures really give us a clear idea of the practical differences between the on-screen and print displays. A standard letter or A4 sheet of paper is reasonably narrow, so by the time the print display has accounted for the menu, only half of the page width is left for the display of the recipe text. This may mean that long recipes need to be printed on two pages, rather than one.

Figure 8.3. The layout appears in Print Preview

Traditionally, sites offer print versions of documents that they expect users to print. However, this approach requires the maintenance of more than one version of the document—and users have to be savvy enough to find and click the **Print** button on the page, rather than simply printing the page using the browser's **Print** button. With the CSS method, the print style sheet will automatically come into play regardless of which print button they click on.

Let's step through the process of developing the print style sheet and linking it to your pages.

## Linking a Print Style Sheet

Open your existing main style sheet and save it as **print.css** so that it becomes your print style sheet. Link this style sheet to your document with the `print` media type, like so:

```
<link rel="stylesheet" type="text/css" href="print.css"
    media="print" />
```

## Creating the Print Styles

If you've saved your existing style sheet as **print.css**, you can use it to decide what needs to be changed in order to create the print style sheet. In my layout, the navigation is contained within a `div`; the section in the style sheet for that element looks like this:

*chapter08/main.css (excerpt)*

```
#navigation {
  width: 200px;
  font: 90% Arial, Helvetica, sans-serif;
  position: absolute;
  top: 41px;
  left: 0;
}
```

The first task we want to do is hide the navigation, as it's useless in the print version of the document. To do this, we replace the properties in the above section of the style sheet with `display: none`:

*chapter08/print.css (excerpt)*

```
#navigation {
  display: none;
}
```

We can now remove any navigation rules that apply to elements within the `navigation` element.

We can also make the content area wider, so that it takes up all the available space on the page. Find the section for the `content` element in your style sheet:

chapter08/main.css *(excerpt)*

```
#content {
  margin-left: 260px;
  margin-right: 60px;
}
```

We can change the left margin to a smaller value, as we no longer need to leave space for the navigation. It's also a good idea to switch from pixel measurements (a screen unit) to points (a print unit), as we discussed in "Should I use pixels, points, ems, or another unit identifier to set font sizes?" in Chapter 2:

chapter08/print.css *(excerpt)*

```
#content {
  margin-left: 20pt;
  margin-right: 30pt;
}
```

If we check the document in Print Preview, as shown in Figure 8.4, or print it via the browser, we'll find that the navigation has disappeared and the content now fills the space much more effectively.

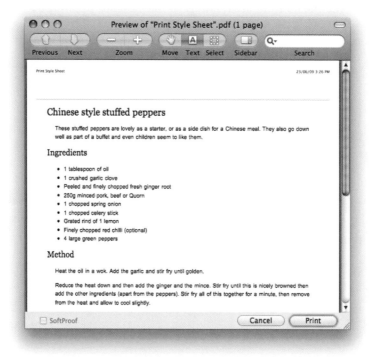

Figure 8.4. The page printing more cleanly after we remove the navigation

The line at the top of Figure 8.4 is the banner's bottom border. We can hide the banner just as we hid the navigation. First, we must find the section for `banner` in the style sheet:

chapter08/main.css *(excerpt)*

```css
#banner {
  height: 40px;
  background-color: #711515;
  border-bottom: 1px solid #ED9F9F;
}
```

Once again, we set the banner to `display: none` and delete the remaining rules associated with this ID:

chapter08/print.css *(excerpt)*

```css
#banner {
  display: none;
}
```

Finally, we can format the text. For print purposes, I normally make any colored text grayscale, unless it's important that the text stays colored. Let's use print-friendly points to size the text, so that our print style sheet renders font sizes reliably across different systems.

Additionally, you might like to consider using a serif font for your printed text, as serif fonts are generally considered easier to read on paper. Here are those changes:

chapter08/print.css *(excerpt)*

```css
#content p, #content li {
  font: 12pt/20pt "Times New Roman", Times, serif;
}
#content p {
  margin-left: 20pt;
}
#content h1, #content h2 {
  font: 16pt Georgia, "Times New Roman", Times, serif;
  color: #4b4b4b;
  background-color: transparent;
}
#content h2 {
  font: 14pt Georgia, "Times New Roman", Times, serif;
  padding-bottom: 2pt;
  border-bottom: 1pt dotted #CCCCCC;
}
```

The much plainer but more readable print layout is shown in its final form in Figure 8.5.

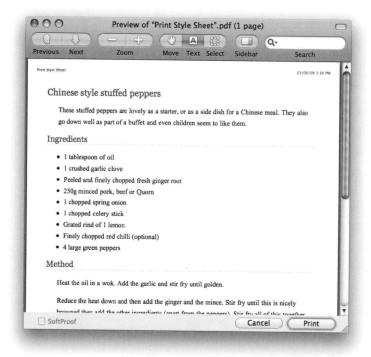

Figure 8.5. Using **Print Preview** to view the page affected by the completed style sheet

 **Print Style Sheets and Table Layouts**

Print style sheets are easy to implement on CSS layouts, but you can also create effective print style sheets for table-based layouts, particularly if you use CSS to set the widths of table cells. You can then hide cells that contain navigation just as we hid the navigation `div` in the above CSS layout.

# How do I add alternative style sheets to my site?

Some modern browsers allow the user to view a list of the style sheets attached to a document, and select the one they want to use to view the site. This can be a simple way to add a style sheet with reversed-out colors, for example.

# Solution

Link your alternative style sheet with `rel="alternative stylesheet"` and give it a descriptive title. The title will display in the browser's menu, so describing the style sheet—for example, "high contrast"—is most helpful for users. You should also give your default style sheet a title to differentiate it from the alternative style sheet:

*chapter08/alternate-stylesheets.html (excerpt)*

```
<link rel="stylesheet" type="text/css" href="main.css"
    title="default" />
<link rel="stylesheet" type="text/css" href="print.css"
    media="print" />
<link rel="alternative stylesheet" type="text/css"
    href="highcontrast.css" title="high contrast" />
```

*chapter08/highcontrast.css*

```
body, html {
  margin: 0;
  padding: 0;
  background-color: #000000;
  color: #FFFFFF;
}
#navigation {
  width: 200px;
  font: 90% Arial, Helvetica, sans-serif;
  position: absolute;
  top: 41px;
  left: 0;
}
#navigation ul {
  list-style: none;
  margin: 0;
  padding: 0;
  border: none;
}
#navigation li {
  border-bottom: 1px solid #ED9F9F;
  margin: 0;
}
#navigation li a:link, #navigation li a:visited {
```

```
    display: block;
    padding: 5px 5px 5px 0.5em;
    border-left: 12px solid #711515;
    border-right: 1px solid #711515;
    color: #FFFFFF;
    background-color: #b51032;
    text-decoration: none;
}
#navigation li a:hover {
    color: #FFFFFF;
    background-color: #711515;
}
#content {
    margin-left: 260px;
    margin-right: 60px;
}
#banner {
    height: 40px;
    background-color: #711515;
    border-bottom: 1px solid #ED9F9F;
    text-align: right;
    padding-right: 20px;
    margin-top: 0;
}
#banner ul {
    margin: 0;
    padding: 0;
}
#banner li {
    display: inline;
}
#banner a:link, #banner a:visited {
    font: 80% Arial, Helvetica, sans-serif;
    color: #FFFFFF;
    background-color: transparent;
}
#content p, #content li {
    font: 80%/1.6em Arial, Helvetica, sans-serif;
}
#content p {
    margin-left: 1.5em;
}
#content h1, #content h2 {
    font: 140% Georgia, "Times New Roman", Times, serif;
```

```
  color: #FFFFFF;
  background-color: transparent;
}
#content h2 {
  font: 120% Georgia, "Times New Roman", Times, serif;
  padding-bottom: 3px;
  border-bottom: 1px dotted #CCCCCC;
}
```

In Figure 8.6, you can see how the page displays when the user selects the alternative style sheet from Firefox's **View** menu.

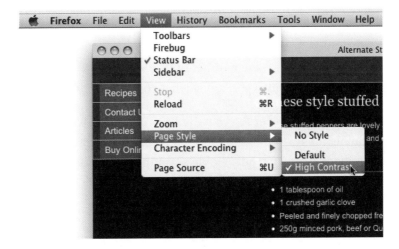

Figure 8.6. Switching to the **High Contrast** style sheet in Firefox

## Discussion

Utilizing this browser functionality is easy, and allows you to add valuable features for users with a minimum of effort. Typically, it takes very little time to create a style sheet that tweaks the color scheme. Simply save your existing style sheet and tweak the fonts, colors, and layout as required.

Unfortunately, browser support for this feature is still limited—and absent in Internet Explorer. However, users who find this functionality beneficial may choose a browser specifically because it gives them access to these features.

### Look How Thoughtful I Am!

As very few sites utilize this feature at present, it would be a good idea to let your users know that you offer alternative style sheets. Perhaps include the information on a separate page that explains how to use the site, which is linked clearly from the home page.

## Zoom Layouts

A step on from simply creating a large-print style sheet is the concept of the **zoom layout**. Popularized by Joe Clark, the zoom layout uses CSS to refactor the page into a single-column layout with high-contrast colors.[11] This is most useful for visitors who use the zoom feature in modern browsers (as it increases the size of the whole layout rather than just the text), or use software that magnifies the screen to make reading easier. When a design is magnified in this way, the sidebars often move off the side of the viewport, resulting in a page that contains only essential content.

Zoom layouts can make it easier for visually impaired users by enlarging the font size and displaying the text in a light color on a dark background—a combination that's easier for many users to read. A style sheet that creates a zoom layout for the design we've been working on throughout this chapter might contain the following rules, and display in the browser as shown in Figure 8.7:

chapter08/zoom.css

```
body, html {
  margin: 1em 2em 2em 2em;
  padding: 0;
  font-size: 140%;
  background-color: #333;
  color: #FFFFFF;
}
#navigation ul {
  list-style: none;
  margin: 0;
  padding: 0;
  border: none;
}
```

---

[11] http://joeclark.org/access/webaccess/zoom/

```
#navigation li {
  float:left;
  width: 20%;
}

#navigation li a:link, #navigation li a:visited {
  color: #FFFF00;
}

#navigation li a:hover {
  text-decoration:none;
}

#content {
  padding: 1em 0 0 0;
  clear:left;
}

#content p, #content li {
  line-height: 1.6em;
}

#content h1, #content h2 {
  font: 140% Georgia, "Times New Roman", Times, serif;
  color: #FFFFFF;
  background-color: transparent;
}

#content h2 {
  font: 120% Georgia, "Times New Roman", Times, serif;
}
```

Figure 8.7. A zoom layout style sheet

# Should I add font–size widgets or other style sheet switchers to my site?

You may come across sites that have added a widget to increase or decrease font size by switching the style sheet. In this chapter we've already covered how to create alternate style sheets; should we provide these style switcher links?

## Solution

Font-size widgets—often seen as a series of the letter "A" in varying sizes—are really redundant if you have built your site well, using font-sizing methods that allow the text to be increased in all browsers. It's seen as more helpful to let your users know how to increase the font size using browser controls, as this will give them the ability to increase the text on most sites, rather than just the ones that offer a widget to do so.

With zoom layouts or other alternate layouts, the guidance is less clear. Modern browsers do allow users to zoom rather than just increase text size and, in an ideal world, all designs would zoom well and there'd be no need to provide alternate style sheets for users wanting to zoom. However, where fixed-width designs are concerned, zooming often results in parts of the design disappearing off screen. I personally think that in this situation, having a different design tailored to the needs of these users is a good thing. You could simply create an alternate style sheet as above and, on a page detailing the accessibility of your site, explain to users which browsers will enable use of alternate style sheets and how to switch to the zoom version, or you could implement a switcher using JavaScript or server-side code. You should, however, only include this functionality if you really need to. Take care to resist the trap of thinking you have to have style switchers, or that they allow you to disregard accessibility in your default design.

# How do I use alternative style sheets without duplicating code?

In the examples we've seen so far in this chapter, we created our alternative style sheet by changing very few properties within the main style sheet. Do we actually need to create a whole new version of the style sheet as an alternative, or is it possible to alter only those styles that *need* to be changed?

## Solution

The answer to this question is to create multiple style sheets: a base style sheet for the properties that never change, a default style sheet that contains the properties that will change, and a style sheet that includes the alternative versions of those properties:

*alternate-stylesheets2.html (excerpt)*

```
<link rel="stylesheet" type="text/css" href="main2.css" />
<link rel="stylesheet" type="text/css" href="defaultcolors.css"
    title="Default" />
<link rel="stylesheet" type="text/css" href="print.css"
```

```
    media="print" />
<link rel="alternative stylesheet" type="text/css"
    href="highcontrast2.css" title="High Contrast" />
```

chapter08/main2.css

```css
body, html {
  margin: 0;
  padding: 0;
}
#navigation {
  font: 90% Arial, Helvetica, sans-serif;
  position: absolute;
  left: 0;
  top: 41px;
}
#navigation ul {
  list-style: none;
  margin: 0;
  padding: 0;
  border: none;
}
#navigation li {
  border-bottom: 1px solid #ED9F9F;
  margin: 0;
}
#navigation li a:link, #navigation li a:visited {
  display: block;
  padding: 5px 5px 5px 0.5em;
  border-left: 12px solid #711515;
  border-right: 1px solid #711515;
  background-color: #B51032;
  color: #FFFFFF;
  text-decoration: none;
}
#navigation li a:hover {
  background-color: #711515;
  color: #FFFFFF;
}
#banner {
  background-color: #711515;
  border-bottom: 1px solid #ED9F9F;
  text-align: right;
  padding-right: 20px;
```

```
    margin-top: 0;
}
#banner ul {
  margin: 0;
}
#banner li {
  display: inline;
}
#banner a:link, #banner a:visited {
  font: 80% Arial, Helvetica, sans-serif;
  color: #FFFFFF
  background-color: transparent;
}
#content p, #content li {
  font: 80%/1.6em Arial, Helvetica, sans-serif;
}
#content p {
  margin-left: 1.5em;
}
#content h1, #content h2 {
  font: 140% Georgia, "Times New Roman", Times, serif;
  color: #B51032;
  background-color: transparent;
}
#content h2 {
  font: 120% Georgia, "Times New Roman", Times, serif;
  padding-bottom: 3px;
  border-bottom: 1px dotted #ED9F9F;
}
```

chapter08/defaultcolors.css

```
body, html {
  background-color: #FFFFFF;
  color: #000000;
}

#content h1, #content h2 {
  color: #B51032;
  background-color: transparent;
}
```

```
#content h2 {
  border-bottom: 1px dotted #ED9F9F;
}
```

chapter08/highcontrast2.css

```
body, html {
  background-color: #000000;
  color: #FFFFFF;
}

#content h1, #content h2 {
  color: #FFFFFF;
  background-color: transparent;
}

#content h2 {
  border-bottom: 1px dotted #CCCCCC;
}
```

## Discussion

To create the **highcontrast.css** file that I used in "How do I add alternative style sheets to my site?" I changed very few of the properties that were in the original style sheet. I changed the base color and background color:

chapter08/main.css *(excerpt)*

```
body, html {
  margin: 0;
  padding: 0;
  background-color: #FFFFFF;
  color: #000000;
}
```

chapter08/highcontrast.css *(excerpt)*

```
body, html {
  margin: 0;
  padding: 0;
```

```
  background-color: #000000;
  color: #FFFFFF;
}
```

I also adjusted the color of the level 1 and 2 headings:

chapter08/main.css *(excerpt)*

```
#content h1, #content h2 {
  font: 140% Georgia, "Times New Roman", Times, serif;
  color: #B51032;
  background-color: transparent;
}

#content h2 {
  font: 120% Georgia, "Times New Roman", Times, serif;
  padding-bottom: 3px;
  border-bottom: 1px dotted #ED9F9F;
}
```

chapter08/highcontrast.css *(excerpt)*

```
#content h1, #content h2 {
  font: 140% Georgia, "Times New Roman", Times, serif;
  color: #FFFFFF;
  background-color: transparent;
}

#content h2 {
  font: 120% Georgia, "Times New Roman", Times, serif;
  padding-bottom: 3px;
  border-bottom: 1px dotted #CCCCCC;
}
```

To avoid making a copy of the entire style sheet in order to create the **highcontrast.css** file, we can remove from the main style sheet those properties that we know we'll need to swap. We'll place them in a new style sheet that determines the default color scheme; our high-contrast style sheet need contain only the altered version of those properties. This way, you avoid having to maintain several different versions of what is, essentially, the same style sheet.

## Summary

In this chapter, we've covered some of the ways in which the use of style sheets can make your site more accessible to a wider range of users. By starting out with an accessible document structure, we're already assisting those who need to use a screen reader to read out the content of the site, and by providing alternative style sheets we can help users with other accessibility needs to customize their experience, making the site easier to use.

# CSS Positioning and Layout

Browser bugs aside, the fundamentals of CSS layout are relatively easy to understand. Once you know the basics, anything more complex is really just repeating the same techniques on various sections of your page.

This chapter will introduce the basics of CSS layout, and explore useful tricks and techniques that you can use to create unique and beautiful sites. These are the essential building blocks—commencement points for your creativity. If you work through the chapter from beginning to end, you'll start to grasp the fundamentals necessary to create workable CSS layouts. The chapter then progresses to more detailed layout examples—so if you're already comfortable with the basics, simply dip into these solutions to find the specific technique you need.

## How do I decide when to use a class and when to use an ID?

At first glance, classes and IDs seem to be used in much the same way: you can assign CSS properties to both classes and IDs, and apply them to change the way (X)HTML elements look. But, in which circumstances are classes best applied? And what about IDs?

## Solution

The most important rule, where classes and IDs are concerned, is that an ID must be only used *once* in a document—as it uniquely identifies the element to which it's applied. Once you've assigned an ID to an element, you cannot use that ID again within that document.

Classes, on the other hand, may be used as many times as you like within the same document. Therefore, if there's a feature on a page that you wish to repeat, a class is the ideal choice.

You can apply both a class and an ID to any given element. For example, you might apply a class to all text input fields on a page; if you want to be able to address those fields using JavaScript, each field will need a separate ID, too. However, no styles need be assigned to that ID.

I tend to use IDs for the main, structural, positioned elements of the page, so I often end up with IDs such as header, content, nav, and footer. Here's an example:

```
<!DOCTYPE html PUBLIC "-//W3C//DTD XHTML 1.0 Strict//EN"
"http://www.w3.org/TR/xhtml1/DTD/xhtml1-strict.dtd">
<html xmlns="http://www.w3.org/1999/xhtml" lang="en-US">
<head>
<title>Absolute positioning</title>
<meta http-equiv="content-type"
    content="text/html; charset=utf-8" />
<link rel="stylesheet" type="text/css" href="position2.css" />
</head>
<body>
    <div id="header"> … </div>
    <div id="content">
        ┊ Main page content here …
    </div>
    <div id="nav"> … </div>
</body>
</html>
```

# Can I make an inline element display as if it were block-level, and vice-versa?

Sometimes, we need to make the browser treat HTML elements differently than it would treat them by default.

## Solution

In Figure 9.1, you can see that we've forced a `div` element to display as an inline element, and a link to display as a block.

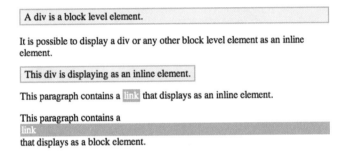

Figure 9.1. Displaying the block-level element inline, while the inline element displays as a block

Here's the markup that achieves this effect:

```
chapter09/inline-block.html
```

```
<!DOCTYPE html PUBLIC "-//W3C//DTD XHTML 1.0 Strict//EN"
  "http://www.w3.org/TR/xhtml1/DTD/xhtml1-strict.dtd">
<html xmlns="http://www.w3.org/1999/xhtml" lang="en-US">
  <head>
    <title>Inline and block level elements</title>
    <meta http-equiv="content-type"
        content="text/html; charset=utf-8" />
    <style type="text/css">
      #one {
        background-color: #CFEAFA;
        border: 2px solid #6CB5DF;
        padding: 2px 6px 2px 6px;
      }
```

```
    #two {
      background-color: #CFEAFA;
      border: 2px solid #6CB5DF;
      padding: 2px 6px 2px 6px;
      display: inline;
    }
    a {
      background-color: #6CB5DF;
      color: #FFFFFF;
      text-decoration: none;
      padding: 1px 2px 1px 2px;
    }
    a.block {
      display: block;
    }
    </style>
  </head>
  <body>
    <div id="one">A div is a block level element.</div>
    <p>It is possible to display a div or any other block level
      element as an inline element. </p>
    <div id="two">This div is displaying as an inline element.
      </div>
    <p>This paragraph contains a
      <a href="http://www.sitepoint.com/">link</a> that
      displays as an inline element.</p>
    <p>This paragraph contains a
      <a class="block" href="http://www.sitepoint.com/">link</a>
      that displays as a block element.</p>
  </body>
</html>
```

## Discussion

Block-level elements are distinguished from inline elements in that they may contain inline elements as well as other block-level elements. They're also formatted differently than inline elements: block-level elements occupy a rectangular area of the page, spanning the entire width of the page by default, whereas inline elements flow along lines of text, and wrap to fit inside the blocks that contain them. HTML elements that are treated as block-level by default include headings (h1, h2, h3, …), paragraphs (p), lists (ul, ol), and various containers (div, blockquote).

In the example above, we see a `div` that displays as normal. As it's a block-level element, it takes up the full width of the parent element, which, in this case, is the `body`. If it were contained within another `div`, or a table cell, it would stretch only to the width of that element.

If we want the `div` to behave differently, we can set it to display inline by applying this CSS property:

```
display: inline;
```

We can cause an inline element to display as if it were a block-level element in the same way. In the above example, note that the `a` element displays as an inline element by default. We often want it to display as a block—for example, when we're creating a navigation bar using CSS. To achieve this, we set the `display` property of the element to `block`. In the example above, this causes the gray box that contains the linked text to expand to the full width of the screen.

# How do margins and padding work in CSS?

What's the difference between the `margin` and `padding` properties, and how do they affect elements?

## Solution

The margin properties add space to the *outside* of an element. You can set margins individually:

```
margin-top: 1em;
margin-right: 2em;
margin-bottom: 0.5em;
margin-left: 3em;
```

You can also set margins using a shorthand property:

```
margin: 1em 2em 0.5em 3em;
```

If all the margins are to be equal, simply use a rule like this:

```
margin: 1em;
```

This rule applies a 1 em margin to all sides of the element.

Figure 9.2 shows what a block-level element looks like when we add margins to it. The code for this page is as follows:

chapter09/margin.html

```
<!DOCTYPE html PUBLIC "-//W3C//DTD XHTML 1.0 Strict//EN"
  "http://www.w3.org/TR/xhtml1/DTD/xhtml1-strict.dtd">
<html xmlns="http://www.w3.org/1999/xhtml" lang="en-US">
  <head>
    <title>Margins</title>
    <meta http-equiv="content-type"
        content="text/html; charset=utf-8" />
    <style type="text/css">
      p {
        background-color: #CFEAFA;
        border: 2px solid #6CB5DF;
      }
      p.margintest {
        margin: 40px;
      }
    </style>
  </head>
  <body>
    <p>This paragraph should be displayed in the default …</p>
    <p>This is another paragraph that has the default …</p>
    <p class="margintest">This paragraph has a 40-pixel …</p>
  </body>
</html>
```

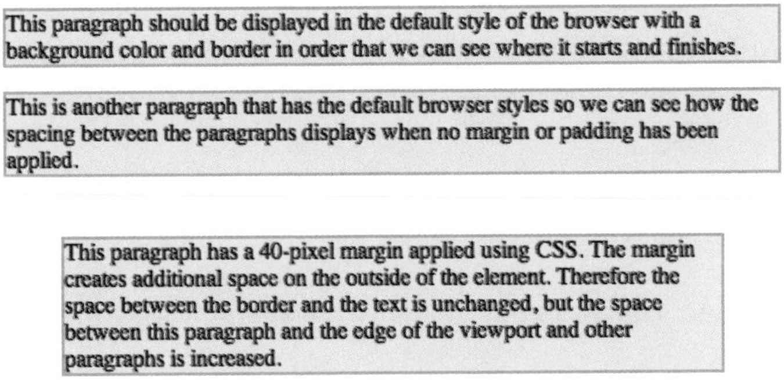

> This paragraph should be displayed in the default style of the browser with a background color and border in order that we can see where it starts and finishes.
>
> This is another paragraph that has the default browser styles so we can see how the spacing between the paragraphs displays when no margin or padding has been applied.
>
> This paragraph has a 40-pixel margin applied using CSS. The margin creates additional space on the outside of the element. Therefore the space between the border and the text is unchanged, but the space between this paragraph and the edge of the viewport and other paragraphs is increased.

Figure 9.2. Applying margins to an element with CSS

The padding properties add space *inside* the element—between its borders and its content. You can set padding individually for the top, right, bottom, and left sides of an element:

```
padding-top: 1em;
padding-right: 1.5em;
padding-bottom: 0.5em;
padding-left: 2em;
```

You can also apply padding using this shorthand property:

```
padding: 1em 1.5em 0.5em 2em;
```

As with margins, if the padding is to be equal all the way around an element, you can simply use a rule like this:

```
padding: 1em;
```

Figure 9.3, which results from the following code, shows what a block looks like with padding applied. Compare it to Figure 9.2 to see the differences between margins and padding:

```
<!DOCTYPE html PUBLIC "-//W3C//DTD XHTML 1.0 Strict//EN"
    "http://www.w3.org/TR/xhtml1/DTD/xhtml1-strict.dtd">
<html xmlns="http://www.w3.org/1999/xhtml" lang="en-US">
  <head>
    <title>Padding</title>
    <meta http-equiv="content-type"
        content="text/html; charset=utf-8" />
    <style type="text/css">
      p {
        border: 2px solid #AAAAAA;
        background-color: #EEEEEE;
      }
      p.paddingtest {
        padding: 40px;
      }
    </style>
  </head>
  <body>
    <p>This paragraph should be displayed in the default …</p>
    <p>This is another paragraph that has the default …</p>
    <p class="paddingtest">This paragraph has 40 pixels …</p>
  </body>
</html>
```

## Discussion

The above solution demonstrates the basics of margins and padding. As we've seen, the margin properties create space between the element to which they're applied and the surrounding elements, while padding creates space *inside* the element to which it's applied. Figure 9.4 illustrates this point.

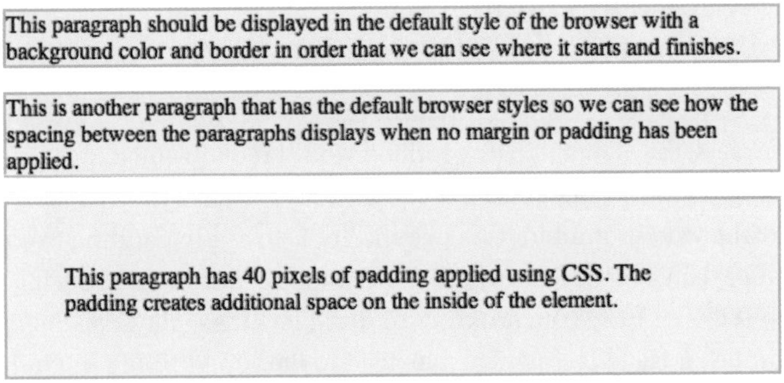

This paragraph should be displayed in the default style of the browser with a background color and border in order that we can see where it starts and finishes.
This is another paragraph that has the default browser styles so we can see how the spacing between the paragraphs displays when no margin or padding has been applied.
This paragraph has 40 pixels of padding applied using CSS. The padding creates additional space on the inside of the element.

Figure 9.3. Applying padding to an element in CSS

margin
16
border
2
padding
40
2
40
627 x 38
40
2
40
2
16

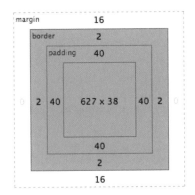

Figure 9.4. Applying margins, padding, and borders

If you're applying margins and padding to a fixed-width element, they'll be added to the specified width to produce the total width for that element. So, if your element has a width of 400 pixels, and you add 40 pixels' worth of padding on all sides, you'll make the element take up 480 pixels of total width (400 pixels wide plus 40 pixels on each side). Add 20 pixels of margins to that, and the element will occupy a width of 520 pixels (a visible width of 480 pixels with 20 pixels of spacing on either side). If you have a very precise layout, remember to calculate your element sizes carefully, including any added margins and padding.

**Quirks Mode May Confuse**

In very old versions of Internet Explorer, namely 5 and 5.5, padding (and borders) are interpreted as being included within the specified width of the element; in these browsers, the element just described would remain 400 pixels in width with the padding included and adding margins would reduce the visible width of the element. One workaround for this peculiarity is to apply padding to a parent element, rather than adding a margin to the element in question. Ensuring compatibility with IE5 is of little concern to most designers these days, so the only time this might be an issue is if you've managed to end up with IE6 in Quirks Mode, as described in Chapter 7.

# How do I wrap text around an image?

With HTML, it's possible to wrap text around an image using the `align` attribute. This attribute was deprecated, but there is a CSS equivalent!

## Solution

Use the CSS `float` property to float an image to the left or right, as shown in Figure 9.5.

Figure 9.5. Floating an image to the left using the `float` property

Here's the code for this page:

```
<!DOCTYPE html PUBLIC "-//W3C//DTD XHTML 1.0 Strict//EN"
  "http://www.w3.org/TR/xhtml1/DTD/xhtml1-strict.dtd">
<html xmlns="http://www.w3.org/1999/xhtml" lang="en-US">
  <head>
    <title>Float</title>
    <meta http-equiv="content-type"
        content="text/html; charset=utf-8" />
    <style type="text/css">
      .featureimg {
        float: left;
        width: 319px;
      }
    </style>
  </head>
  <body>
    <h1>Chinese-style stuffed peppers</h1>
    <img src="peppers1.jpg" width="319" height="213" alt="peppers"
        class="featureimg" />
    <p>These stuffed peppers are lovely as a starter, or as a …</p>

    ⋮ More paragraphs

  </body>
</html>
```

## Discussion

The float property takes the element out of the document flow and *floats* it against the edge of the block-level element that contains it. Other block-level elements will then ignore the floated element and render as if it's absent. Inline elements such as content, however, will make space for the floated element, which is why we can use float to cause our text to wrap around an image.

As we can see clearly in Figure 9.5, the text bumps right up against the side of the image. If we add a border to that image, the text will collide against the side of the border.

To create space between our image and the text, we need to add a margin to the image. Since the image is aligned against the left-hand margin, we only need to add right and bottom margins to move the text away from the image slightly:

chapter09/float2.html *(excerpt)*

```
.featureimage {
  float: left;
  width: 319px;
  border: 2px solid #000000;
  margin-right: 20px;
  margin-bottom: 6px;
}
```

Figure 9.6 shows the resulting display, with extra space around the floated image.

## Chinese style stuffed peppers

These stuffed peppers are lovely as a starter, or as a side dish for a Chinese meal. They also go down well as part of a buffet and even children seem to like them.

Heat the oil in a wok. Add the garlic and stir fry until golden.

Reduce the heat down and then add the ginger and the mince. Stir fry until this is nicely browned then add the other ingredients (apart from the peppers). Stir fry all of this together for a minute, then remove from the heat and allow to cool slightly.

Core and remove the seeds of the peppers and cut them into quarters.

Divide the mince mixture between these quarters and arrange the peppers in an oven proof dish

Figure 9.6. Adding right and bottom margins to an image to improve the display

# How do I stop the next element moving up when I use float?

Floating an image or other element causes it to be ignored by block-level elements, although the text and inline images contained in those elements will appear to wrap around the floated element. How can you force elements on your page to display below the floated element?

## Solution

The CSS property clear allows you to make a given element display beneath any floated elements as if they'd remained unfloated in the first place. In this example, we apply this property with a value of both to the first paragraph that follows the list of ingredients:

chapter09/float-clear.html

```
<!DOCTYPE html PUBLIC "-//W3C//DTD XHTML 1.0 Strict//EN"
  "http://www.w3.org/TR/xhtml1/DTD/xhtml1-strict.dtd">
<html xmlns="http://www.w3.org/1999/xhtml" lang="en-US">
  <head>
    <title>float and clear</title>
    <meta http-equiv="content-type"
        content="text/html; charset=utf-8" />
    <style type="text/css">
      .featureimg {
        float: right;
        width: 319px;
        margin-left: 20px;
        margin-bottom: 6px;
        border: 1px solid #000000;
      }
      .clear {
        clear: both;
      }
    </style>
  </head>
  <body>
    <h1>Chinese style stuffed peppers</h1>
    <img src="peppers1.jpg" width="319" height="213" alt="peppers"
        class="featureimg" />
```

```
<ul>
  <li>1 tablespoon of oil</li>
  <li>1 crushed garlic clove</li>
  <li>Peeled and finely chopped fresh ginger root</li>
  <li>250g minced pork, beef or Quorn</li>
  <li>1 chopped spring onion</li>
  <li>1 chopped celery stick</li>
  <li>Grated rind of 1 lemon</li>
  <li>Finely chopped red chilli (optional)</li>
  <li>4 large green peppers</li>
</ul>
<p class="clear">These stuffed peppers are lovely as a…</p>

⋮ More paragraphs

  </body>
</html>
```

As shown in Figure 9.7 where we've floated the image to the right of the page, this markup causes the paragraph to be pushed down so that it begins below the floated image.

**Chinese style stuffed peppers**

- 1 tablespoon of oil
- 1 crushed garlic clove
- Peeled and finely chopped fresh ginger root
- 250g minced pork, beef or Quorn
- 1 chopped spring onion
- 1 chopped celery stick
- Grated rind of 1 lemon
- Finely chopped red chilli (optional)
- 4 large green peppers

These stuffed peppers are lovely as a starter, or as a side dish for a Chinese meal. They also go down well as part of a buffet and even children seem to like them.

Heat the oil in a wok. Add the garlic and stir fry until golden.

Figure 9.7. The first paragraph displays clear of the floated image

# Discussion

The `float` property takes an element out of the flow of the document: the block-level elements that appear after it will simply ignore the floated element. This effect can be seen more clearly if we apply a border to the elements in our document, as illustrated in Figure 9.8, which adds a two-pixel border to the `ul` and `p` elements in the page.

The floated image basically sits on top of the block elements. The text within those elements wraps around the image, but the elements themselves will ignore the fact that the floated element is there. This means that, in our example, if the height of the ingredients list is less than that of the image, the paragraph after the list of ingredients will wrap around the image, also shown in Figure 9.8.

Figure 9.8. Applying a two-pixel border to the `ul` and `p` elements

## Chinese style stuffed peppers

- 1 tablespoon of oil
- 1 crushed garlic clove
- Peeled and finely chopped fresh ginger root
- 250g minced pork, beef or Quorn
- 1 chopped spring onion
- 1 chopped celery stick
- Grated rind of 1 lemon
- Finely chopped red chilli (optional)
- 4 large green peppers

These stuffed peppers are lovely as a starter, or as a side dish for a Chinese meal. They also go down well as part of a buffet and even children seem to like them.

Heat the oil in a wok. Add the garlic and stir fry until golden.

Figure 9.9. Using the clear property to clear the paragraph from the float

To make the paragraph begin at a point below that at which the image finishes, we can use the clear property:

chapter09/float-clear.html *(excerpt)*

```
.clear {
  clear: both;
}
```

We apply this CSS class to the first <p> tag after the ingredients list:

chapter09/float-clear.html *(excerpt)*

```
<p class="clear">These stuffed peppers are lovely as a
    starter, or as a side dish for a Chinese meal. They also go
    down well as part of a buffet and even children seem to like
    them.</p>
```

If we leave the borders in place and reload the document as in Figure 9.9, we can see that the paragraph begins below the pepper image, as does its border.

The clear property can also take values of left or right, which are useful if you want to clear an element only from left or right floats, respectively. The value you're most likely to use, though, is both. Be aware that both float and clear can trigger bugs, particularly in Internet Explorer. You may recall we mentioned the "disappearing content" behavior of Internet Explorer 6 in Chapter 7.

# How do I align a site's logo and slogan to the left and right?

If you've ever used tables for layout, you'll know how easy it is to create the type of effect shown in Figure 9.10 with a two-column table. This method allows you to align the contents of the left-hand table cell to the left, and those of the right-hand cell to the right. Fortunately, the same end result is achievable using CSS.

Stage & Screen                    theatre and film reviews

Figure 9.10. Aligning the logo and slogan left and right, respectively, using CSS

## Solution

We can use `float` to create this type of layout:

chapter09/slogan-align.html *(excerpt)*

```
<body>
  <div id="header">
    <img src="stage-logo.gif" width="187" height="29"
        alt="Stage &amp; Screen" class="logo" />
    <span class="slogan">theatre and film reviews</span>
  </div>
</body>
```

chapter09/slogan-align.css

```
body {
  margin: 0;
  padding: 0;
  background-color: #FFFFFF;
  color: #000000;
```

```
    font-family: Arial, Helvetica, sans-serif;
    border-top: 2px solid #2A4F6F;
}
#header {
    border-top: 1px solid #778899;
    border-bottom: 1px dotted #B2BCC6;
    height: 3em;
}
#header .slogan {
    font: 120% Georgia, "Times New Roman", Times, serif;
    color: #778899;
    background-color: transparent;
    float: right;
    width: 300px;
    margin-right: 2em;
    margin-top: 0.5em;
}
#header .logo {
    float: left;
    width: 187px;
    margin-left: 1.5em;
    margin-top: 0.5em;
}
```

## Discussion

The float property allows us to align the elements in our header with either side of the viewport. Before adding the float, our elements will display next to each other, as in Figure 9.11.

The elements appear side by side because the HTML that marks them up dictates nothing about their positions on the page. Thus, they appear one after the other.

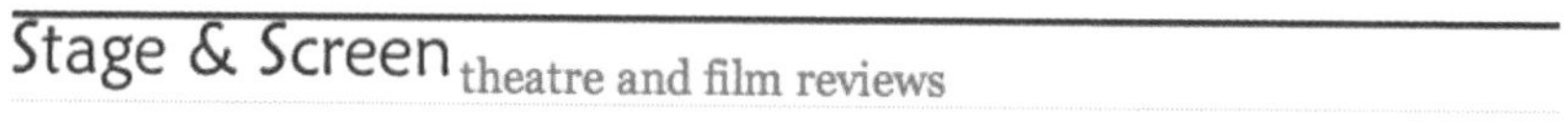

Stage & Screen theatre and film reviews

Figure 9.11. The elements displaying at their default positions

Let's take a look at the markup that controls the slogan's alignment:

chapter09/slogan-align.html *(excerpt)*

```
<div id="header">
  <img src="stage-logo.gif" width="187" height="29"
      alt="Stage &amp; Screen" class="logo" />
  <span class="slogan">theatre and film reviews<span>
</div>
```

By floating the class `logo` to the left and `slogan` to the right, we can move the elements to the left and right of the display. I've also added a rule to align the text in our slogan to the right; without this line, the text that comprises our slogan will still be left-aligned within the `span` element that we floated to the right! Figure 9.12 shows the result.

## Stage & Screen                    theatre and film reviews

Figure 9.12. Applying `float` to make the elements display as desired

To provide some space around the elements, let's add a margin to the top and left of the logo, and the top and right of the slogan:

chapter09/slogan-align.css *(excerpt)*

```
#header .slogan {
  font: 120% Georgia, "Times New Roman", Times, serif;
  color: #778899;
  background-color: transparent;
  float: right;
  width: 300px;
  text-align: right;
  margin-right: 2em;
  margin-top: 0.5em;
}
#header .logo {
  float: left;
  width: 187px;
  margin-left: 1.5em;
  margin-top: 0.5em;
}
```

One aspect to be aware of when you're using this technique is that, once you've floated all the elements within a container, that container will no longer be "held open" by anything, so it will collapse to zero height, as Figure 9.13 shows.

## Stage & Screen          theatre and film reviews

Figure 9.13. Floating the elements causing the header to collapse

To demonstrate this point, I've added a large border to my header in Figure 9.14. Here, there are no floated elements, so the header surrounds the elements.

Stage & Screen theatre and film reviews

Figure 9.14. Showing the size of the header when there are no floated elements

Once I float the elements right and left, the header loses its height, because the elements have been taken out of the document flow. The thick red line at the top of Figure 9.13 is actually the header's border.

To avoid this problem, you can set an explicit height for the block:

chapter09/slogan-align.css *(excerpt)*

```
#header {
  border-top: 1px solid #778899;
  border-bottom: 1px dotted #B2BCC6;
  height: 3em;
}
```

The block now occupies the desired area of the page, as Figure 9.15 shows.

## Stage & Screen          theatre and film reviews

Figure 9.15. The page displaying normally after a height is set for the header <div>

When you're setting heights in this kind of situation, keep in mind the potential impact that user-altered text sizes may have on your layout. Using ems is a handy way to set heights: they'll expand relative to the text size, so they can accommodate larger text sizes without running the risk of having the floated element burst out of the box.

If you were less sure about the amount of text in this box, you would need to use a clearing technique as we discussed when we learned about floated and cleared elements.

# How do I set an item's position on the page using CSS?

It's possible to use CSS to specify exactly where on the page an element should display.

## Solution

With CSS, you can place an element on the page by positioning it from the top, right, bottom, or left using **absolute positioning**. The two blocks shown in Figure 9.16 have been placed with absolute positioning.

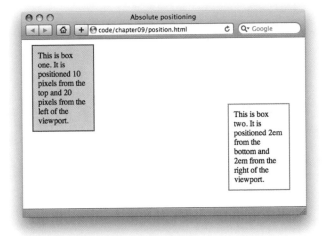

Figure 9.16. Placing boxes using absolute positioning

The code for this page is as follows:

chapter09/position.html

```
<!DOCTYPE html PUBLIC "-//W3C//DTD XHTML 1.0 Strict//EN"
  "http://www.w3.org/TR/xhtml1/DTD/xhtml1-strict.dtd">
<html xmlns="http://www.w3.org/1999/xhtml" lang="en-US">
  <head>
    <title>Absolute positioning</title>
    <meta http-equiv="content-type"
        content="text/html; charset=utf-8" />
    <link rel="stylesheet" type="text/css" href="position.css" />
  </head>
  <body>
    <div id="box1">This is box one. It is positioned 10 pixels
        from the top and 20 pixels from the left of the viewport.
    </div>
    <div id="box2">This is box two. It is positioned 2em from the
        bottom and 2em from the right of the viewport.</div>
  </body>
</html>
```

chapter09/position.css

```
#box1 {
  position: absolute;
  top: 10px;
  left: 20px;
  width: 100px;
  background-color: #B0C4DE;
  border: 2px solid #34537D;
}
#box2 {
  position: absolute;
  bottom: 2em;
  right: 2em;
  width: 100px;
  background-color: #FFFAFA;
  border: 2px solid #CD5C5C;
}
```

# Discussion

Setting an element's `position` property to `absolute` removes it completely from the document flow. As an example, if I add several paragraphs of text to the example document shown above, the two boxes will sit on top of the content, as shown in Figure 9.17.

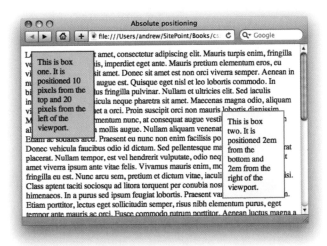

Figure 9.17. The main content ignoring the positioned boxes

In the markup that I used to produce this display, the paragraphs follow the absolutely positioned `divs`; however, because the `divs` have been removed from the document flow, the paragraphs begin at the top-left corner, just as they would if there were no boxes.

As we'll see in "How do I create a liquid, two-column layout with the menu on the left and the content on the right?", we can create space for absolutely positioned areas by placing them within the margins or padding of other elements. What may be less obvious from this example, though, is that elements need not be positioned relative to the edges of the document (although this approach is quite common). Elements can also be positioned within other elements with the same degree of precision.

Figure 9.18 depicts a layout that contains two boxes. In this example, box two is nested inside box one. Because box one is also positioned absolutely, the absolute positioning of box two sets its position relative to the edges of box one.

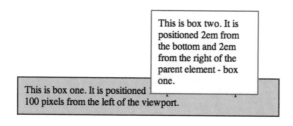

Figure 9.18. Positioning box two relative to box one

Here's the markup that produces the display:

```
                                    chapter09/position2.html (excerpt)
<div id="box1">This is box one. It is positioned 100 pixels from the
    top and 100 pixels from the left of the viewport.
    <div id="box2">This is box two. It is positioned 2em from the
        bottom and 2em from the right of the parent element - box one.
    </div>
</div>
```

```
                                            chapter09/position2.css
#box1 {
  position: absolute;
  top: 100px;
  left: 100px;
  width: 400px;
  background-color: #B0C4DE;
  border: 2px solid #34537D;
}
#box2 {
  position: absolute;
  bottom: 2em;
  right: 2em;
  width: 150px;
```

```
  background-color: #FFFAFA;
  border: 2px solid #CD5C5C;
}
```

To demonstrate this point further, let's add a `height` of 300 pixels to the CSS for box1:

```
#box1 {
  position: absolute;
  top: 100px;
  left: 100px;
  width: 400px;
  height: 300px;
  background-color: #B0C4DE;
  border: 2px solid #34537D;
}
```

You'll now see box two render entirely within box one, as shown in Figure 9.19, rather than appearing to stick out the top of it. This display results because box two is positioned with respect to the bottom and right-hand edges of box one.

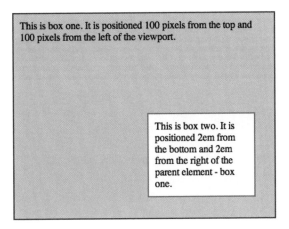

Figure 9.19. Box two rendering within box one

### Positioning Starts with the Parent

It's important to note that the parent element (box1) must be positioned using CSS in order for the child element (box2) to base its position on that parent.

If the parent element's position property is left unset, then the child's position will be based on the edges of the nearest positioned ancestor element—the parent's parent, and so on—or else the body element (in other words the edges of the document). In the above example, if the parent element had remained unpositioned the child element would have been positioned according to the edges of the document, since no further ancestor elements exist.

# How do I center a block on the page?

One common page layout uses a fixed-width, centered box to contain the page content, like the one shown in Figure 9.20. How can we center this box on the page using CSS?

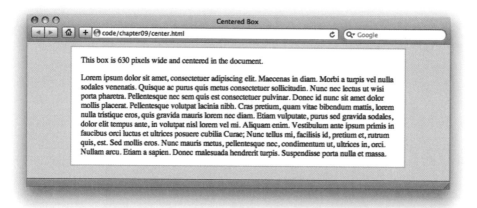

Figure 9.20. Centering a fixed-width box using CSS

## Solution

You can use CSS to center a fixed-width box by setting its left and right margins to auto:

chapter09/center.html

```
<!DOCTYPE html PUBLIC "-//W3C//DTD XHTML 1.0 Strict//EN"
  "http://www.w3.org/TR/xhtml1/DTD/xhtml1-strict.dtd">
<html xmlns="http://www.w3.org/1999/xhtml" lang="en-US">
  <head>
    <title>Centered Box</title>
    <meta http-equiv="content-type"
        content="text/html; charset=utf-8" />
    <link rel="stylesheet" type="text/css" href="center.css" />
  </head>
  <body>
    <div id="content">
      <p>This box is 630 pixels wide and centered in the document.
      </p>
      <p>Lorem ipsum dolor sit amet, consectetuer adipiscing …
      </p>
    </div>
  </body>
</html>
```

chapter09/center.css

```
body {
  background-color: #CCD3D9;
  color: #000000;
}
#content {
  width: 630px;
  margin-left: auto;
  margin-right: auto;
  border: 2px solid #A6B2BC;
  background-color: #FFFFFF;
  color: #000000;
  padding: 0 20px 0 20px;
}
```

## Discussion

This technique allows you to center boxes easily, and is ideal if you need to center a content block on a page.

When we set both the left and right margins to auto, we're asking the browser to calculate equal values for each margin, thereby centering the box. In "How do I create a liquid, two-column layout with the menu on the left and the content on the right?", we'll see how to create a layout inside a container that has been centered in this way.

**Internet Explorer 5.x**

In the past, this technique required additional CSS to work around a bug in Internet Explorer 5.x because that browser prevented the margins from centering content. Setting text-align: center; on the body, then setting it to text-align: left; on the content div was the standard way to circumvent the problem. If you still have to support this ol' workhorse of a browser, that's how you do it.

# How do I create boxes with rounded corners?

There are a number of approaches you can use to create rounded corners on boxes. Here, we'll look at three different ways of achieving this effect.

## Solution 1: The CSS3 `border-radius` Property

There's a property called border-radius that allows you to specify by how much to round the corners of the border around a block element. This property will be part of the CSS3 recommendation when it's finalized.[1] Unfortunately, no browser yet supports the CSS3 border-radius property, but thankfully both Safari and Firefox have enabled experimental support in the form of vendor-specific extensions.[2] Even better, because the extensions are actually a part of the browser rendering engines, any browser that uses either the Gecko engine (like Camino) or the WebKit engine (like Chrome) will also support these properties. This solution, illustrated in Figure 9.21, works only in up-to-date versions of Safari, Firefox, Camino, and Chrome, as opposed to Opera or Internet Explorer. Here's the markup and CSS:

---

[1] http://www.w3.org/TR/css3-border/#the-border-radius
[2] http://reference.sitepoint.com/css/vendorspecific/

chapter09/corners1.html

```
<!DOCTYPE html PUBLIC "-//W3C//DTD XHTML 1.0 Strict//EN"
  "http://www.w3.org/TR/xhtml1/DTD/xhtml1-strict.dtd">
<html xmlns="http://www.w3.org/1999/xhtml" lang="en-US">
  <head>
    <title>Rounded Corners</title>
    <meta http-equiv="content-type"
    content="text/html; charset=utf-8" />
    <link rel="stylesheet" type="text/css" href="corners1.css" />
  </head>
  <body>
    <div class="curvebox">
      <p>Lorem ipsum dolor sit amet, consectetuer adipiscing</p>
    </div>
  </body>
</html>
```

chapter09/corners1.css

```
.curvebox {
  width: 250px;
  padding: 1em;
  background-color: #B0C4DE;
  color: #33527B;
  -moz-border-radius: 25px;
  -webkit-border-radius: 25px;
}
```

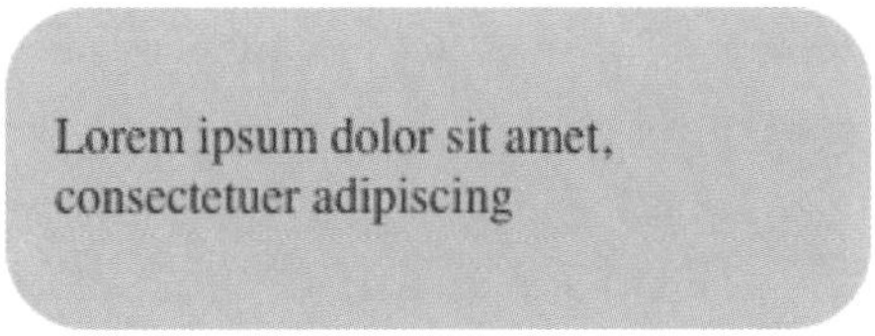


Figure 9.21. Rounded corners, CSS3-style

This example creates rounded corners without a single image! The CSS property that creates those nicely rounded corners on the box borders is:

```
-moz-border-radius: 25px;
-webkit-border-radius: 25px;
```

Remove these lines from the CSS, as I've done in Figure 9.22, and you'll see that the box displays with the usual square corners (as it does in browsers that are yet to have support).

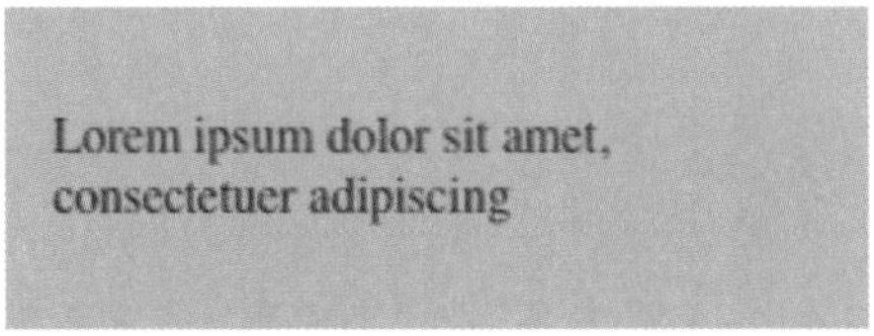

Lorem ipsum dolor sit amet,
consectetuer adipiscing

Figure 9.22. The box display in non-supporting browsers

Obviously, it's currently only of use to site visitors who use Gecko-based or WebKit-based browsers, so most web designers will look to a different solution.

## Solution 2: Images and Additional Markup

A solution that works in multiple browsers uses additional images and markup to create the rounded effect. First, create the corner images using a graphics program. You'll need a small image for each corner of the box. The easiest way to create these is to divide a circle into quarters so that you end up with a set, as shown in Figure 9.23.

Figure 9.23. Rounded-corner images

The markup for this example is as follows. The top-left and bottom-left images are included in the document itself, within top and bottom divs:

chapter09/corners2.html

```
<!DOCTYPE html PUBLIC "-//W3C//DTD XHTML 1.0 Strict//EN"
    "http://www.w3.org/TR/xhtml1/DTD/xhtml1-strict.dtd">
<html xmlns="http://www.w3.org/1999/xhtml" lang="en-US">
  <head>
    <title>Rounded corners</title>
    <meta http-equiv="Content-Type"
        content="text/html; charset=utf-8" />
    <link rel="stylesheet" type="text/css" href="corners2.css" />
  </head>
  <body>
    <div class="rndbox">
      <div class="rndtop"><img src="topleft.gif" alt="" width="30"
          height="30" /></div>
      <p>Lorem ipsum dolor sit amet, consectetuer adipiscing</p>
      <div class="rndbottom"><img src="bottomleft.gif" alt=""
          width="30" height="30" /></div>
    </div>
  </body>
</html>
```

The top-right and bottom-right images are included as background images in the CSS for the divs, with the classes rndtop and rndbottom:

chapter09/corners2.css *(excerpt)*

```
.rndbox {
  background: #C6D9EA;
  width: 300px;
  font: 0.8em Verdana, Arial, Helvetica, sans-serif;
  color: #000033;
}
.rndtop {
  background: url(topright.gif) no-repeat right top;
}
.rndbottom {
  background: url(bottomright.gif) no-repeat right top;
}
.rndbottom img {
```

```
  display:block;
}
.rndbox p {
  margin: 0 0.4em 0 0.4em;
}
```

Together, the images, markup, and CSS create a curved box like the one shown in Figure 9.24.

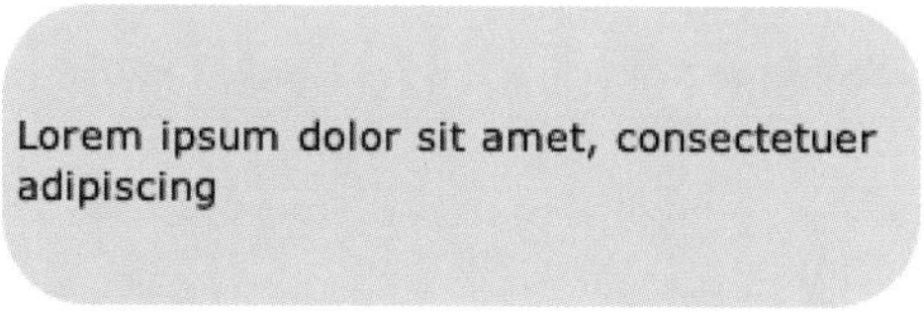

> Lorem ipsum dolor sit amet, consectetuer adipiscing

Figure 9.24. A curved box created by using markup and images

## Solution 3: Using JavaScript

Adding markup and images to your code can be an unattractive option, especially if you have a lot of boxes requiring rounded corners. To deal with this problem, many people have come up with solutions that use JavaScript to add the rounded corners to otherwise square boxes. The beauty of this is that even if users have JavaScript disabled, they see a perfectly usable site—it merely lacks the additional style of the curved edges.

Various methods have been devised to achieve rounded corners using JavaScript, but here we'll look at just one—NiftyCube—as it's very easy to drop into your code and make a start. The script is included in the code archive for this book, but if you'd like the latest version, download NiftyCube from the NiftyCube web site, and unzip the zip file.[3] You'll find lots of example pages in the zip archive, but all you need to implement this effect in your own pages is the JavaScript file **niftycube.js** and the CSS file **niftyCorners.css**. Copy these files into your site. Our starting point is a square-cornered box created by the following markup:

---

[3] http://www.html.it/articoli/niftycube/

```
<!DOCTYPE html PUBLIC "-//W3C//DTD XHTML 1.0 Strict//EN"
  "http://www.w3.org/TR/xhtml1/DTD/xhtml1-strict.dtd">
<html xmlns="http://www.w3.org/1999/xhtml" lang="en-US">
  <head>
    <title>Rounded Corners</title>
    <meta http-equiv="content-type"
        content="text/html; charset=utf-8" />
    <link rel="stylesheet" type="text/css" href="corners3.css" />
  </head>
  <body>
    <div class="curvebox">
      <p>Lorem ipsum dolor...</p>
    </div>
  </body>
</html>
```

You have a reasonable amount of freedom in terms of the way you style your box, with one exception—the padding inside your box *must* be specified in pixels. If you use any other unit, such as ems, then your corners will fail to render properly in Internet Explorer. The result of our work is pictured in Figure 9.25.

```
.curvebox {
  width: 250px;
  padding: 20px;
  background-color: #B0C4DE;
  color: #33527B;
}
```

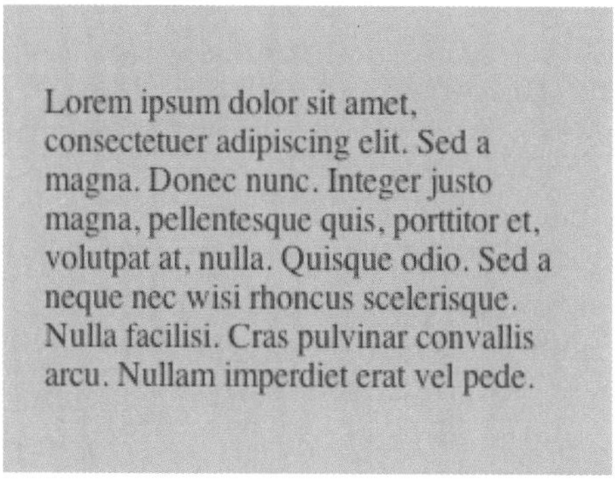

Lorem ipsum dolor sit amet, consectetuer adipiscing elit. Sed a magna. Donec nunc. Integer justo magna, pellentesque quis, porttitor et, volutpat at, nulla. Quisque odio. Sed a neque nec wisi rhoncus scelerisque. Nulla facilisi. Cras pulvinar convallis arcu. Nullam imperdiet erat vel pede.

Figure 9.25. The square box

To add rounded corners to this box using NiftyCube, link the JavaScript file to the head of your document, then write a simple function to tell the script that you wish to round the corners of the class `curvebox`:

chapter09/corners3.html

```
<!DOCTYPE html PUBLIC "-//W3C//DTD XHTML 1.0 Strict//EN"
  "http://www.w3.org/TR/xhtml1/DTD/xhtml1-strict.dtd">
<html xmlns="http://www.w3.org/1999/xhtml" lang="en-US">
  <head>
    <title>Rounded Corners</title>
    <meta http-equiv="content-type"
        content="text/html; charset=utf-8" />
    <link rel="stylesheet" type="text/css" href="corners3.css" />
    <script type="text/javascript" src="niftycube.js">
    </script>
    <script type="text/javascript">
      window.onload=function(){
        Nifty("div.curvebox");
      }
    </script>
  </head>
  <body>
    <div class="curvebox">
      <p>Lorem ipsum dolor sit amet, consectetuer adipiscing…</p>
```

```
      </div>
    </body>
  </html>
```

This markup produces the display shown in Figure 9.26.

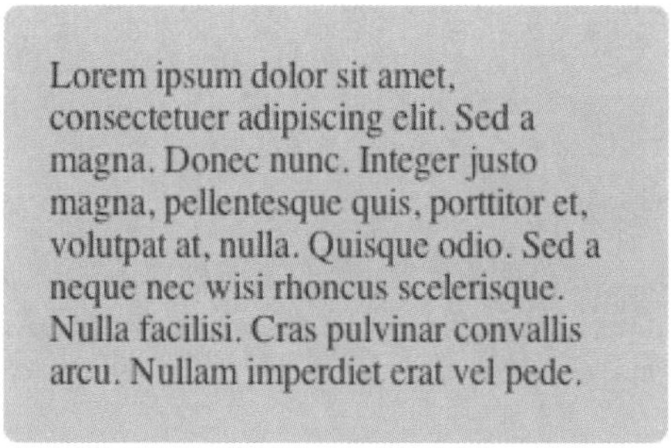

Lorem ipsum dolor sit amet, consectetuer adipiscing elit. Sed a magna. Donec nunc. Integer justo magna, pellentesque quis, porttitor et, volutpat at, nulla. Quisque odio. Sed a neque nec wisi rhoncus scelerisque. Nulla facilisi. Cras pulvinar convallis arcu. Nullam imperdiet erat vel pede.

Figure 9.26. Rounded corners without images or extra markup

# Discussion

While numerous solutions are available to help you create rounded corners without JavaScript, they all require you to insert additional markup or ensure that your markup is structured in a certain way.[4] If you only have a few boxes whose corners you want to round—perhaps a main layout container or a couple of larger boxes—the additional images and markup will only be a minor imposition. But if your layout includes many rounded corners, peppering your markup with extra divs and images may be an extremely undesirable option. The JavaScript method allows cleaner HTML code, but as with all JavaScript solutions, it only works when the user has JavaScript enabled.

Personally, I feel that using JavaScript in this way—to plug the holes in CSS support—is legitimate. As long as you've checked that your layout remains clear and easy to use without the rounded corners, those without JavaScript will continue to use your site. If you do use this JavaScript solution on a project, be sure to check the whole site with JavaScript turned off, to make sure that the users still have a positive experience on the site.

---

[4] One attempt at generating rounded corners using semantic markup and no JavaScript is Spanky Corners [http://tools.sitepoint.com/spanky/], created by SitePoint's Alex Walker.

# How do I create a liquid, two-column layout with the menu on the left and the content on the right?

Web page layouts like that shown in Figure 9.27, displaying a menu on the left and a large content area to the right, are extremely common. Let's discover how to build this layout using CSS.

Figure 9.27. Building a liquid two-column layout using CSS

## Solution

Here's the markup and CSS that produces the display shown in Figure 9.27:

```
<!DOCTYPE html PUBLIC "-//W3C//DTD XHTML 1.0 Strict//EN"
  "http://www.w3.org/TR/xhtml1/DTD/xhtml1-strict.dtd">
<html xmlns="http://www.w3.org/1999/xhtml" lang="en-US">
  <head>
    <title>Stage &amp; Screen - theatre and film reviews</title>
    <meta http-equiv="content-type"
        content="text/html; charset=utf-8" />
    <link rel="stylesheet" type="text/css" href="2col.css" />
  </head>
  <body>
    <div id="header">
      <img src="stage-logo.gif" width="187" height="29"
          alt="Stage &amp; Screen" class="logo" />
      <span class="strapline">theatre and film reviews</span>
    </div>
    <div id="content">
      <h1>Welcome to Stage &amp; Screen</h1>
      <p>Lorem ipsum dolor sit amet, consectetuer adipiscing …</p>
      ⋮
    </div>
    <div id="nav">
      <ul>
        <li><a href="#">Play Reviews</a></li>
        <li><a href="#">Film Reviews</a></li>
        <li><a href="#">Post a Review</a></li>
        <li><a href="#">About this site</a></li>
        <li><a href="#">Contact Us</a></li>
      </ul>
      <h2>Latest Reviews</h2>
      <ul>
        <li><a href="#">Angels &amp; Demons</a></li>
        <li><a href="#">Star Trek</a></li>
        <li><a href="#">Up</a></li>
        <li><a href="#">Land of the Lost</a></li>
      </ul>
    </div>
  </body>
</html>
```

```css
body {
  margin: 0;
  padding: 0;
  background-color: #FFFFFF;
  color: #000000;
  font-family: Arial, Helvetica, sans-serif;
  border-top: 2px solid #2A4F6F;
}
#header {
  border-top: 1px solid #778899;
  border-bottom: 1px dotted #B2BCC6;
  height: 3em;
}
#header .strapline {
  font: 120% Georgia, "Times New Roman", Times, serif;
  color: #778899;
  background-color: transparent;
  float: right;
  width: 300px;
  text-align: right;
  margin-right: 2em;
  margin-top: 0.5em;
}
#header .logo {
  float: left;
  width: 187px;
  margin-left: 1.5em;
  margin-top: 0.5em;
}
#nav {
  position: absolute;
  top: 5em;
  left: 1em;
  width: 14em;
}
#nav ul {
  list-style: none;
  margin: 0;
  padding: 0;
}
#nav li {
  font-size: 80%;
```

```
    border-bottom: 1px dotted #B2BCC6;
    margin-bottom: 0.3em;
}
#nav a:link, #nav a:visited {
  text-decoration: none;
  color: #2A4F6F;
  background-color: transparent;
}
#nav a:hover {
  color: #778899;
}
#nav h2 {
  font: 110% Georgia, "Times New Roman", Times, serif;
  color: #2A4F6F;
  background-color: transparent;
  border-bottom: 1px dotted #CCCCCC;
}
#content {
  margin-left: 16em;
  margin-right: 2em;
}
h1 {
  font: 150% Georgia, "Times New Roman", Times, serif;
}
#content p {
  font-size: 80%;
  line-height: 1.6em;
}
```

## Discussion

Our starting point for this layout is the header that we created in "How do I align a site's logo and slogan to the left and right?". We've added to that layout some content, which resides within a div whose ID is content. The navigation for the page comprises two unordered lists that are contained in a div with the ID nav. As you'd expect, without any positioning applied, these blocks will display below the heading in the order in which they appear in the document (as depicted in Figure 9.28).

Figure 9.28. The content and navigation displaying without positioning information

At this point, the CSS looks like this:

```
                                              chapter09/2col.css (excerpt)
body {
  margin: 0;
  padding: 0;
  background-color: #FFFFFF;
  color: #000000;
  font-family: Arial, Helvetica, sans-serif;
  border-top: 2px solid #2A4F6F;
}
#header {
  border-top: 1px solid #778899;
  border-bottom: 1px dotted #B2BCC6;
  height: 3em;
}
```

```
#header .slogan {
  font: 120% Georgia, "Times New Roman", Times, serif;
  color: #778899;
  background-color: transparent;
  float: right;
  width: 300px;
  text-align: right;
  margin-right: 2em;
  margin-top: 0.5em;
}
#header .logo {
  float: left;
  width: 187px;
  margin-left: 1.5em;
  margin-top: 0.5em;
}
```

## Sizing and Positioning the Menu

Let's use absolute positioning to position the menu just under the heading bar, and give it an appropriate width:

chapter09/2col.css *(excerpt)*

```
#nav {
  position: absolute;
  top: 5em;
  left: 1em;
  width: 14em;
}
```

As you can see in Figure 9.29, this code causes the menu to appear over the text content, as the absolute positioning we've applied has removed it from the flow of the document.

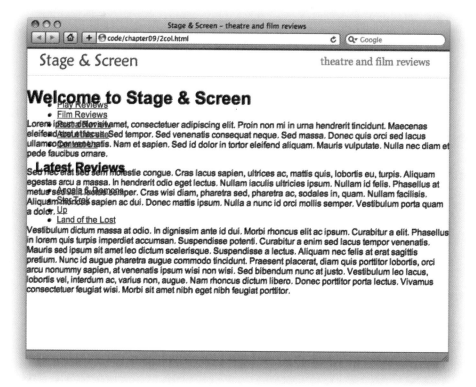

Figure 9.29. Positioning the menu absolutely

## Positioning the Content

As we're aiming to maintain a liquid layout, it's undesirable to assign a fixed width to the content and, in fact, it's unnecessary anyway. The problem with the content is that it appears where we want the menu to sit. To solve this problem, we can simply apply a large left-hand margin to the content area to allow space for the menu. The results are shown in Figure 9.30:

```
#content {
  margin-left: 16em;
  margin-right: 2em;
}
```

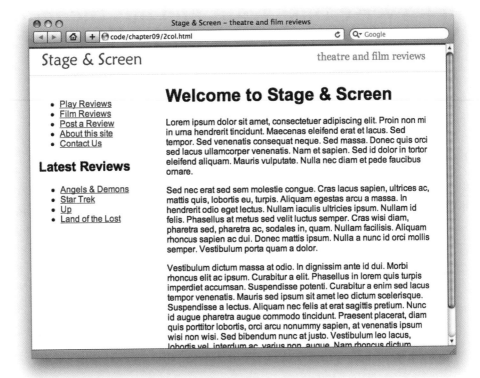

Figure 9.30. Adding margins to the content

Now that all the elements are laid out neatly, we can work on the styling of individual elements, using CSS to create the layout we saw back in Figure 9.27. The completed CSS style sheet is given at the start of this solution.

### Ems for Positioning Text Layouts

I used ems to position the elements in this layout. The em unit will resize as the text resizes, which should help us avoid any problems with overlapping text if users resize fonts in their browsers. For layouts that are predominantly text-based, the em is an excellent choice for setting the widths of boxes and margins. However, care should be taken if your design involves many images, as they lack the ability to resize with text. In this instance you may prefer to use pixels to position elements in cases where you need precise control over the elements' locations on the page.

# Can I reverse this layout and put the menu on the right?

Can the technique presented in "How do I create a liquid, two-column layout with the menu on the left and the content on the right?" be used to create a layout in which the menu is positioned on the right?

## Solution

Yes, exactly the same technique can be used! You'll need to position your menu from the top and right, and give the content area a large right margin so that the menu has sufficient space in which to display. The result is shown in Figure 9.31.

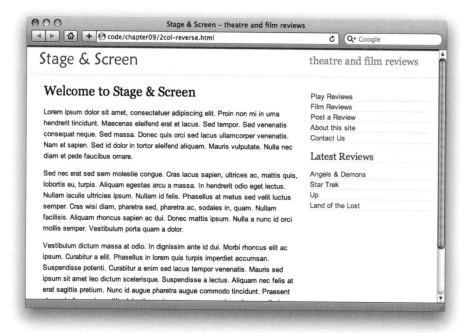

Figure 9.31. Building a two-column layout so that the menu appears on the right

## Discussion

Positioning the menu on the right requires no change to the markup of the original document. All we need to do is change the positioning properties for nav, and the margins on content:

chapter09/2col-reverse.css

```
#nav {
  position: absolute;
  top: 5em;
  right: 1em;
  width: 14em;
}
#content {
  margin-left: 2em;
  margin-right: 16em;
}
```

The advantage of using absolute positioning can be seen clearly here. It's of no consequence where our menu appears in the markup: the use of absolute positioning means it will be removed from the document flow and we can place it wherever we like on the page. This can be of great benefit for accessibility purposes, as it allows us to place some of the less-important items (such as lists of links to other sites, advertising, and so on) right at the end of the document code. This way, those who employ screen readers to use the site are saved from having to hear these unnecessary items read aloud each time they access a page. Yet you, as the designer, are still able to position these items wherever you like for visual effect.

# How do I create a fixed-width, centered, two-column layout?

You can use CSS to create a two-column layout that's contained within a centered div on the page.

## Solution

Creating a two-column, fixed-width, centered layout is slightly trickier than a fixed-width, left-aligned, or liquid layout; that's because there is no absolute reference point from the left-hand or right-hand side of the viewport that you can use to position the elements horizontally. However, there are a couple of different ways in which we can deal with this complication in order to achieve the kind of layout shown below.

Whichever layout method you choose, the HTML is the same:

*chapter09/2col-fixedwidth.html*

```html
<!DOCTYPE html PUBLIC "-//W3C//DTD XHTML 1.0 Strict//EN"
  "http://www.w3.org/TR/xhtml1/DTD/xhtml1-strict.dtd">
<html xmlns="http://www.w3.org/1999/xhtml" lang="en-US">
  <head>
    <title>Recipe for Success | Perfect Pizza</title>
    <link href="2col-fixedwidth.css" rel="stylesheet"
        type="text/css" />
    <meta http-equiv="content-type"
        content="text/html; charset=utf-8" />
  </head>
  <body>
    <div id="wrapper">
      <div id="header">
        <h1>Perfect Pizza</h1>
      </div>
      <div id="content">
        <h2>Choosing Your Toppings</h2>
        <p>Sed nec erat sed sem molestie congue. Cras lacus …</p>
        ⋮
      </div>
      <div id="nav">
        <ul>
          <li><a href="#">Prepare the Dough</a></li>
          <li class="cur"><a href="#">Choose Your Toppings</a></li>
          <li><a href="#">Pizza Ovens</a></li>
          <li><a href="#">Side Salads</a></li>
        </ul>
      </div>
    </div>
  </body>
</html>
```

The first and simplest option to achieve this layout is to place the content and navigation elements within the centered block, using absolute and relative positioning, respectively:

chapter09/2col-fixedwidth.css

```css
body {
  margin: 0;
  padding: 0;
  font-family: Arial, Helvetica, sans-serif;
  background-color: #FFFFFF;
}
#wrapper {
  position: relative;
  width: 760px;
  margin-right: auto;
  margin-left: auto;
  margin-bottom: 1em;
}
#header {
  background-image: url(kitchen.jpg);
  background-repeat: no-repeat;
  height: 200px;
  position: relative;
}
#header h1 {
  margin: 0;
  padding: 0.3em 10px 0.3em 0;
  text-align: right;
  width: 750px;
  font-weight: normal;
  color: #FFFFFF;
  font-size: 190%;
  position: absolute;
  bottom: 0;
  left: 0;
  background-image: url(black80percent.png);
}
#content {
  margin-left: 250px;
  width: 500px;
  padding: 0 10px 0 0;
}
#content h2 {
```

```
    font-size: 120%;
    color: #3333FF;
    background-color: transparent;
    margin: 0;
    padding: 1.4em 0 0 0;
}
#content p {
    font-size: 80%;
    line-height: 1.6;
}
#nav {
    position: absolute;
    top: 200px;
    left: 0;
    width: 230px;
}
#nav ul {
    list-style: none;
    margin: 3em 0 0 0;
    padding: 0;
    border: none;
}
#nav li {
    font-size: 85%;
}
#nav a:link, #nav a:visited {
    color: #555555;
    background-color: transparent;
    display: block;
    padding: 1em 0 0 10px;
    text-decoration: none;
    min-height: 40px;
}
#nav a:hover, #nav li.cur a:link, #nav li.cur a:visited {
    color: #FFFFFF;
    background-image: url(arrow.gif);
    background-repeat: no-repeat;
}
```

As you can see from Figure 9.32, this gives us a very simple layout. Adding more design features, such as a background image behind the content or a border wrapping the whole layout, will require a different method.

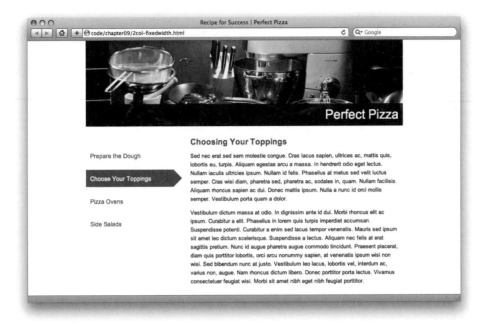

Figure 9.32. The fixed-width, centered layout

An alternative approach is to simply float the navigation and content against the left and right sides of the centered block, respectively. Floating the elements will give you more flexibility if you need to add other elements to the layout, such as a footer, or if you want to add a border around the layout. If you float the left and right columns, you can add a footer and apply `clear: both` to place it beneath the two columns, regardless of their heights. This dynamic placement of the footer within the document flow is impossible if the columns are absolutely positioned. We've also taken advantage of the floated layout and added a border around the entire layout:

chapter09/2col-fixedwidth-float.css

```
body {
  margin: 0;
  padding: 0;
  font-family: Arial, Helvetica, sans-serif;
  background-color: #FFFFFF;
}
#wrapper {
```

```
    position: relative;
    width: 760px;
    margin-right: auto;
    margin-left: auto;
    margin-bottom: 1em;
    background-image: url(sidebar.gif);
    background-repeat: repeat-y;
    border-right: 1px solid #888888;
    border-bottom: 1px solid #888888;
}
#header {
    background-image: url(kitchen.jpg);
    background-repeat: no-repeat;
    height: 200px;
    position: relative;
}
#header h1 {
    margin: 0;
    padding: 0.3em 10px 0.3em 0;
    text-align: right;
    width: 750px;
    font-weight: normal;
    color: #FFFFFF;
    font-size: 190%;
    position: absolute;
    bottom: 0;
    left: 0;
    background-image: url(black80percent.png);
}
#content {
    float: right;
    width: 500px;
    padding: 0 10px 0 0;
}
#content h2 {
    font-size: 120%;
    color: #3333FF;
    background-color: transparent;
    margin: 0;
    padding: 1.4em 0 0 0;
}
#content p {
    font-size: 80%;
    line-height: 1.6;
```

```
}
#nav {
  float: left;
  width: 230px;
}
#nav ul {
  list-style: none;
  margin: 3em 0 0 0;
  padding: 0;
  border: none;
}
#nav li {
  font-size: 85%;
}
#nav a:link, #nav a:visited {
  color: #555555;
  background-color: transparent;
  display: block;
  padding: 1em 0 0 10px;
  text-decoration: none;
  min-height: 40px;
}
#nav a:hover, #nav li.cur a:link, #nav li.cur a:visited {
  color: #FFFFFF;
  background-image: url(arrow.gif);
  background-repeat: no-repeat;
}
#footer {
  clear: both;
  font-size: 80%;
  padding: 1em 0 1em 0;
  margin-left: 250px;
  color: #999999;
  background-color: transparent;
}
```

The result is shown in Figure 9.33.

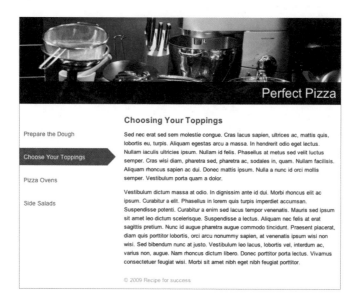

Figure 9.33. The floated, fixed-width, centered layout with a border

# Discussion

For the purposes of this discussion, we'll ignore purely aesthetic-style properties such as borders, colors, and fonts, so that we can concentrate on the layout.

Both versions of this layout begin with a centered div, similar to the layouts we worked with in "How do I center a block on the page?". This div is given the ID wrapper:

```
chapter09/2col-fixedwidth.css or chapter09/2col-fixedwidth-float.css (excerpt)

body {
  margin: 0;
  padding: 0;
    ⋮
}

#wrapper {
  width: 760px;
  margin-right: auto;
```

```
    margin-left: auto;
    ⋮
}
```

The result of applying these styles is shown in Figure 9.34.

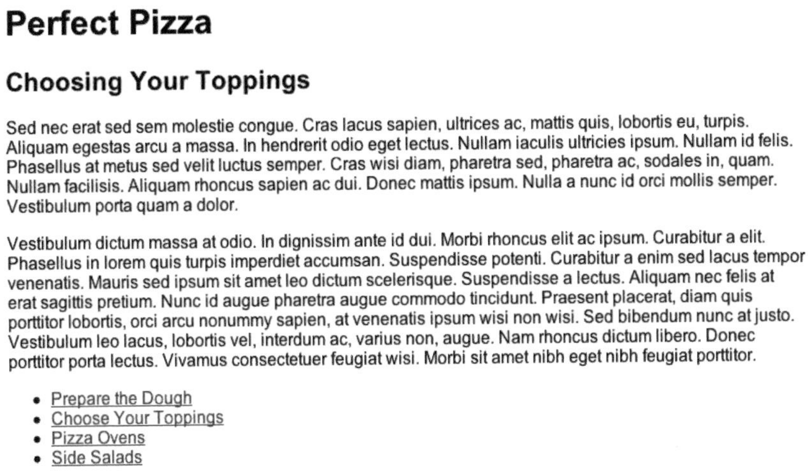

## Perfect Pizza

### Choosing Your Toppings

Sed nec erat sed sem molestie congue. Cras lacus sapien, ultrices ac, mattis quis, lobortis eu, turpis. Aliquam egestas arcu a massa. In hendrerit odio eget lectus. Nullam iaculis ultricies ipsum. Nullam id felis. Phasellus at metus sed velit luctus semper. Cras wisi diam, pharetra sed, pharetra ac, sodales in, quam. Nullam facilisis. Aliquam rhoncus sapien ac dui. Donec mattis ipsum. Nulla a nunc id orci mollis semper. Vestibulum porta quam a dolor.

Vestibulum dictum massa at odio. In dignissim ante id dui. Morbi rhoncus elit ac ipsum. Curabitur a elit. Phasellus in lorem quis turpis imperdiet accumsan. Suspendisse potenti. Curabitur a enim sed lacus tempor venenatis. Mauris sed ipsum sit amet leo dictum scelerisque. Suspendisse a lectus. Aliquam nec felis at erat sagittis pretium. Nunc id augue pharetra augue commodo tincidunt. Praesent placerat, diam quis porttitor lobortis, orci arcu nonummy sapien, at venenatis ipsum wisi non wisi. Sed bibendum nunc at justo. Vestibulum leo lacus, lobortis vel, interdum ac, varius non, augue. Nam rhoncus dictum libero. Donec porttitor porta lectus. Vivamus consectetuer feugiat wisi. Morbi sit amet nibh eget nibh feugiat porttitor.

- Prepare the Dough
- Choose Your Toppings
- Pizza Ovens
- Side Salads

Figure 9.34. Centering the content on the page

Now, in "How do I create a liquid, two-column layout with the menu on the left and the content on the right?" we saw that we could use absolute positioning to control the navigation's location, and apply enough margin to the content of the page so that there'd be no overlap between the two blocks. The only difference in this layout is that we need to position the navigation within the centered `wrapper` block, so we're unable to give it an absolute position on the page.

Instead of using `absolute`, you can set an element's `position` property to `relative` which, unlike absolute positioning, keeps the element within the document flow; instead, it lets you shift the element from the starting point of its default position on the page. If no coordinates are provided in order to shift the element, it will actually stay exactly where the browser would normally position it. However, unlike an element that lacks having a `position` value specified, a relatively positioned element will provide a new **positioning context** for any absolutely positioned elements within it.

In plain English, an element with `position: absolute` that's contained within an element with `position: relative` will base its position on the edges of that parent element, instead of the edges of the browser window. This is exactly what we need to use to position the navigation within the centered block in this example.

The first step is to set the `position` property of `wrapper` to `relative`:

chapter09/2col-fixedwidth.css *(excerpt)*

```
#wrapper {
  position: relative;
  text-align: left;
  width: 760px;
  margin-right: auto;
  margin-left: auto;
    ⋮
}
```

We then use absolute positioning to set the location of the `navigation` block:

chapter09/2col-fixedwidth.css *(excerpt)*

```
#navigation {
  position: absolute;
  top: 200px;
  left: 0;
  width: 230px;
}
```

Finally, we add a margin to the main content of the page to make space for the newly positioned navigation area:

chapter09/2col-fixedwidth.css *(excerpt)*

```
#content {
  margin-left: 250px;
  padding: 0 10px 0 0;
}
```

As long as the content of the page occupies more vertical space than the navigation, this layout will work just fine. Unfortunately, since the `navigation` block is absolutely positioned, it's unable to affect the height of the `wrapper` block, so if the content is shorter than the navigation, the `wrapper` block will be too short to contain the navigation. We can see this effect by adding a two-pixel, red border to the wrapper, and adding text to the sidebar so that it becomes longer than the content. In Figure 9.35, you can clearly see that the content in the sidebar extends below the `wrapper` element.

Figure 9.35. The content in the sidebar extending below the bottom of the `wrapper` block

The alternative method of using floated blocks to achieve our design goals is more complex, but it overcomes the limitation I just mentioned, enabling us to position a footer below the columns regardless of which column is the longest. First, we float the `navigation` block left and the `content` block right:

chapter09/2col-fixedwidth-float.css *(excerpt)*

```
#content {
  float: right;
  width: 500px;
  padding: 0 10px 0 0;
}

#navigation {
  float: left;
  width: 230px;
}
```

This should give us the same layout as the positioned example offered. However, if we now look at the layout with the red border on the wrapper, you'll find that the red border only wraps the header area of the page. The wrapper no longer wraps!

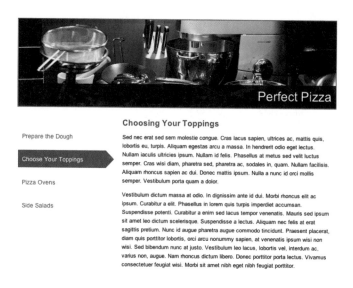

Figure 9.36. Floating the navigation left and the content right

One of the reasons we wanted to use a floated layout, however, is to add a footer. I will add this to the document below the floated columns:

chapter09/2col-fixedwidth-float.html *(excerpt)*

```html
<div id="nav">
  <ul>
    <li><a href="#">Prepare the Dough</a></li>
    <li class="cur"><a href="#">Choose Your Toppings</a></li>
    <li><a href="#">Pizza Ovens</a></li>
    <li><a href="#">Side Salads</a></li>
  </ul>
</div>
<div id="footer">&copy; 2009 Recipe for success</div>
</div>
</body>
</html>
```

Reload the page, and as you can see in Figure 9.37, the border of the `wrapper` block now cuts through the page content. This occurs because we floated most of the block's contents, removing them from the document flow. The only element inside `wrapper` that's still within the document flow is the `footer` block, which can be seen in the bottom-left corner of the `wrapper` block, where it has been pushed by the floated blocks.

If we set the `clear` property of the `footer` block to `both`, the footer will drop down below both of the floated blocks; this forces the `wrapper` to accommodate both the navigation and the content—no matter which is taller. The page now renders as shown in Figure 9.38:

chapter09/2col-fixedwidth-float.css *(excerpt)*

```css
#footer {
  clear: both;
  ⋮
}
```

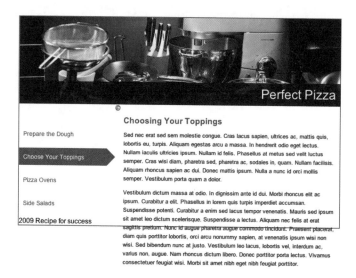

Figure 9.37. After adding the footer

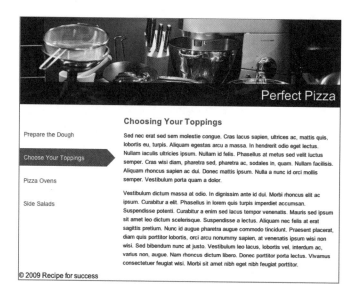

Figure 9.38. The footer set to `clear: both`

# How do I create a full-height column?

If you've tried to add a background to a side column like the one shown in "How do I create a fixed-width, centered, two-column layout?", you may have discovered you're unable to make the column extend to the full height of the taller column next to it, forcing your background to look a little strange. For example, applying a background image to the navigation element will simply display the background behind the navigation list, rather than stretching it down the column to the end of the content, as shown in Figure 9.39.

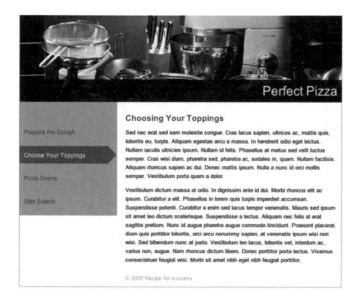

Figure 9.39. The gray background displaying only behind the navigation content

## Solution

The solution to this problem is to apply the background image to a page element that does extend the full height of the longer column, but displays at the same width as our navigation, making it look as though the background is on the navigation column. In this case, we can apply the background image to wrapper, as Figure 9.40 illustrates:

chapter09/2col-fixedwidth-float.css *(excerpt)*

```
#wrapper {
  position: relative;
  text-align: left;
  width: 760px;
  margin-right: auto;
  margin-left: auto;
  margin-bottom: 1em;
  background-image: url(sidebar.gif);
  background-repeat:repeat-y;
  border-right: 1px solid #888888;
  border-bottom: 1px solid #888888;
}
```

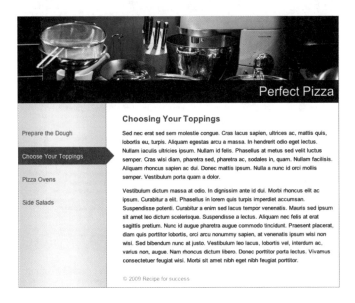

Figure 9.40. The background appearing to be attached to the navigation column

## Discussion

This simple technique can be used to great effect in your layouts. In this example, I chose to apply the image to the wrapper block, as I want the background to extend right down to the end of the content; the solid image on my header background hides the sidebar background image as it extends all the way to the top of the page. You could also use this technique to have the background stop above the footer, or after a certain section of content: simply apply the background to an element that contains the section of content you want.

### Creating Gradient Backgrounds

I've used a repeating background image here as my image is the same all the way down the page. You could also use a tall image with a gradient fading to your background color and set it to `no-repeat`.

# How do I add a drop shadow to my layout?

Drop shadows are commonly used on layouts—particularly on content boxes within a layout. Let's add a drop shadow to a fixed width layout such as the one we worked with in the section called "How do I create a full-height column?".

## Solution

We can add a drop shadow to the edges of this layout using two images: one for the background, and one to create the shadow effect at the bottom of the layout. Figure 9.41 shows the effect we're working to create.

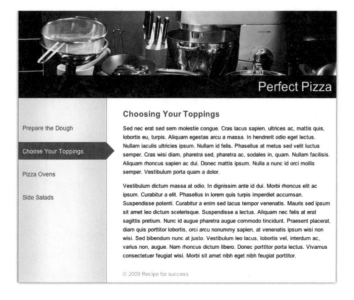

Figure 9.41. A drop shadow

To create this effect, we need to add some markup that will provide us with hooks to which we can add the two images.

The first image, which I've named **shadow-bg.jpg** and can be seen in Figure 9.42, is a background image that we'll apply to the div with an ID of wrapper. This image is the left and right drop shadow, and it repeats down the page. The second image, **shadow-bottom.jpg**, we'll apply to the bottom of our layout.

Figure 9.42. The files used to create the drop shadow effect

I've increased the width of my wrapper block by 20 pixels because I want the content area to stay the same width, but I need to allow room for the shadow on either side of the content. I've also added the shadow image as a background image on this element:

```
                                        chapter09/2col-fixedwidth-shadow.css (excerpt)

#wrapper {
  position: relative;
  text-align: left;
  width: 780px;
  margin-right: auto;
  margin-left: auto;
  background-image: url(shadow-bg.jpg);
  background-repeat: repeat-y;
}
```

Next, I wrap an additional div—which I've named wrapper2—around the content, navigation, and footer elements, just inside the wrapper block:

```
<!DOCTYPE html PUBLIC "-//W3C//DTD XHTML 1.0 Strict//EN"
  "http://www.w3.org/TR/xhtml1/DTD/xhtml1-strict.dtd">
<html xmlns="http://www.w3.org/1999/xhtml" lang="en-US">
  <head>
    <title>Recipe for Success | Perfect Pizza</title>
    <link href="2col-fixedwidth-shadow.css" rel="stylesheet"
        type="text/css" />
    <meta http-equiv="content-type"
        content="text/html; charset=utf-8" />
  </head>
  <body>
    <div id="wrapper"><div id="wrapper2">
      <div id="header">
        <h1>Perfect Pizza</h1>
      </div>
      <div id="content">
        <h2>Choosing Your Toppings</h2>
        <p>Sed nec erat sed sem molestie congue. Cras lacus …</p>
        <p>Vestibulum dictum massa at odio. In dignissim …</p>
      </div>
      <div id="nav">
        <ul>
          <li><a href="#">Prepare the Dough</a></li>
          <li class="cur"><a href="#">Choose Your Toppings</a></li>
          <li><a href="#">Pizza Ovens</a></li>
          <li><a href="#">Side Salads</a></li>
        </ul>
      </div>
      <div id="footer">&copy; 2009 Recipe for success</div>
    </div></div>
  </body>
</html>
```

I add to this div the sidebar background image that I've moved from the outer wrapper. I also add some padding to this div to push the page contents away from the drop shadow:

chapter09/2col-fixedwidth-shadow.css *(excerpt)*

```
#wrapper2 {
  background-image: url(sidebar.gif);
  background-repeat:repeat-y;
  margin: 0 10px 0 10px;
}
```

Finally, I need to add the bottom of the drop shadow. I add another `div` element with an `id` of `btm` to the code just before the closing `</div>` of the outer wrapper:

chapter09/2col-fixedwidth-shadow.html *(excerpt)*

```
<div id="footer">&copy; 2009 Recipe for success</div>
</div>
<div id="btm"></div></div>
</body>
</html>
```

Now I simply add the drop shadow bottom image as a background image to this div and give it a height equal to the size of the background image:

chapter09/2col-fixedwidth-shadow.css *(excerpt)*

```
#btm {
  background-image: url(shadow-bottom.jpg);
  background-repeat: no-repeat;
  display: block;
  height: 13px;
}
```

Voilá—our drop shadow is complete!

# How do I create a three-column CSS layout?

Many designs fall into a three-column model. As demonstrated in Figure 9.43, you might need a column for navigation, one for content, and one for additional items such as advertising or highlighted content on the site. Let's see how we can accomplish this type of layout using CSS.

Figure 9.43. A three-column layout developed in CSS

# Solution

A three-column, liquid layout is easily created using a simple technique, similar to the one we used to build the two-column layout in "How do I create a liquid, two-column layout with the menu on the left and the content on the right?":

```
                                                    chapter09/3col.html
<!DOCTYPE html PUBLIC "-//W3C//DTD XHTML 1.0 Strict//EN"
  "http://www.w3.org/TR/xhtml1/DTD/xhtml1-strict.dtd">
<html xmlns="http://www.w3.org/1999/xhtml" lang="en-US">
  <head>
    <title>Recipe for Success</title>
    <meta http-equiv="content-type"
        content="text/html; charset=utf-8" />
    <link rel="stylesheet" type="text/css" href="3col.css" />
  </head>
  <body>
    <div id="content">
      <h1>Recipe for Success</h1>
      <p>Lorem ipsum dolor sit amet, consectetuer adipiscing …</p>
```

```
      <p>Quisque sodales imperdiet enim. Quisque cursus …</p>
    </div>
    <div id="side1">
      <form method="post" action="" id="searchform">
        <h3><label for="keys">Search the Recipes</label></h3>
        <div>
          <input type="text" name="keys" id="keys" class="txt" />
          <br />
          <input type="submit" name="Submit" value="Submit" />
        </div>
      </form>
      <ul>
        <li><a href="#">About Us</a></li>
        <li><a href="#">Recipes</a></li>
        <li><a href="#">Articles</a></li>
        <li><a href="#">Buy Online</a></li>
        <li><a href="#">Contact Us</a></li>
      </ul>
    </div>
    <div id="side2">
      <h3>Please Visit our Sponsors</h3>
      <div class="adbox"><p>Lorem ipsum dolor sit amet …</p></div>
      <div class="adbox"><p>Sed mattis, orci eu porta …</p></div>
      <div class="adbox"><p>Quisque mauris nunc, mattis …</p></div>
    </div>
  </body>
</html>
```

chapter09/3col.css

```
body {
  margin: 0;
  padding: 0;
  background-image: url(tomato_bg.jpg);
  background-repeat: no-repeat;
  background-color: #FFFFFF;
}
p {
  font: 80%/1.8em Verdana, Geneva, Arial, Helvetica, sans-serif;
  padding-top: 0;
  margin-top: 0;
}
form {
  margin: 0;
```

```
  padding: 0;
}
#content {
  margin: 66px 260px 0px 240px;
  padding: 10px;
}
#content h1 {
  text-align: right;
  padding-right: 20px;
  font: 150% Georgia, "Times New Roman", Times, serif;
  color: #901602;
}
#side1 {
  position: absolute;
  width: 200px;
  top: 30px;
  left: 10px;
  padding: 70px 10px 10px 10px;
}
#side2 {
  position: absolute;
  width: 220px;
  top: 30px;
  right: 10px;
  padding: 70px 10px 10px 10px;
  border-left: 1px dotted #CCCCCC;
  background-image: url(sm-tomato.jpg);
  background-position: top right;
  background-repeat: no-repeat;
}
#side2 h3 {
  font: 110% Georgia, "Times New Roman", Times, serif;
  margin: 0;
  padding-bottom: 4px;
}
.adbox {
  padding: 2px 4px 2px 6px;
  margin: 0 0 10px 0;
  border: 1px dotted #B1B1B1;
  background-color: #F4F4F4;
}
#side1 h3 {
  font: 110% Georgia, "Times New Roman", Times, serif;
  color: #621313;
```

```
    background-color: transparent;
    margin: 0;
    padding-bottom: 4px;
}
#side1 .txt {
    width: 184px;
    background-color: #FCF5F5;
    border: 1px inset #901602;
}
#side1 ul {
    list-style: none;
    margin-left: 0;
    padding-left: 0;
    width: 184px;
}
#side1 li {
    font: 80% Verdana, Geneva, Arial, Helvetica, sans-serif;
    margin-bottom: 0.3em;
    border-bottom: 1px solid #E7AFAF;
}
#side1 a:link, #side1 a:visited {
    text-decoration: none;
    color: #901602;
    background-color: transparent;
}
#side1 a:hover {
    color: #621313;
}
```

## Discussion

This layout uses a simple technique. We start with the unstyled document shown in Figure 9.44, which has three divs: one with ID content, one with ID side1, and one with ID side2.

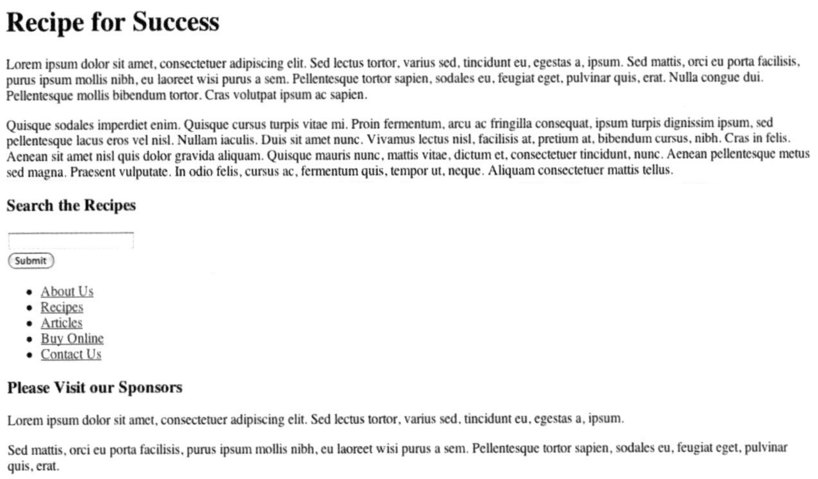

## Recipe for Success

Lorem ipsum dolor sit amet, consectetuer adipiscing elit. Sed lectus tortor, varius sed, tincidunt eu, egestas a, ipsum. Sed mattis, orci eu porta facilisis, purus ipsum mollis nibh, eu laoreet wisi purus a sem. Pellentesque tortor sapien, sodales eu, feugiat eget, pulvinar quis, erat. Nulla congue dui. Pellentesque mollis bibendum tortor. Cras volutpat ipsum ac sapien.

Quisque sodales imperdiet enim. Quisque cursus turpis vitae mi. Proin fermentum, arcu ac fringilla consequat, ipsum turpis dignissim ipsum, sed pellentesque lacus eros vel nisl. Nullam iaculis. Duis sit amet nunc. Vivamus lectus nisl, facilisis at, pretium at, bibendum cursus, nibh. Cras in felis. Aenean sit amet nisl quis dolor gravida aliquam. Quisque mauris nunc, mattis vitae, dictum et, consectetuer tincidunt, nunc. Aenean pellentesque metus sed magna. Praesent vulputate. In odio felis, cursus ac, fermentum quis, tempor ut, neque. Aliquam consectetuer mattis tellus.

**Search the Recipes**

Submit

- About Us
- Recipes
- Articles
- Buy Online
- Contact Us

**Please Visit our Sponsors**

Lorem ipsum dolor sit amet, consectetuer adipiscing elit. Sed lectus tortor, varius sed, tincidunt eu, egestas a, ipsum.

Sed mattis, orci eu porta facilisis, purus ipsum mollis nibh, eu laoreet wisi purus a sem. Pellentesque tortor sapien, sodales eu, feugiat eget, pulvinar quis, erat.

Figure 9.44. The unstyled XHTML document

We create the three columns using the following CSS fragments. We place both the left-hand and right-hand columns with absolute positioning: side1 is positioned from the left edge of the page, side2 from the right. We also add some significant top padding to these columns to make room for background images that will act as headings:

chapter09/3col.css *(excerpt)*

```css
#side1 {
  position: absolute;
  width: 200px;
  top: 30px;
  left: 10px;
  padding: 70px 10px 10px 10px;
}
```

chapter09/3col.css *(excerpt)*

```css
#side2 {
  position: absolute;
  width: 220px;
  top: 30px;
  right: 10px;
```

```
    padding: 70px 10px 10px 10px;
    ⋮
}
```

The `content` block simply sits between the two absolutely positioned columns, with margins applied to the content to give the columns the room they need:

chapter09/3col.css *(excerpt)*

```
#content {
    margin: 66px 260px 0px 240px;
    padding: 10px;
}
```

Figure 9.45 shows what the page looks like with these initial positioning tasks complete.

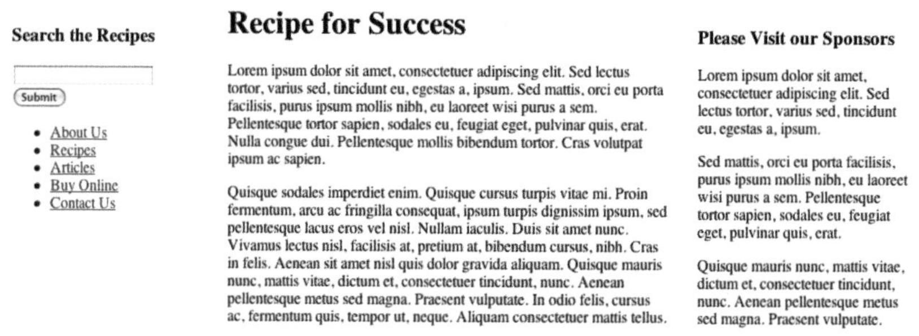

**Search the Recipes**

[ Submit ]

- About Us
- Recipes
- Articles
- Buy Online
- Contact Us

## Recipe for Success

Lorem ipsum dolor sit amet, consectetuer adipiscing elit. Sed lectus tortor, varius sed, tincidunt eu, egestas a, ipsum. Sed mattis, orci eu porta facilisis, purus ipsum mollis nibh, eu laoreet wisi purus a sem. Pellentesque tortor sapien, sodales eu, feugiat eget, pulvinar quis, erat. Nulla congue dui. Pellentesque mollis bibendum tortor. Cras volutpat ipsum ac sapien.

Quisque sodales imperdiet enim. Quisque cursus turpis vitae mi. Proin fermentum, arcu ac fringilla consequat, ipsum turpis dignissim ipsum, sed pellentesque lacus eros vel nisl. Nullam iaculis. Duis sit amet nunc. Vivamus lectus nisl, facilisis at, pretium at, bibendum cursus, nibh. Cras in felis. Aenean sit amet nisl quis dolor gravida aliquam. Quisque mauris nunc, mattis vitae, dictum et, consectetuer tincidunt, nunc. Aenean pellentesque metus sed magna. Praesent vulputate. In odio felis, cursus ac, fermentum quis, tempor ut, neque. Aliquam consectetuer mattis tellus.

**Please Visit our Sponsors**

Lorem ipsum dolor sit amet, consectetuer adipiscing elit. Sed lectus tortor, varius sed, tincidunt eu, egestas a, ipsum.

Sed mattis, orci eu porta facilisis, purus ipsum mollis nibh, eu laoreet wisi purus a sem. Pellentesque tortor sapien, sodales eu, feugiat eget, pulvinar quis, erat.

Quisque mauris nunc, mattis vitae, dictum et, consectetuer tincidunt, nunc. Aenean pellentesque metus sed magna. Praesent vulputate.

Figure 9.45. Three columns appearing with the initial CSS positioning

With our three columns in place, we can simply style the individual elements as required for the design in question. I've used background images of tomatoes on the body and on `side2`, as you can see previously in Figure 9.43.

# How do I add a footer to a liquid layout?

If you've experimented at all with absolute positioning, you may have begun to suspect that an absolutely positioned layout will make it impossible to add a footer that will always stay beneath all three columns, no matter which is the longest. Well, you'd be right!

To add a footer to our three-column layout we'll need to use a floated layout. A floated, liquid layout presents an additional problem in contrast to the standard floated, fixed-width layout. When we float an element in our layout, we need to give it a width. Now, in a fixed-width layout we know what the actual width of each column is, so we can float each column and give it a width. In a liquid layout such as the one we saw in "How do I create a three-column CSS layout?", we have two columns whose widths we know (the sidebars), and one unknown—the main content area, which expands to fill the space.

## Solution

In order to solve the problem of needing to have a flexible column in a floated layout, we need to build a slightly more complex layout, using negative margins to create space for a fixed-width column in a flexible content area. We'll also need to add some markup to our layout in order to give us some elements to float:

```
chapter09/3col-alt.html
<!DOCTYPE html PUBLIC "-//W3C//DTD XHTML 1.0 Strict//EN"
  "http://www.w3.org/TR/xhtml1/DTD/xhtml1-strict.dtd">
<html xmlns="http://www.w3.org/1999/xhtml" lang="en-US">
  <head>
    <title>Recipe for Success</title>
    <meta http-equiv="content-type"
        content="text/html; charset=utf-8" />
    <link rel="stylesheet" type="text/css" href="3col-alt.css" />
  </head>
  <body>
    <div id="wrapper">
      <div id="content">
        <div id="side1">
          <form method="post" action="" id="searchform">
            <h3><label for="keys">Search the Recipes</label></h3>
```

```
      <div>
          <input type="text" name="keys" id="keys"
              class="txt" /><br />
          <input type="submit" name="Submit" value="Submit" />
      </div>
    </form>
    <ul>
      <li><a href="#">About Us</a></li>
      <li><a href="#">Recipes</a></li>
      <li><a href="#">Articles</a></li>
      <li><a href="#">Buy Online</a></li>
      <li><a href="#">Contact Us</a></li>
    </ul>
  </div>
  <div id="main">
    <h1>Recipe for Success</h1>
    <p>Lorem ipsum dolor sit amet, consectetuer …</p>
    <p>Quisque sodales imperdiet enim. Quisque …</p>
  </div>
</div>
</div>

<div id="side2">
  <h3>Please Visit our Sponsors</h3>
  <div class="adbox"><p>Lorem ipsum dolor sit amet …</p></div>
  <div class="adbox"><p>Sed mattis, orci eu porta …</p></div>
  <div class="adbox"><p>Quisque mauris nunc, mattis …</p></div>
</div>
<div id="footer">
  ⋮ footer content…
</div>
  </body>
</html>
```

Within our CSS, we give the new `wrapper` block a width of 100% and a negative right margin of −230 pixels. This use of negative margins enables us to give the sidebar a variable width that's 230 pixels less than the width of the browser window.

We can then float our sidebars into position, to the left and right of the content:

*chapter09/3col-alt.css (excerpt)*

```css
body {
  margin: 0;
  padding: 0;
}
#wrapper {
  width:100%;
  float:left;
  margin-right: -230px;
  margin-top: 66px;
}
#content {
  margin-right: 220px;
}
#main {
  margin-left: 220px;
}
#side1 {
  width:200px;
  float:left;
  padding: 0 10px 0 10px;
}
#side2 {
  width: 190px;
  padding: 80px 10px 0 10px;
  float:right;
}
#footer {
  clear:both;
  border-top: 10px solid #CECECE;
}
```

As you can see in Figure 9.46, this CSS positions the columns where we need them, and our new footer falls neatly below the three columns. This solution can also be used for a two-column layout; you can change the order of columns by floating elements to the right instead of the left. With a little experimentation, you should be able to make the layout behave as you need it to, even if it seems a little counter-intuitive at first!

**Search the Recipes**

( Submit )

- About Us
- Recipes
- Articles
- Buy Online
- Contact Us

## Recipe for Success

Lorem ipsum dolor sit amet, consectetuer adipiscing elit. Sed lectus tortor, varius sed, tincidunt eu, egestas a, ipsum. Sed mattis, orci eu porta facilisis, purus ipsum mollis nibh, eu laoreet wisi purus a sem. Pellentesque tortor sapien, sodales eu, feugiat eget, pulvinar quis, erat. Nulla congue dui. Pellentesque mollis bibendum tortor. Cras volutpat ipsum ac sapien.

Quisque sodales imperdiet enim. Quisque cursus turpis vitae mi. Proin fermentum, arcu ac fringilla consequat, ipsum turpis dignissim ipsum, sed pellentesque lacus eros vel nisl. Nullam iaculis. Duis sit amet nunc. Vivamus lectus nisl, facilisis at, pretium at, bibendum cursus, nibh. Cras in felis. Aenean sit amet nisl quis dolor gravida aliquam. Quisque mauris nunc, mattis vitae, dictum et, consectetuer tincidunt, nunc. Aenean pellentesque metus sed magna. Praesent vulputate. In odio felis, cursus ac, fermentum quis, tempor ut, neque. Aliquam consectetuer mattis tellus.

**Please Visit our Sponsors**

Lorem ipsum dolor sit amet, consectetuer adipiscing elit. Sed lectus tortor, varius sed, tincidunt eu, egestas a, ipsum.

Sed mattis, orci eu porta facilisis, purus ipsum mollis nibh, eu laoreet wisi purus a sem. Pellentesque tortor sapien, sodales eu, feugiat eget, pulvinar quis, erat.

Quisque mauris nunc, mattis vitae, dictum et, consectetuer tincidunt, nunc. Aenean pellentesque metus sed magna. Praesent vulputate.

Figure 9.46. The columns floated into place

# How do I create a thumbnail gallery with CSS?

If you need to display a collection of images—perhaps for a photo album—a table may seem like the easiest way to go. However, the layout shown in Figure 9.47 was achieved using CSS; it provides some significant benefits that table versions lack.

Figure 9.47. Building an image gallery of thumbnails using CSS

## Solution

This solution uses a simple list for the album images, and positions them using CSS:

chapter09/gallery.html

```html
<!DOCTYPE html PUBLIC "-//W3C//DTD XHTML 1.0 Strict//EN"
  "http://www.w3.org/TR/xhtml1/DTD/xhtml1-strict.dtd">
<html xmlns="http://www.w3.org/1999/xhtml" lang="en-US">
  <head>
    <title>CSS photo album</title>
    <meta http-equiv="content-type"
        content="text/html; charset=utf-8" />
    <link href="gallery.css" rel="stylesheet" type="text/css" />
  </head>
  <body>
    <ul id="albumlist">
      <li><img src="thumb1.jpg" alt="Candle" width="240"
          height="160" />A light in the darkness</li>
      <li><img src="thumb2.jpg" alt="Pete Ryder" width="240"
          height="160" />Pete Ryder</li>
      <li><img src="thumb3.jpg" alt="La Grande Bouffe" width="240"
          height="160" />La Grande Bouffe</li>
      <li><img src="thumb4.jpg" alt="sculpture" width="240"
          height="160" />Sculpture</li>
      <li><img src="thumb5.jpg" alt="Duck stretching wings"
          width="240" height="160" />Splashing about</li>
      <li><img src="thumb6.jpg" alt="Duck" width="240"
          height="160" />Duck</li>
      <li><img src="thumb7.jpg" alt="Red leaves" width="240"
          height="160" />Red</li>
      <li><img src="thumb8.jpg" alt="Autumn leaves" width="240"
          height="160" />Autumn</li>
    </ul>
  </body>
</html>
```

chapter09/gallery.css

```css
body {
  background-color: #FFFFFF;
  color: #000000;
  margin: 0;
```

```
    padding: 0;
}
#albumlist {
  list-style-type: none;
}
#albumlist li {
  float: left;
  width:240px;
  margin-right: 6px;
  margin-bottom: 10px;
  font: bold 0.8em Arial, Helvetica, sans-serif;
  color: #333333;
}
#albumlist img {
  display: block;
  border: 1px solid #333300;
}
```

## Discussion

Our starting point for this layout is the creation of an unordered list—within it, we'll store each image in a `li` element, along with an appropriate image caption. Without the application of CSS, this list will display as shown in Figure 9.48:

chapter09/gallery.html *(excerpt)*

```html
<ul id="albumlist">
  <li><img src="thumb1.jpg" alt="Candle" width="240"
      height="160" />A light in the darkness</li>
  <li><img src="thumb2.jpg" alt="Pete Ryder" width="240"
      height="160" />Pete Ryder</li>
  <li><img src="thumb3.jpg" alt="La Grande Bouffe" width="240"
      height="160" />La Grande Bouffe</li>
  <li><img src="thumb4.jpg" alt="sculpture" width="240"
      height="160" />Sculpture</li>
  <li><img src="thumb5.jpg" alt="Duck stretching wings"
      width="240" height="160" />Splashing about</li>
  <li><img src="thumb6.jpg" alt="Duck" width="240"
      height="160" />Duck</li>
  <li><img src="thumb7.jpg" alt="Red leaves" width="240"
      height="160" />Red</li>
```

```
    <li><img src="thumb8.jpg" alt="Autumn leaves" width="240"
        height="160" />Autumn</li>
  </ul>
```

Note that I've applied an ID of albumlist to the list that contains the photos.

Figure 9.48. The unstyled list of images

To create the grid-style layout of the thumbnails, we're going to position the images by using the float property on the li elements that contain them. Add these rules to your style sheet:

```
#albumlist {
  list-style-type: none;
}
#albumlist li {
  float: left;
  width:240px;
}
#albumlist img {
  display: block;
}
```

All we're aiming to achieve with these rules is to remove the bullet points from the list items and float the images left, as shown in Figure 9.49. Also, by setting the images to display as blocks, we force their captions to display below them.

Your pictures should now have moved into position. If you resize the window, you'll see that they wrap to fill the available width. If the window becomes too narrow to contain a given number of images side by side, the last image simply drops down to start the next line.

Figure 9.49. The page display after the images are floated left

We now have our basic layout—let's add to it to make it more attractive. For example, we could insert some rules to create space between the images in the list, and specify a nice font for the image captions:

chapter09/gallery.css *(excerpt)*

```css
#albumlist li {
  float: left;
  width:240px;
  margin-right: 6px;
  margin-bottom: 10px;
  font: bold 0.8em Arial, Helvetica, sans-serif;
  color: #333333;
}
```

We could also add borders to the images:

chapter09/gallery.css *(excerpt)*

```
#albumlist img {
  border: 1px solid #333300;
}
```

The flexibility of this layout method makes it particularly handy when you're pulling your images from a database—it's unnecessary to calculate the number of images, for example, so that you can build list items on the fly as you create your page.

All the same, this wrapping effect may sometimes be unwanted. You can stop unwanted wrapping by setting the width of the list tag, `<ul>`:

```
#albumlist {
  list-style-type: none;
  width: 600px;
}
```

This rule forcibly sets the width to which the images may wrap, producing the display shown in Figure 9.50.

Figure 9.50. The images ceasing to wrap after we set the width of the containing `<ul>` tag

# How do I use CSS Tables for Layout?

In the section called "How do I create a full-height column?" I mentioned that there's no method in CSS to create full-height columns. Perhaps I should have said there's no method currently supported in all common browsers for creating full height columns, as I'm about to demonstrate a method of doing just this using CSS tables.

## Solution

The term **CSS tables** refers to the table-related `display` property values specified in CSS 2.1; for example `table`, `table-row`, and `table-cell`. Using these display values you can make any HTML element act like the equivalent table-related element when displayed.

The minimum browser versions that support CSS tables are Firefox 2, Opera 9.5, Safari 3, Chrome 1, and Internet Explorer 8. Unfortunately this method fails to work in Internet Explorer 6 or 7, so you'll have to decide how useful this technique is to you.

CSS tables solve problems associated with laying out elements in proper grids, as well as the issue of being unable to display a full-height background. Specifying the value `table` for the `display` property of an element allows you to display that element and its descendants as though they were table elements which, crucially, allows us to define boundaries of a cell element in relation to other elements next to it.

Let's return to the two-column, fixed-width layout and create a full-height column without the pretend background trick. The below markup is our HTML document made ready for displaying the columns as table cells:

chapter09/2col-fixedwidth-tables.html *(excerpt)*

```
<!DOCTYPE html PUBLIC "-//W3C//DTD XHTML 1.0 Strict//EN"
  "http://www.w3.org/TR/xhtml1/DTD/xhtml1-strict.dtd">
<html xmlns="http://www.w3.org/1999/xhtml" lang="en-US">
  <head>
    <title>Recipe for Success | Perfect Pizza</title>
    <link href="2col-fixedwidth-table.css" rel="stylesheet"
        type="text/css" />
```

```
      <meta http-equiv="content-type"
          content="text/html; charset=utf-8" />
  </head>
  <body>
    <div id="wrapper">
      <div id="header">
        <h1>Perfect Pizza</h1>
      </div>
      <div id="main">
        <div id="nav">
          <ul>
            <li><a href="#">Prepare the Dough</a></li>
            <li class="cur"><a href="#">Choose Your Toppings</a>
            </li>
            <li><a href="#">Pizza Ovens</a></li>
            <li><a href="#">Side Salads</a></li>
          </ul>
        </div>
        <div id="content">
          <h2>Choosing Your Toppings</h2>
          <p>Sed nec erat sed sem molestie congue. Cras lacus …</p>
          <p>Vestibulum dictum massa at odio. In dignissim …</p>
          <div id="footer">&copy; 2009 Recipe for success</div>
        </div>
      </div>
    </div>
  </body>
</html>
```

You can see that I've added an additional div element with an id of main that wraps the content and nav elements. I've also had to place the markup for navigation above the markup for content; one drawback of using CSS tables is that the source order for your column content must match the order in which you want them to display. Finally, because I no longer need to specify clear: both; for the footer element in order to clear the previously floated columns, I can place it inside the main content div.

I only need to make a few small changes to the CSS. First, I can take the sidebar background image out of the wrapper element as we're able to apply this to the column directly; I set the display property of the new main div to table, and the content and nav elements are set to table-cell. I can now add my sidebar background image directly to the nav element and remove the margin-left and clear properties from the footer element, as it no longer needs to act as a clearing element as it did for the floated layout. Here are the CSS changes:

```
#wrapper {
  position: relative;
  text-align: left;
  width: 760px;
  margin-right: auto;
  margin-left: auto;
  margin-bottom: 1em;
  border-right: 1px solid #888888;
  border-bottom: 1px solid #888888;
}
  ⋮
#main {
  display: table;
}
#content {
  display: table-cell;
  width: 500px;
  padding: 0 10px 0 20px;
}
  ⋮
#nav {
  display: table-cell;
  width: 230px;
  background-image: url(sidebar.gif);
  background-repeat:repeat-y;
}
  ⋮
#footer {
  font-size: 80%;
  padding: 1em 0 1em 0;
  color: #999999;
  background-color: transparent;
}
```

The layout should now look identical to the floated layout described in the section called "How do I create a full-height column?", but without having to resort to using floated elements and dealing with all the problems that introduces. The CSS table version is much simpler and more intuitive.

If you recall from the section called "How do I add a footer to a liquid layout?", adding a footer to a three-column liquid layout introduced a lot of complexity and forced us to use counter-intuitive negative margins. If we attempt the same layout using CSS tables you'll see the solution is far simpler. Here is the markup for the CSS table version of our three-column liquid layout:

chapter09/3col-table.html *(excerpt)*

```
<!DOCTYPE html PUBLIC "-//W3C//DTD XHTML 1.0 Strict//EN"
  "http://www.w3.org/TR/xhtml1/DTD/xhtml1-strict.dtd">
<html xmlns="http://www.w3.org/1999/xhtml" lang="en-US">
  <head>
    <title>Recipe for Success</title>
    <meta http-equiv="content-type"
        content="text/html; charset=utf-8" />
    <link rel="stylesheet" type="text/css" href="3col-table.css" />
  </head>
  <body>
    <div id="wrapper">
      <div id="content">
        <div id="side1">
          <form method="post" action="" id="searchform">
            <h3><label for="keys">Search the Recipes</label></h3>
            <div>
              <input type="text" name="keys" id="keys"
                  class="txt" /><br />
              <input type="submit" name="Submit" value="Submit" />
            </div>
          </form>
          <ul>
            <li><a href="#">About Us</a></li>
            <li><a href="#">Recipes</a></li>
            <li><a href="#">Articles</a></li>
            <li><a href="#">Buy Online</a></li>
            <li><a href="#">Contact Us</a></li>
          </ul>
        </div>
        <div id="main">
          <h1>Recipe for Success</h1>
          <p>Lorem ipsum dolor sit amet, consectetuer …</p>
```

```
          <p>Quisque sodales imperdiet enim. Quisque …</p>
        </div>
        <div id="side2">
          <h3>Please Visit our Sponsors</h3>
          <div class="adbox"><p>Lorem ipsum dolor sit …</p></div>
          <div class="adbox"><p>Sed mattis, orci eu  …</p></div>
          <div class="adbox"><p>Quisque mauris nunc,  …</p></div>
        </div>
      </div>
    </div>
    <div id="footer">
      ⋮ footer content…
    </div>
  </body>
</html>
```

The first aspect you should notice is that it's straightforward in comparison to the floated layout version. Next the CSS:

chapter09/3col-table.css *(excerpt)*

```
#wrapper {
  width:100%;
}
#content {
  display: table;
  width: 100%;
}
#main {
  display: table-cell;
}
#side1 {
  display: table-cell;
  width:200px;
  padding: 0 10px 0 10px;
}
#side2 {
  display: table-cell;
  width: 190px;
  padding: 80px 10px 0 10px;
}
```

```
#footer {
  border-top: 10px solid #CECECE;
}
```

The CSS is equally straightforward: no margins, floating, or clearing required. The layout displays in the same way as a single-row table with three cells. The footer sits nicely below the three columns.

## Discussion

You may have noticed that there is no element set to display as a table row. In a simple layout the browser will add in a pretend table row, known as an **anonymous table element**, to surround the table cell elements. If your layout is any more complex though, I'd recommend you add in extra elements to display as the table rows as well. It's just the most error-free way to create a CSS table layout.

While certainly attractive to use, the lack of support from IE6 and IE7 is a problem. If you want the best of both worlds then it's possible to use conditional comments to supply IE6 and IE7 with the CSS they require. I think we'll be seeing a lot more of CSS tables in the future, especially as IE6 and IE7 usage starts to drop. If you want to know more about the technique and how to deal with those older browsers, then please see the book I co-wrote with Kevin Yank, *Everything You Know About CSS is Wrong* also published by Sitepoint.[5]

## Summary

This chapter should have given you some starting points and ideas for your own layouts. By combining other solutions in this book, such as the innovative use of navigation and images, with your own creativity, you should be able to come up with myriad designs based on the layouts we've explored here. As with tables, most CSS layouts are really just variations on a theme.

Once you have a grasp of the basics, and you've learned the rules, you'll find that you really are limited only by your imagination. For inspiration, and to see what other designers are doing with CSS layouts, have a look at the CSS Zen Garden.[6]

---

[5] http://www.sitepoint.com/books/csswrong1/

[6] http://www.csszengarden.com/

# Index

## Symbols

!important keyword, 15

\# ID prefix, 10

## A

<a> elements (*see* links)

absolute keyword font sizes, 27

absolute positioning, 307, 309

   advantages, 331

   three-column liquid layouts, 351, 355

   two-column fixed-width layouts, 333, 339

   two-column liquid layouts, 327

   within other elements, 309, 339

access keys, 201–204

accessibility

   (*see also* text-only devices)

   absolute positioning and, 331

   access keys, use of, 203

   advantages of CSS, 217

   <blockquote> elements and, 49

   designing in, 144

   <fieldset> and <legend> elements, 199

   image text and, 81

   image-based navigation, 131

   pixel sizing and, 23

   problems with implicit labels, 191

   problems with tabular layouts, 139

   reliance on color and, 181

   tabular data, 141

   testing in text-only browsers, 257

   what to be aware of, 256

accesskey attribute, 203

accounts data spreadsheet, 140

:active pseudo-class, 13, 32, 33, 125

adjacent selectors, 12

Adobe BrowserLab, 225

align attribute alternatives, 296

alignment

   of form fields, 191, 195, 196

   of site logo and slogan in headers, 303

   of tabular data, 151

   of text, 45, 46, 49

   in two-column liquid layouts, 322, 330

alt text, 260

alternating column colors, 160

alternating row colors, 152, 155, 207

alternative style sheets, 274

   alerting users, 278

   avoiding code duplication, 281

   print style sheets, 263

anchor elements (*see* links)

anonymous table elements, 371

applying styles

   determining which, 15

arrow key navigation, 259

@media at-rule, 262

attribute selectors, 117, 207

   identifying input types with, 185

attributes, HTML

   (*see also* class attributes; ID attributes)

   deprecated attributes, 296

   for tabular data, 143

aural media type, 262

author's web site, 258

auto setting, margin properties, 312, 314

# THE ART & SCIENCE OF CSS

BY **CAMERON ADAMS**
**JINA BOLTON**
**DAVID JOHNSON**
**STEVE SMITH**
**JONATHAN SNOOK**

CREATE INSPIRATIONAL STANDARDS-BASED WEB DESIGN

# THE PRINCIPLES OF
# BEAUTIFUL
# WEB DESIGN

BY **JASON BEAIRD**

# SIMPLY
# JAVASCRIPT

BY **KEVIN YANK**
& **CAMERON ADAMS**

**THE CSS ANTHOLOGY**
101 ESSENTIAL TIPS, TRICKS & HACKS

CD-ROM

The CD-ROM is not missing.
Download all the code in this book from:
http://www.sitepoint.com/books/cssant3/code.php